Building
Partnerships for
Service-Learning

Building Partnerships for Service-Learning

Barbara Jacoby and Associates

JOSSEY-BASS
A Wiley Imprint
www.josseybass.com

Published by Jossey-Bass
A Wiley Imprint
989 Market Street, San Francisco, CA 94103-1741   www.josseybass.com

Jossey-Bass books and products are available through most bookstores. To contact Jossey-Bass
directly call our Customer Care Department within the U.S. at 800-956-7739, outside the U.S.
at 317-572-3986 or fax 317-572-4002.

Jossey-Bass also publishes its books in a variety of electronic formats. Some content that
appears in print may not be available in electronic books.

Library of Congress Cataloging-in-Publication Data
Jacoby, Barbara.
  Building partnerships for service-learning / Barbara Jacoby and
associates.—1st ed.
    p. cm.—(The Jossey-Bass higher and adult education series)
Includes bibliographical references and index.
  ISBN 0-7879-5890-5 (alk. paper)
  1. Student service—United States. 2. Student volunteers in social
service—United States. 3. Experiential learning—United States.
I. Title. II. Series.
  LC221 .J33 2003
  378.1'03—dc 21   2002152153

Printed in the United States of America
FIRST EDITION
HB Printing   10 9 8 7 6 5 4 3 2 1

The Jossey-Bass
Higher and Adult Education Series

To Pearl and Herb Gendler—
my beloved parents, whose
extraordinary partnership
since 1943 continues to inspire
many current and potential partners.

Contents

Foreword

What a difference six years can make! Service-learning has come a long way since 1996, when Barbara Jacoby and associates published *Service-Learning in Higher Education*. As Jacoby writes in this extraordinarily useful volume, *Building Partnerships for Service-Learning*, "the number of students, institutions, and communities involved [in service-learning] has grown dramatically" (p. 2). Campus Compact, the national coalition of more than 850 college and university presidents committed to the civic purposes of higher education, recently found a significant increase in service-learning on college and university campuses. Among the 327 campuses that responded to a survey distributed in 2001, 14 percent reported an increase of 10 percent or more in the number of faculty involved in service-learning from 2000 to 2001, with 51 percent noting a smaller increase of a few additional faculty each year. Eighty-seven percent of the respondents offered service-learning courses in 2001, an 8 percent increase from 2000 (Campus Compact, 2002).

Clearly, these statistics represent significant progress. But far more service-learning in far more colleges and universities is still needed if service-learning is to become truly central to the academic enterprise. How to develop more service-learning courses, however, is no longer the most pressing question facing service-learning practitioners and the service-learning movement in general. It has been replaced by a much more fundamental, much more difficult problem: How can service-learning most effectively contribute to changing American higher education, and the American schooling system in general, for the better? Recognition that the service-learning movement thus far has had only a limited impact on changing higher education and increasing student civic engagement perhaps accounts for this change of focus. In her 2001 study for the Grantmaker Forum on Community and National Service, Cynthia Gibson, for example, questioned the impact service-learning and other engaged pedagogies actually have had on the American university. Weaving together her own words with those of Barry Checkoway and Kevin Mattson, Gibson writes:

> Other higher education leaders have echoed Derek Bok's concern that universities are disassociated with the civic missions on which they were founded—missions that assumed responsibility for preparing students for active participation in a democratic society and developing students' knowledge for the improvement of communities. Currently, it is "hard to find top administrators with consistent commitment to this mission; few faculty members consider it central to their role, and community groups that approach the university for assistance often find it difficult to get what they need." In short, the university has primarily become "a place for professors to get tenured and students to get credentialed" [Gibson, 2001, p. 11].

An abiding belief that service-learning can and should do more animates the work of Barbara Jacoby and her colleagues. They would like service-learning to live up "to its potential to lead institutions of higher education to transform themselves into fully engaged citizens of their communities and world" (p. xvii). In other words, the goal of this book is to help service-learning practitioners better contribute to creating a truly engaged, truly democratic American higher education system, which, in turn, will contribute to a truly democratic society. This volume argues that "strong, democratic partnerships" will help service-learning address "the most serious issues facing communities and society at large" (p. 314).

In my judgment, Jacoby has it exactly right. Creating effective, democratic, mutually beneficial, mutually respectful partnerships should be a primary, if not the primary, agenda for service-learning in the first decade of the twenty-first century. It should be a primary agenda because, by working to create partnerships of that kind, service-learning practitioners will necessarily be working to transform higher education in America. Quite simply, as they currently function, colleges and universities do not and cannot make significant contributions to American democracy. Given their elitist, self-referential, conflict-riven, competitive culture, they may actually contribute to civic disengagement and the weakening of community ties, rather than to creating a robust participatory civic life. A radically different higher education system is needed. Neither internal tinkering nor disparate, unconnected, unintegrated service-learning projects will help create that system. To the contrary, significant, serious partnerships designed to achieve a significant, serious goal are required if fundamental progress toward creating a truly engaged, truly democratic civic university is to be made.

"It is not possible to run a course aright when the goal itself is not rightly placed," wrote Francis Bacon in *Novum Organum* in 1620 (Benson, 1972, p. xi). As noted above, for Jacoby, as well as a number of other contributors to this volume, the "rightly placed goal" for service-learning is helping to create a truly democratic society. For that to occur, Jacoby calls on universities to focus their attention on improving democracy and the quality of life in their local communities. Here Jacoby is echoing one of John Dewey's most significant propositions: "Democracy must begin at home, and its home is the neighborly community" (Dewey, 1927/1954, p. 213). Democracy, Dewey emphasized, has to be built on face-to-face interactions in which human beings work together cooperatively to solve the ongoing problems of life. In effect, Jacoby has updated Dewey and proposed that: Democracy must begin at home, and its home is the engaged neighborly college or university and its local community partners.

The benefits of a local community focus for college and university service-learning courses and programs are obvious. Ongoing, continuous interaction is facilitated through work in an easily accessible local setting. Relationships of trust, so essential for effective partnerships and effective learning, are also built through day-to-day work on problems and issues of mutual concern. In addition, the local community also provides a setting in which a number of service-learning courses can work together and produce substantive results. Work in a college or university's local community also allows for interaction across schools and disciplines, creating interdisciplinary learning opportunities. And finally, the local community is a real-world site in which community members and academics can pragmatically determine whether the work is making a real difference, and whether the neighborhood and the institution are better as a result of common efforts.

Needless to say, "community-focused service-learning partnerships" (to coin a phrase) is not the usual practice. As Susan Jones notes in Chapter Eight on exemplary partnerships with community agencies: "Little in the research and literature on service-learning provides evidence that the accomplishment of indistinguishable consequences [between the higher education institutions and the community], or true reciprocity, is actually achieved" (p. 153). Jacoby and her colleagues persuasively make a case for a different kind of service-learning. In their view, service-learning functions as a community-building and democracy-building activity, involving not only student reflection on the service experience but also the provision of genuine service to the community, as well as the development of democratic, respectful relationships between students and the community members with whom they work. Jacoby and her colleagues also make the case that service-learning should attempt to solve, not merely address or learn from, community problems.

For a number of years (seventeen to be exact) my colleagues, students, and I have been trying to do that kind of service-learning at the University of Pennsylvania. To describe our work, we use the term "strategic academically based community service," a form of service-learning that involves the integration of research, teaching, and service. It focuses on helping to solve significant structural problems at Penn and in its local community—problems such as elitist, nondemocratic schooling, failing public schools, poor health care, and poverty. We have tried, are trying, and have made progress, but we have very, very far to go, both at Penn and in its local community, West Philadelphia. We have learned in practice how hard it is to overcome the dead hand of academic tradition, which strongly favors so-called "pure" over applied research, and individual, entrepreneurial, discipline-focused projects over cooperative, real-world, community problem-solving work. Simply put, engaging the entire range of a college or university's resources to help create democratic neighborly communities requires lots of hard thinking, doing, reflecting, learning, and relearning.

I learned a great deal from Jacoby and her colleagues on ways to get us from here to there, namely, from the "somewhat engaged" to the "truly engaged" college and university. In effect, this book answers the implementation question, helping the reader learn how to create partnerships with community organizations, pre-K–12 schools, and students, for example. And that is an invaluable service. As the distinguished systems theorists C. West Churchman and Ian Mitroff emphasize, "implementation . . . is one of the most difficult problems humans face," particularly the problem of "how to change people and human institutions" (1998, p. 117).

An avid builder of partnerships at the University of Maryland and the community, Barbara Jacoby is extraordinarily well qualified to be lead author of a volume designed to increase our understanding of partnerships, as well as provide us with useful knowledge for building better partnerships. And she has assembled a similarly qualified group of coauthors who have done exemplary work building partnerships and teaching and writing about service-learning. Among the powerful insights that many of the authors developed over their years of experience, perhaps the most significant is that sustained, effective collaboration between academics and community members is crucial for advancing both knowledge and human welfare. I agree strongly that multiple perspectives and approaches are needed to improve both communities and higher education institutions. Knowledge, quite simply, resides in many places, not just in the academy. Providing strategies for democratizing and integrating the production and use of knowledge may indeed be one of the volume's most important contributions.

Thinking and writing about building partnerships for service-learning may not be easy, but it is much, much easier than actually building real partnerships between colleges and universities and their communities. Will the ideas and strategies presented in this volume bear fruit on campuses and communities, helping to generate much better service-learning and new and better partnerships? My hunch is that they will. I am certain, however, that effectively implementing "community-focused service-learning partnerships" would help American colleges and universities better educate students to be lifelong, moral, democratic citizens in a democratic society.

IRA HARKAVY
Associate Vice President and Director
Center for Community Partnerships
University of Pennsylvania

References

Benson, L. *Toward the Scientific Study of History.* Philadelphia: Lippincott, 1972.

Campus Compact. *Highlights and Trends in Student Service and Service-Learning.* Retrieved August 18, 2002 from [http://www.compact.org/newscc/stats2001/].

Churchman, C. W., and Mitroff, I. I. "The Management of Science and the Mismanagement of the World." In W. N. Dunn (ed.), *The Experimenting Society: Essays in Honor of Donald T. Campbell.* New Brunswick, N.J.: Transaction, 1998.

Dewey, J. *The Public and Its Problems.* Denver, Colo.: Alan Swallow, 1927/1954.

Gibson, C. *From Inspiration to Participation: A Review of Perspectives on Youth Civic Engagement.* Berkeley, Calif.: The Grantmaker Forum on Community and National Service, 2001.

Preface

Since the publication of *Service-Learning in Higher Education: Concepts and Practices* in 1996, much has come clear to this avid observer, practitioner, and advocate of service-learning. Service-learning has become institutionalized, as we like to say, on many more campuses. The numbers of students participating in both curricular and cocurricular service-learning have skyrocketed. Thanks to our colleagues who are active researchers and reflective analysts, we now have substantial evidence of the outcomes of service-learning and numerous guidelines and models of good practice. Even more significantly, it is widely recognized that service-learning is located squarely at the intersection of two powerful movements: the intentional orientation of undergraduate education toward active learning and the call for the civic renewal of higher education—the engaged campus.

Through high-quality service-learning, students perform activities that directly address human and community needs. In addition, students engage in critical reflection about what social responsibility means to them and how they will make socially responsible choices throughout all aspects of their lives. Communities benefit from new energy brought to bear on their problems and enhanced capacity to capitalize on their assets. When service-learning lives up to its potential to lead institutions of higher education to transform themselves into fully engaged citizens of their communities and the world, its ability to bring about positive social change is limitless.

What else has become evident is that service-learning is all about partnerships. And so partnerships had to be the subject of this book. Although much has been written about campus-community partnerships, many of us are all too familiar with examples of "partnerships in name only," in which the partnership essentially exists in a grant application or university promotional brochure. Too many communities have complained of being used as "learning laboratories" or having been "partnered to death" by universities. On the other hand, very little has been written about the other partnerships that are required to support strong and effective service-learning. These include, but are not limited to, partnerships within a single institution of higher education; among institutions; with schools, community agencies, and neighborhoods; with national and regional associations; and with governmental and nongovernmental organizations in the United States and abroad. Service-learning partnerships are complex, interdependent, fluid, dynamic, and delicate.

This book is about how service-learning should be, must be, if it is to fulfill its potential for both service and learning. In discussions with campus and association leaders of service-learning about the conceptual design of this book, more than one called for a book that is "inspirational rather than mechanical." Yet, they agreed, inspiration without the benefit of what we have learned through experience is not enough. The premise here is that the way to advance service-learning, to secure its future, and to maximize its benefits is through the creation and sustainability of a wide range of authentic, democratic, reciprocal partnerships. Stated simply, "You can take service-learning to the next level by taking partnerships to the next level" (Bailis, 2000, p. 3).

Audiences

Building Partnerships for Service-Learning was intentionally written for several audiences. Potential service-learning partners encompass a wide range of individuals with different perspectives and motivations, as well as different levels of knowledge about, and experience in, service-learning. This book will assist college presidents and senior academic officers to discover the key roles they can and should play in the development and sustenance of service-learning partnerships and why they should do so. As more and more institutions of higher education seek to reclaim their civic role—to become engaged in their communities—service-learning partnerships readily open the door to broader, more profound, and more transformative partnerships. The book elucidates how academic deans, department chairs, and faculty can enhance research, teaching, and learning by engaging in partnerships for service-learning. It also enables student leaders and student affairs professionals to assume their rightful places as partners in developing and implementing service-learning experiences that promote many facets of student learning and development.

Although its primary focus is on those within the higher education community, on campuses and in associations, this book is also valuable for community leaders, K–12 educators, nonprofit agency staff, and corporate sector representatives who may wish to consider entering into service-learning partnerships with colleges and universities. It will explain the often confusing landscape of higher education to those who do not work within it: "So you want to work with a university. . . . [T]his is what you'll face" (E. Hollander, personal communication, October 2000.) For our international colleagues it offers a comprehensive examination of service-learning partnerships in the United States together with specific insights on forming high-quality international partnerships. The book also contains important implications for public policy makers, foundation leaders, and government officials whose understanding and support of service-learning partnerships are critical if they are to be sustainable over time and successful in meeting human and community needs.

Overview of the Contents

The first three chapters provide the fundamentals of partnerships for service-learning: principles, relationships, and assessment. Chapter One places partnerships for service-learning in the context of today's higher education and offers three frameworks, or sets of principles, to guide the development of authentic, democratic partnerships. In Chapter Two, Sandra Enos and Keith Morton discuss the complex dynamics of relationships between campuses and communities and the differences between transactional and transformative relationships. Sherril B. Gelmon, in Chapter Three, proposes assessment as a means of building service-learning partnerships.

The next three chapters describe the kinds of partnerships within higher education that provide the foundation for high-quality, sustainable service-learning. In Chapter Four, Cathy McHugh Engstrom explores partnerships between academic and student affairs and advocates for the formation of collaborative partnerships. Irene Fisher and Shannon Wilson, in Chapter Five, propose benchmarks for the development of service-learning partnerships with students and examine a wide range of outstanding examples of such partnerships. Chapter Six, by Jennifer M. Pigza and Marie L. Troppe, offers three models for campuswide infrastructure for service-learning and civic engagement, together with benchmarks for use in institutional self-assessment. In Chapter Seven, James Birge, Brooke Beaird, and Jan Torres address the principles and practices of building service-learning partnerships between and among institutions of higher education.

The next chapters focus on partnerships involving colleges and a range of external entities. Chapter Eight, by Susan R. Jones, urges colleges to develop truly reciprocal partnerships with community agencies, arguing that equality in these relationships is both important and possible. In Chapter Nine, Terry Pickeral discusses the history, current state of practice, and future of service-learning partnerships between K–12 and higher education, offering recommendations for moving partnerships to greater scope, depth, and quality. Janni Sorenson, Kenneth M. Reardon, and Cathy Klump present, in Chapter Ten, a case study of a service-learning course that evolved into outstanding partnerships to rebuild urban neighborhoods struggling with poverty and neglect. In Chapter Eleven, Philip Nyden challenges higher education, despite its traditional research culture, to engage in collaborative action research through service-learning partnerships.

The chapters that follow further expand the partnership paradigm in exciting ways. Stacey Riemer and Joshua McKeown, in Chapter Twelve, address the challenges and benefits of involving corporate partners in service-learning. Linda A. Chisholm's Chapter Thirteen spurs us to create international partnerships for service-learning in response to rapidly increasing globalization. In Chapter Fourteen, Elizabeth Hollander and Matthew Hartley examine the relationship between civic renewal and service-learning and how placing service-learning in a civic frame affirms its purpose and centrality in higher education. The final chapter sets forth a mandate for action to secure the future of partnerships for service-learning.

Acknowledgments

This book has been inspired and enriched by many people. I am indebted to all of them.

First, I thank and appreciate the chapter authors for so generously sharing their knowledge and experience with us. It has been an honor to work with such an amazing group of thinkers, educators, and professionals.

Much of the inspiration for this book came from a lively meeting hosted by Campus Compact that included its incredible staff and Providence friends. The impetus to make this volume into a vehicle that encourages colleges and universities to enter into authentic, democratic service-learning partnerships with communities that advance the common good and enable higher education to fulfill its public purpose came from them. For this, I am deeply grateful.

I thank the wonderful staff of Commuter Affairs and Community Service at the University of Maryland for their constant support and assistance with this project. Leslie Stubbs and David Palomino did a tremendous amount of hard work in preparing the manuscript. John Garland gallantly assisted with the final details. This book would not have been possible without them.

The guidance of David Brightman at Jossey-Bass was invaluable throughout the journey. Melissa Kirk and Elisa Rassen were also helpful. Roger Nozaki, Debbie White, and Bruce Behringer were instrumental in the development of the chapter on corporate partners.

With great love and appreciation, I thank my husband and partner of thirty-one years, Steve Jacoby. No matter how discouraged I get along the way, he always cheers me up, puts things in perspective, and remains my loyal fan.

Last but surely not least, as I always try to do, I acknowledge those "who went before." In this case, I ask that we raise our collective glass in a toast to the many dedicated individuals who have nurtured, supported, and ventured into partnerships for service-learning.

BARBARA JACOBY
October 2002

Reference

Bailis, L. N. *Taking Service-Learning to the Next Level: Emerging Lessons from the National Community Development Program.* Springfield, Va.: National Society for Experiential Education, 2000.

The Authors

Barbara Jacoby is director of Commuter Affairs and Community Service and adviser to the president for America Reads*America Counts at the University of Maryland–College Park. She also serves as director of the National Clearinghouse for Commuter Programs, the only national organization that exists solely to provide information and assistance to professionals in designing programs and services for commuter students. She is affiliate associate professor of college student personnel at the University of Maryland. She earned her B.A. (1971), M.A. (1972), and Ph.D. (1978) degrees in French language and literature at the University of Maryland.

Jacoby is the author of *Service-Learning in Higher Education: Concepts and Practices* (1996), *Involving Commuter Students in Learning* (2000), and *The Student as Commuter: Developing a Comprehensive Institutional Response* (1989). She has written many articles and book chapters on topics that include service-learning in higher education, enhancing the educational experience of college students, and the future of student affairs. She has been featured on three national teleconferences on commuter students and adult learners. Jacoby has consulted extensively at colleges and universities across the country and has made numerous keynote speeches and presentations. She is active in promoting service-learning on her campus, in the state of Maryland, and nationally.

Over the years she has held many leadership positions in the American College Personnel Association and the National Association of Student Personnel Administrators. She has also served on the board of directors of the Council for the Advancement of Standards in Higher Education since 1980. Her Services, Programs, Advocacy, and Research (SPAR) model—a comprehensive approach to meeting the needs of diverse student populations—has been adopted for use by a number of institutions. Jacoby's institution and professional associations have recognized her outstanding contributions on several occasions.

Brooke Beaird is associate director of Campus Compact and former executive director of the Colorado Campus Compact. Prior to becoming the first director of the Colorado Compact in 1992, Beaird was assistant director of Campus Compact and directed the Campus Partners in Learning, a national mentoring project. Beaird has been responsible for both national and state programs in service-learning and has managed substantial grants from both federal and private sources. His work at the state and national levels has involved running programs for presidents, faculty, and students engaged in campus-based service. Beaird served on the Colorado governor's Commission on National and Community Service and its Executive Committee. He has a B.A. degree in English from Centenary College of Louisiana (1967) and an M.A. degree in business and economics from the University of Texas–Austin (1969). He has completed all but the dissertation in the higher education administration doctoral program at the University of Denver.

James Birge has been executive director of the Pennsylvania Campus Compact since 1997. His interests lie in educating men and women to take leadership roles in a changing society. He has worked with the people in rural Coahuila, Mexico, and with the homeless in Denver. Birge received a Ph.D. degree in leadership studies from Gonzaga University in 2000. His dissertation topic was "Academic Presidents as Public Leaders." His undergraduate degree (1984) is in education from Westfield State College in Massachusetts, and his master's degree (1987) is in counseling from Plymouth State College in New Hampshire. Prior to working for Campus Compact, he was the coordinator of the Center for Service Learning at Regis University in Denver.

Linda A. Chisholm is currently president of the International Partnership for Service-Learning, which she cofounded with Howard A. Berry in 1982. She holds a B.A. degree in history (1962) from the University of Tulsa, an M.A. degree in renaissance and reformation studies (1972) from the University of Tulsa, and a Ph.D. degree in history and higher education research from Columbia University (1982). She is former president of the Association of Episcopal Colleges and was the founder and first general secretary of the international organization Colleges and Universities of the Anglican Communion. Chisholm has been awarded honorary degrees from the General Theological Seminary in New York (Doctor of Divinity, 1995) and Cuttington University College in Liberia (Doctor of Humane Letters, 2001), and the University Fellowship from the University of Surrey Roehampton in London (2000). She recently authored *Charting a Hero's Journey* (2000). Chisholm coauthored two books with Howard A. Berry, *Service-Learning in Higher Education Around the World: An Initial Look* (1999) and *Students Tell Students: How to Serve and Learn Abroad Effectively* (1992).

Cathy McHugh Engstrom is associate professor in higher education at Syracuse University and coordinator of the master's program in student affairs/higher education. She received her Ph.D. degree in counseling and personnel services from the University of Maryland–College Park (1991) and her M.S. degree in higher education administration from the University of Vermont (1981). Issues of representation, diversity, power and authority, collaboration, and learning are embedded in her research and writing activities, including her work on student affairs–academic affairs partnerships and innovative pedagogies to promote student learning. Prior to joining the faculty, Engstrom worked as a student affairs administrator for more than fourteen years at the University of California–Davis, the University of Maryland–College Park, and Virginia Polytechnic Institute and State University. She authored a chapter with Vincent Tinto, "Developing Partnerships with Academic Affairs to Promote Student Learning," in Barr and Desler's *Handbook of Student Affairs Administration* (2000).

Sandra Enos is assistant professor of sociology at Rhode Island College. Prior to becoming a faculty member, she directed the Project to Integrate Service with Academic Study at Campus Compact from 1994 to 1996. Early in her career, she served as a VISTA volunteer in rural Alabama. She has also worked in child welfare, adult corrections, and as a policy aide in the office of the governor of the state of Rhode Island. She is the author of *Mothering from the Inside: Parenting in a Women's Prison* (2001) and several articles on service-learning in sociology. With Marie L. Troppe, Enos coauthored the chapter "Service-Learning in the Curriculum" for *Service-Learning in Higher Education: Concepts and Practices* (Jacoby, 1996). She earned her B.A. degree (1971) in sociology from Rhode Island College, her M.A. degree (1974) in sociology and interdisciplinary urban affairs from Brown University, and her Ph.D. degree in sociology from the University of Connecticut.

Irene S. Fisher is special assistant to the president for campus-community partnerships at the University of Utah. She served as founding director of the Lowell Bennion Community Service Center at the University of Utah from 1987 to 2001. From 1996 to 2001 she was volunteer executive director of the Utah Campus Compact and adjunct faculty member in the University of Utah's graduate school of social work and the department of family and consumer studies. She formerly directed Utah Issues Information Program, an advocacy organization for low-income issues. Fisher served as chair of the Coalition for Utah's Future, the League of Women Voters of Salt Lake City, and Utah Children. She received her B.A. degree (1959) in speech communication and elementary education from Northern State College in South Dakota and an honorary doctorate of humane letters from the University of Utah (2001). She authored the chapter "Integrating Service-Learning Experiences into Postcollege Choices" in *Service-Learning in Higher Education: Concepts and Practices* (Jacoby, 1996).

Sherril B. Gelmon is professor of public health at Portland State University and Campus Compact engaged scholar on assessment. She holds a doctorate of public health in health policy from the University of Michigan (1990), a masters of health science from the University of Toronto (1983), and undergraduate degrees in physical therapy from the universities of Toronto (1978) and Saskatchewan (1976). Prior to joining Portland State University, she served as executive director of the Accrediting Commission on Education for Health Services Administration (1988–1994) and director of academic affairs for the Association of University Programs in Health Administration (1988–1994), and as coordinator of the planning directorate for the University of Toronto Faculty of Medecine (1984–1988). She was the national evaluation director for both the Health Professions Schools in Service to the Nation program and the Community Based Quality Improvement in Health Professions Education initiative. She also served as project director for the Task Force on the Accreditation of Health Professions Education for the Pew Health Professions Commission. She has served as an examiner with the Malcolm Baldrige National Quality Award Program for the U.S. Department of Commerce since 1999. Gelmon is the lead author of *Assessing Service-Learning and Civic Engagement: Principles and Techniques* published by Campus Compact in 2001.

Matthew Hartley is assistant professor of education at the University of Pennsylvania in the graduate school of education. He completed his Ed.D. degree at Harvard University's graduate school of education in administration, planning, and social policy (2001), where he served as a teaching fellow, research assistant, and editor and cochair of the *Harvard Educational Review*. Prior to that, he was the founding director of community service learning at Bradford College in Bradford, Massachusetts. Hartley received his M.Ed. degree at the Harvard University graduate school of education (1994) and his B.A. degree at Colby College in art history (1986).

Elizabeth Hollander is executive director of Campus Compact, a national coalition of more than 850 college and university presidents who support the expansion of opportunities for public and community service in higher education and the importance of integrating service into academic study. Hollander served as executive director of the Monsignor John J. Egan Urban Center at DePaul University. She was also president of the Government Assistance Program in Illinois and director of planning for the city of Chicago. She is a fellow of the National Academy of Public Administration and serves on its Civic Engagement Panel. Hollander also serves on the boards of the Woodstock Institute in Chicago, the American Association of Colleges and Universities Diversity Web, the advisory board of the online *Journal of College and Character,* the American Committee of the International Consortium on Higher

Education, the selection committee for the Jimmy and Rosalynn Carter Partnership Award for Campus-Community Collaboration, and the Truman Regional Scholarship Committee. In 2001, Hollander received an honorary doctorate from Millikin University in Illinois. She received a B.A. degree cum laude in political science from Bryn Mawr College (1961).

Susan R. Jones is assistant professor in the school of educational policy and leadership and director of the student personnel assistantship program at Ohio State University. She earned her B.A. degree (1978) in sociology at Saint Lawrence University, her M.Ed. degree (1981) in higher education and student affairs at the University of Vermont, and her Ph.D. degree (1995) in college student personnel at the University of Maryland–College Park. Before joining the faculty at Ohio State, she held a number of student affairs positions including dean of students at Trinity College of Vermont and assistant director of campus programs and the Stamp Student Union at the University of Maryland. Jones's research interests and publications focus on identity development, service-learning, and student affairs administration. She is on the editorial board of the *Journal of College Student Development*. She has twice served as an Ohio Campus Compact faculty fellow and was the recipient of a Scholarship of Engagement grant. She is a previous board member of the National Association for Women in Education and is currently on the board of trustees of Project Open Hand, an AIDS service organization in Columbus, Ohio.

Cathy Klump is national housing organizer for the National Training and Information Center in Chicago, a thirty-year-old nonprofit organization that provides training, technical assistance, and community organizing support for grassroots community organizations. From 1999 to 2001 Klump was director of the Neighborhood Technical Assistance Center in East St. Louis. She also served as vice-chair of the East St. Louis Action Research Project at the University of Illinois at Urbana-Champaign and assisted in developing three comprehensive neighborhood revitalization plans in partnership with hundreds of community leaders. Klump holds an M.A. degree (1999) and B.A. degree (1997) in urban and regional planning from the University of Illinois. She received the Michael J. Carroll Award for Community Development in 1998.

Joshua McKeown is director of student services and programs at the Syracuse University School of Management. He is a doctoral student in higher education at the Syracuse University school of education. He has more than seven years of experience in career services, corporate relations, student recruiting, and student services. He has published several articles on career services, presented on student services for part-time students at national conferences, and addressed civic organizations on community service projects involving M.B.A. students. His research interests focus on student development through international experiences. He received his B.A. degree in international relations from Syracuse University (1992) and his M.B.A. degree from Clarkson University (1994).

Keith Morton is associate professor of American studies in English and director of the Feinstein Institute for Public Service at Providence College. His B.A. degree (1979) is in English and history from the University of Massachusetts at Amherst; his M.A. (1982) and Ph.D. (1986) degrees are in American studies from the University of Minnesota. He has worked in the areas of community development, community service, and community theory for the past fifteen years. Prior to joining Providence College in 1994, he was program director and then executive director of the University of Minnesota YMCA and director of Campus Compact's Project on Integrating Service with Academic Study. His interests are the history of community, community development, and how people make meaning out of experience.

Philip Nyden is professor of sociology and director of the Center for Urban Research and Learning at Loyola University in Chicago. In the late 1980s he helped to establish the Policy Research and Action Group in Chicago. Nyden has worked with the Leadership Council for Metropolitan Open Communities, the Organization of the NorthEast, the Evanston Human Relations Commission, and the Human Relations Foundation on a variety of projects aimed at promoting diverse neighborhoods, improving access to quality affordable housing, understanding the needs of youth and families, and enhancing business development in economically diverse communities. Books authored or coauthored include *Building Community: Social Research in Action* (1997), *Challenging Uneven Development: An Urban Agenda for the 1990s* (1991), and *Chicago: Race, Class, and the Response to Urban Decline* (1987). Nyden also recently coauthored *Black, White, and Shades of Brown,* a Leadership Council report on access to economic opportunity in Chicago's suburbs. He received his B.A. degree from Drew University (1972). His M.A. (1973) and Ph.D. (1979) degrees are in sociology from the University of Pennsylvania.

Terry Pickeral is executive director of the National Center for Learning and Citizenship, which provides leadership in service-learning, citizenship, and state and district policy. He leads several national service-learning and citizenship initiatives, including Learning In Deed, Every Student A Citizen, and Schools as Citizens. He coauthored and coedited several service-learning resource books for the Campus Compact National Center for Community Colleges and completed a Corporation for National and Community Service Fellowship. Pickeral received his M.A. degree (1977) in sociology from the University of British Columbia and his B.A. degree (1974) in sociology from the University of Hawaii.

Jennifer M. Pigza is a Ph.D. candidate in education policy and leadership at the University of Maryland–College Park, where she also works as a coordinator of community service programs in the office of Commuter Affairs and Community Service. She teaches courses in leadership and community service as well as a seminar for undergraduate teaching assistants for service-learning. In 1999–2000 she and Marie L. Troppe coordinated the University of Maryland's Engaged Campus project for Campus Compact. Pigza has been involved in leadership positions in the American College Personnel Association as a state division president and conference planning team member. Prior to her work in higher education, Pigza spent four years with the Jesuit Volunteer Corps: East. She received her M.Ed. degree (1996) in higher education and student affairs administration at the University of Vermont and her B.A. degree (1990) in English literature at Loyola College in Maryland.

Kenneth M. Reardon is an associate professor in city and regional planning at Cornell University. He currently serves as faculty coordinator for the College of Architecture, Art, and Planning's Rochester Research Action Project. Before coming to Cornell, he was associate professor in urban and regional planning at the University of Illinois–Urbana-Champaign, where he initiated the East St. Louis Action Research Project and directed it for nearly ten years. Reardon received the President's Award for Public Service from the American Institute of Certified Planners (AICP) in 2000 and the Ernest A. Lynton Award from the New England Research Center on Higher Education in 2001. He has published more than forty book chapters and journal articles on participatory planning and design, citizen empowerment, and community-university partnerships. He serves on the editorial board of the *Journal of Planning Literature* and the *AICP Casebook Series* and is a member of the national steering committee of the Planners Network. Reardon earned his B.A. degree in sociology from the University of Massachusetts–Amherst (1976), his M.A. degree in urban planning from Hunter College of the City University of New York (1982), and his Ph.D. degree in city and regional planning from Cornell University (1990).

Stacy Riemer is associate director of the Center for Public and Community Service and an adjunct instructor in the higher education program at Syracuse University. Currently a doctoral candidate in the higher education program at Syracuse, she has more than eight years of experience in higher education administration and teaching. Her experience includes program development in student services and activities, as well as service-learning. She has presented on community service as a component of leadership development, incorporating a service component into learning communities, reflection strategies as qualitative assessment, and learning communities for graduate students. Her current research is on the experiences of college student literacy tutors working in the public schools. Riemer's B.S. degree is from St. John Fisher College in management (1992), and her M.S. degree is from the University of Rochester in higher education (1995).

Janni Sorensen is a Ph.D. candidate in urban and regional planning at the University of Illinois at Urbana-Champaign. She has worked as senior graduate research assistant with the university's East St. Louis Project since 1998. She has taught the neighborhood planning workshop course at the University of Illinois. Her master's degree is in urban planning from Aalborg University, Denmark (1997). Her B.S. degree (1995) is also from Aalborg University.

Jan Torres is projects and budget director for Campus Compact and has been with Campus Compact since 1992. She was project director for the Campus Partners in Learning project, funded by the Carnegie Corporation, and also served as project director for $2.6 million in grants from the Corporation for National and Community Service. She was network director for the state compacts until 1998. Prior to coming to Campus Compact, Torres managed a three-year, $1.4 million federal grant that focused on building coalitions in the Hispanic community and providing intervention programs for at-risk Hispanic youth. She has an extensive community development background and is the author of several publications, including two editions of an award-winning resource manual on substance abuse and community resources and *Learning to Manage Federal Grants,* published by Campus Compact. She was the editor for *Establishing and Sustaining an Office of Community Service* and *Benchmarks for Campus/Community Partnerships,* also published by Campus Compact. She holds a B.S. degree (1964) in nutrition and diet therapy from Hunter College in New York.

Marie L. Troppe is coordinator of service-learning in the office of Commuter Affairs and Community Service at the University of Maryland–College Park. She consults with faculty on service-learning pedagogy and teaches a seminar for undergraduate teaching assistants in service-learning. Previously she served as project associate for Campus Compact's Project on Integrating Service with Academic Study and as assistant director of Georgetown University's Volunteer and Public Service Center. Her articles on service-learning have appeared in the *Journal of Business Ethics* and *Metropolitan Universities.* She coauthored with Sandra Enos the chapter "Service-Learning in the Curriculum," which appeared in *Service-Learning in Higher Education: Concepts and Practices* (Jacoby, 1996). Troppe is currently a Ph.D. student in English at the University of Maryland. She received her M.A. degree (1992) in English from Georgetown University and her B.A. degree (1988) in English literature from the Catholic University of America.

Shannon Huff Wilson is service-learning coordinator at Horizonte Instruction and Training Center, a nontraditional high school in Salt Lake City. She completed her B.S. degree (1997) in university studies (psychology of gifted women) at the University of Utah. She was a student project director for the Mayor's Youth Volunteer Council at the University of Utah's Bennion Community Service Center. Wilson received the Barbara Tanner Fellowship from the Bennion Center, which initiated her work at Horizonte Instruction and Training Center. With her support, Horizonte was named a national service-learning leader school by the Corporation for National and Community Service for 1999–2000. Wilson was involved with the leader school selection process for 2000–01.

Building
Partnerships for
Service-Learning

Chapter One

Fundamentals of Service-Learning Partnerships

Barbara Jacoby

High-quality service-learning that is beneficial to all parties involved must be built on a solid foundation of carefully developed partnerships. It has been said that "service-learning and partnerships are two sides of the same coin" (Bailis, 2000, p. 5). This chapter provides an overview of service-learning and its status in higher education today. It then outlines why service-learning must be based on a web of democratic and reciprocal partnerships. In addition, three frameworks that contain guidelines for the development and sustenance of strong partnerships for service-learning are offered.

Service-Learning Today

The Preface to *Service-Learning in Higher Education: Concepts and Practices* takes the stance that service-learning has "tremendous potential" to enable colleges and universities to meet their goals for student learning and development while making unique contributions to addressing community, national, and global needs (Jacoby, 1996, p. xvii). In the few years since the book was published, much has been accomplished to tap the vast potential of service-learning.

Regarding both the curriculum and the cocurriculum, we talk much more about service-learning with its underlying concepts of reflection and reciprocity than about the one-directional practices of volunteerism and community service. The number of students, institutions, and communities involved has grown dramatically, prompting John DiBiaggio, then president of Tufts University, to open his keynote address to the March 2001 national conference of the American Association of Higher Education by stating that "service-learning has taken off." We have more research about its effects, more models and principles to guide its practice, more support from national organizations, and more financial and other involvement of government and foundations. We are more certain of the powerful ways in which service-learning contributes to what has become an even clearer and sharper focus on the quality and coherence of the student learning experience and the achievement of desired learning outcomes. We have more purposefully integrated service-learning into academic courses and majors as well as into initiatives such as living-learning programs, course-based learning communities, new student orientation, leadership development, and multicultural education.

As more and more colleges and universities actively embrace the concept of "the engaged campus" and make civic education a priority, service-learning is increasingly cited as a driver of the civic engagement of higher education (Hollander, Saltmarsh, and Zlotkowski, 2001; Bringle, 2001). Peter Magrath defines engaged institutions as those that "work with their community as partners to discover new knowledge, promote learning, and apply it throughout their region" (London, 2002, p. 12). Service-learning can be a relatively low-risk way for institutions to begin partnering with communities and others to work together to identify shared concerns and to provide specific relief. Service-learning also enables institutional leaders to view civic engagement as more than traditional, narrowly defined outreach or public service. Democratic service-learning partnerships can lead institutions away from viewing engagement as "something carried out *on behalf of* the community instead of *in partnership with* the community" (London, 2000, p. 4). In many instances, service-learning partnerships have served as the catalyst for broader and deeper engagement and civic responsibility by colleges and universities.

Service-learning has encouraged colleges and universities of all types to reexamine and bolster their missions to prepare students to become civically engaged citizens. Both educators and the general public are concerned that studies reveal that, although youth involvement in community service has increased in recent years, their interest and participation in our democratic institutions have decreased dramatically (Cone, Cooper, and Hollander, 2001; Sax, Astin, Korn, and Mahoney, 1999). We know that service-learning can enhance students' critical thinking skills and that the combination of community service, academic knowledge, and reflection can help students develop an understanding of the root causes of social problems. Conceptualizing service-learning in terms of civic education enables educators to "make room in our practices and in our curriculum for conversations where students name for themselves what it is they are doing and its connections to community, citizenship, and democratic politics" (Morton and Battistoni, 1995, p. 18).

Service-learning has even led to reconsideration of the fundamental tenets of the faculty promotion and tenure process. Several persuasive arguments have been advanced that encourage institutions to include participatory action research as legitimate faculty scholarship (Boyer, 1990; Troppe, 1994; Nyden, this volume). Assessment of teaching is being expanded to include multiple methods of measuring achievement of learning outcomes, and definitions of faculty service are being broadened to include work that enhances the quality of life in surrounding communities (Morton, 1996).

In addition, higher education's leaders are talking about how colleges and universities can and should model democratic leadership and participation. According to Astin (1999): "If those in higher education want students to acquire the democratic virtues of honesty, tolerance, empathy, generosity, teamwork, cooperation, service, and social responsibility, then they must model these same qualities not only in individual professional conduct but also in their curriculum, teaching techniques, and institutional policies" (p. 37). Astin goes on to state that in order to model democratic behavior, "we have available a wonderfully simple and powerful tool: service learning" (p. 40).

In this book, as in the 1996 volume, service-learning is defined as follows: "Service-learning is a form of experiential education in which students engage in activities that address human and community needs together with structured opportunities intentionally designed to promote student learning and development. Reflection and reciprocity are key concepts of service-learning" (Jacoby, 1996,

p. 5). The hyphen in *service-learning* symbolizes the symbiotic relationship between service and learning (S. Migliore, personal communication, April 1995). The term *community* in the definition of service-learning refers to local neighborhoods, the state, the nation, and the global community. The human and community needs that service-learning addresses are those needs that are *defined by the community* (Jacoby, 1996).

As a form of experiential education, service-learning is based on the pedagogical principle that learning and development do not necessarily occur as a result of experience itself but as a result of reflection explicitly designed to foster learning and development (Jacoby, 1996). The other essential concept of service-learning is reciprocity: "All parties in service-learning are learners and help determine what is to be learned. Both the server and those served teach, and both learn" (Kendall, 1990, p. 22). Service-learning thus stands in contrast to the traditional, paternalistic, one-way approach to service, where one person or group has resources that they share with a person or group that they assume lacks resources. Reciprocity also eschews the traditional concept of volunteerism, which is based on the idea that a more competent person comes to the aid of a less competent person. In the old paradigm, volunteers often attempt to solve other people's problems before fully understanding the situation or its causes. Service-learning encourages students to do things *with* others rather than *for* them. Everyone should expect to change in the process (Karasik, 1993).

Service-Learning in Higher Education (Jacoby, 1996) notes that service-learning is a program, a philosophy, and a pedagogy. As a program, service-learning emphasizes the accomplishment of tasks to meet human and community needs in combination with "intentional learning goals and with conscious reflection and critical analysis" (Kendall, 1990, p. 20). Tasks in which participants engage are often direct services, such as tutoring, work in soup kitchens and homeless shelters, assistance in hospitals, environmental cleanups, and renovation and construction of homes and community facilities. Students involved in service-learning also do advocacy and policy-level work on such issues as housing, poverty, the environment, education, and human services. Service-learning programs have different goals and different approaches. Some may view service-learning as discipline-based. As such, programs may be designed to enable students to achieve greater depth in a particular field of knowledge and to apply their knowledge to address real community issues. In addition, they may seek to engage students in exploring the public purpose of their discipline. Other service-learning programs, both curricular and cocurricular, may have goals in the areas of leadership, ethical development, spiritual development, critical thinking, analytical or creative writing, citizenship or civic education, social justice, or increased understanding of human difference and commonality. Service and reflection activities are thus designed to focus on different learning outcomes (Jacoby, 1996).

Service-learning is a philosophy of "human growth and purpose, a social vision, an approach to community, and a way of knowing" (Kendall, 1990, p. 23). It is the element of reciprocity that elevates it to the level of philosophy, "an expression of values—service to others, community development and empowerment, reciprocal learning—which determines the purpose, nature and process of *social and educational exchange* between learners (students) and the people they serve" (Stanton, 1990, p. 67). Service-learning is a philosophy of reciprocity, which implies a concerted effort to move from charity to justice, from service to the elimination of need (Jacoby, 1996).

Service-learning is also a pedagogy that is grounded in experience as a basis for learning and on the centrality and intentionality of reflection designed to enable learning to occur. It is based on the work of researchers and theorists on learning, including John Dewey, Jean Piaget, Kurt Lewin, Donald Schön, and David Kolb, who believe that we learn through combinations of action and reflection. Kolb's (1984) model outlines the learning experience as a constantly revisited four-step cycle: concrete experience, reflection on the experience, synthesis and abstract conceptualization, and active experimentation that tests the concepts in new situations. Reflection stimulates the learner to integrate observations and implications with existing knowledge and to formulate concepts and questions to deepen the learner's understanding of the world and the root causes of the need for service (Jacoby, 1996). In this sense, service-learning as pedagogy relates to service-learning as philosophy.

Why *Partnerships* for Service-Learning?

Because service-learning educators and advocates are, by definition, reflective practitioners, there is a shared realization that there is much more to be done to fully realize the vast potential of service-learning and a shared commitment to do it. Service-learning is different from many educational endeavors in that it cannot happen within the confines of a classroom, a discipline, or even a campus (Jacoby, 1996). As a program, a philosophy, and a pedagogy, service-learning must be grounded in a network, or web, of authentic, democratic, reciprocal partnerships. By necessity, service-learning involves a range of partnerships within and across the institution; with other institutions, schools, community service providers, and community members; also with governments on all levels, national and regional associations, foundations; and, in some cases, with governmental and nongovernmental organizations around the world.

In the series of seminars on higher education and public life held between 1998 and 2001 by the Kettering Foundation, participants lamented the fact that service-learning programs are often conceived of as "benefits bestowed *on* the community *by* the university" (London, 2001, p. 10). As a result, it is not at all uncommon for local residents to view their area college or university as separate and distinct from the rest of the community and to regard academics with suspicion, even scorn. The way around this problem is "to dispense with the traditional *outreach* paradigm that seeks to provide services to the community, *on behalf of* the community. What is needed instead is an engagement model that looks for opportunities to partner *with* communities to meet collective needs. To be effective, the process must be reciprocal: it must serve the community while establishing learning opportunities and a framework for academic research on the part of the institution" (p. 13).

One can differentiate partnerships from other types of institutional relationships by asking the question, Who benefits? "If the answer is not 'all parties,' the arrangement is not a true partnership" (Grobe, 1990, p. 6). As Lloyd clarifies, "What binds people together most effectively are shared goals. Organizations also need to see a clear self-interest in collective action to sustain their interests over any length of time" (cited in Hollander and Hartley, 2000, p. 355). Truly reciprocal partnerships are also termed *collaborations,* defined as "a mutually beneficial and well defined relationship [that] includes a commitment to: a definition of mutual goals; a jointly developed structure and shared responsibility; mutual authority and accountability for success; and sharing not only of responsibilities but also of the rewards" (Mattessich and Monsey, 1992, p. 7). All individuals and institutions involved in partnerships, or collaborations, learn about themselves and others in the process and are affected, likely changed, in the process.

In early discussions with leaders in the service-learning field, questions arose regarding the appropriateness and accuracy of the use of *partnership* to describe relationships between universities and communities. In other words, is the power differential between institutions of higher education and communities too great to even permit a truly equal relationship to develop? It should be noted that some chapters in this book distinguish between partnerships and collaborations, while others use these terms interchangeably. Despite these issues, this book generally uses the term *partnership,* because it is as appropriate for its purpose as any other and is used as "coin of the realm" by the majority of service-learning practitioners and advocates.

Among many definitions, the working definition of partnership put forth by the Community-Campus Partnerships for Health is as good as any for the purposes of this book. A partnership is "a close mutual cooperation between parties having common interests, responsibilities, privileges and power" (Community-Campus Partnerships for Health, 2001). The Center for the Advancement of Collaborative Strategies in Health at the New York Academy of Medicine elaborates on this definition as follows: "A successful collaborative process enables a group of people and organizations to combine their complementary knowledge, skills, and resources so they can accomplish more together than they can on their own. We call this unique combining power 'partnership synergy'" (Center for the Advancement of Collaborative Strategies in Health, 2002, p. 2). The center does not view a partnership as simply an exchange of resources among participants. Rather, the partners work together to create something new and valuable, a whole that is greater than the sum of the parts. Partnership synergy enables a partnership to think and act in ways that surpass the capacities of the individual participants: "When a collaborative process achieves a high level of synergy, the partnership is able to think in new and better ways about how it can achieve its goals; carry out more comprehensive, integrated interventions; and strengthen its relationship with the broader community" (Center for the Advancement of Collaborative Strategies in Health, 2002, p.2).

Guidelines and Frameworks for Service-Learning Partnerships

It is quite clear that there can be no recipe or formula for successful, sustainable, democratic partnerships for service-learning. Because the work of service-learning is complex and multidimensional, it must be undergirded by a web of strong, interconnected partnerships. The complicated relationships that are internal to the potential partnering entities add yet another layer of complexity. Ramaley (2000a) explains: "Often partnerships are fragmented by competing interests within the community, or on campus, or both" (p. 3).

In addition, there are few models of sustained and truly reciprocal partnerships between colleges and communities. There are even fewer examples of multisector partnerships. We are still cautiously testing the waters, most often dipping our toes in gingerly. As such, I have resisted the temptation to select a single framework or set of principles as a standard for the service-learning partnerships described in this book. Likewise, I feel it unwise to select a single theoretical lens through which to conceptualize partnerships for service-learning. In this spirit, I encouraged the chapter authors to ground their work in the principles and theoretical perspectives that seemed most appropriate to them. It is significant, however, that there are similarities among the several lists of characteristics of high-quality partnerships that have emerged in the last five years. Three such lists, or frameworks, are offered below. It is also notable that there are differences in emphasis among them. The recently published frameworks are clearly inspired by sets of principles now widely regarded as classic, including Robert Sigmon's three principles (1979) and the *Principles of Good Practice for Combining Service and Learning,* commonly referred to as the "Wingspread principles" (Porter Honnet and Poulsen, 1989).

It is important to note that although they are intended to inspire cross-sector partnerships, all three sets of principles described in this chapter focus primarily on colleges and universities. Torres explains the reasons for this approach:

> Campuses are our primary constituency and would benefit most from the expertise gathered. Forming partnerships with communities is difficult terrain for colleges and universities to travel. Although many college and university mission statements include public service as a priority, there are a number of obstacles that compete with that mission, such as the emphasis on research, publishing, and numerous disciplinary requirements. Moreover, the cooperative, collaborative model is not native to the university. Campuses are more likely to think of themselves as curators of knowledge rather than as students with much to learn from their neighbors. In true partnerships, all participants will both teach, learn, exchange resources, and reap mutual benefits [2000, p. 3].

Campus Compact Benchmarks for Campus/Community Partnerships

In 1998, Campus Compact staff convened a meeting of practitioners with expertise in campus-community partnerships at the Johnson Foundation's Wingspread Conference Center in Racine, Wisconsin, to "examine the anatomy of campus/community collaborations" (Torres, 2000, p. 1). The benchmarks that resulted represent the eight essential features of *genuine democratic* partnerships identified at the Wingspread conference. These features are loosely grouped into three overlapping stages of partnership development (see Exhibit 1.1).

The Campus Compact benchmarks explicitly state the fundamental purpose of campus-community partnerships as "critical to sustaining the health of our democracy" (Torres, 2000, p. 2). Rather than focusing only on service-learning partnerships, the benchmarks address both broader and deeper issues: "to identify benchmarks for critical components of a genuine democratic partnership

Exhibit 1.1. Campus Compact Benchmarks
for Campus/Community Partnerships

STAGE I: DESIGNING THE PARTNERSHIP

Genuine democratic partnerships are:

Founded on a shared vision and clearly articulated values.

✓ Partnerships proceed from the idea that participants are members of a common community that they seek to improve for the sake of their own and each other's benefit. In collaborative conversation, partners develop a vision of how their immediate environment—the community in which they live and work—can be strengthened. Resources and skills are pooled and used to help the partnership realize its vision.

Genuine democratic partnerships are:

Beneficial to partnering institutions.

The work of a partnership holds tangible incentives for partners. It satisfies some of their unique self-interests as well as the shared interests of the group. Concrete benefits are an important piece of why institutions remain faithful to a partnership.

STAGE II: BUILDING COLLABORATIVE RELATIONSHIPS

Genuine democratic partnerships that build strong collaborative relationships are:

Composed of interpersonal relationships based on trust and mutual respect.

Strong relationships take time to build and energy to maintain, but partnerships cannot exist without them. Genuine democratic partnerships value the bonds that form between people, and acknowledge that the building of strong communities happens through networks of individual relationships that deepen with time and experiences shared. Strong collaborative relationships are intentional and are characterized by the following: trust and mutual respect; equal voice; shared responsibilities; risks and rewards; forums to support frequent and open communication; clear lines of accountability; shared vision; and mutual interest.

Genuine democratic partnerships that build strong collaborative relationships are:

✓ **Multidimensional: they involve the participation of multiple sectors that act in service of a complex problem.**

Multidimensional relationships are those formed between diverse institutions in order to address a neighborhood problem, or network of problems, that no one institution can resolve on its own. They necessitate the participation of multiple sectors of society and are inclusive. Partnering institutions actively seek out the unique assets of each partner; each partner provides a contribution that enables the partnership to have comprehensive problem-solving strategies. Partnering institutions should, however, be prepared for the culture clash that may occur when a multisector approach is used.

Genuine democratic partnerships that build strong collaborative relationships are:

Clearly organized and led with dynamism.

Partnerships function best when participants understand their individual responsibilities and how these relate to the work as a whole. A combination of clear lines of accountability and energetic leadership fuels a partnership with the clarity of purpose and the inspiration necessary to effect change.

STAGE III: SUSTAINING PARTNERSHIPS OVER TIME

Genuine democratic partnerships that will be sustained over time are:

Integrated into the mission and support systems of the partnering institutions.

The most effective way to sustain a partnership is to secure the support of influential neighborhood institutions, and to spread the work of the partnership throughout your own institution. Successful partnerships are aligned with their institutional missions, frequently linked to the academic curriculum and have full institutional support. The important questions to ask are: What does your institution value, and how does the work of the partnership relate to those values? To what degree should the work of a partnership link to the curriculum, and how might this link be made? Ideally, a partnership both reflects and influences the priorities of its sponsoring institution.

Genuine democratic partnerships that will be sustained over time are:

Sustained by a "partnering process" for communication, decision making, and the initiation of change.

A strong partnership process provides ample opportunity for the sharing of opinions and ideas. This solidifies the commitment of partners to collaborate over time, and facilitates their ability to change direction and redefine their work as the world around them changes. Three major elements form the basis of a strong partnership process: a method for revisiting the premises of the partnership; a structure that allows for evolution and growth; and practices that support frequent communication both within the partnership and in the immediate community.

Genuine democratic partnerships that will be sustained over time are:

Evaluated regularly with a focus on both methods and outcomes.

A partnership can be evaluated on several levels simultaneously—the impact on participating groups (particularly the community), the products of a partnership, and the processes by which work is accomplished. The results of evaluation can be used to guide future work and modify existing practices. Sometimes evaluation can provide a context to convene partners and stakeholders. In this way, the activity itself serves the important purpose of bringing participants together in analytical conversation.

Source: Torres, 2000, pp. 5–7. Used with permission.

with communities; to discuss ways to integrate these partnerships with the academic mission of the university; and to develop strategies for sustaining the partnerships" (Torres, 2000, p. 1). The intention of Campus Compact is clearly to "examine the anatomy of campus/ community collaborations" (Torres, 2000, p. 1). The benchmarks seek to harness the power of genuine democratic partnerships to transform the partnering institutions and to "invest the campus with a desire for community action" (Torres, 2000, p.2).

More specifically, Campus Compact aims to increase civic participation and to redefine both how cities and towns solve problems and how universities use the knowledge they generate and teach. There is a clear statement of the importance of the development of a shared vision of the future and of the partners as members of a shared community (Torres, 2000). Further, the benchmarks emphasize that partners from different sectors each possess "a different kind of access to . . . social systems" and that "collaboration among these diverse parties holds the potential to transform the systems that perpetuate inequity" (p. 16). The concept of equity is profound, reaching far beyond mere equality among service-learning partners.

Although campuses and communities are necessary members of these partnerships, the principles are general enough to inform collaborations with the private sector, government agencies, and others. And although service-learning is fundamental to the partnerships described by Campus Compact, the benchmarks are designed to "extend the reach of service-learning" toward "fully engaged campuses" (p. 2). Multisector partnerships, especially those that transform the partners in ways that increase their capacity to bring their resources to bear on mutually defined problems, have far more potential to address problems at higher levels and in more comprehensive ways.

The Campus Compact benchmarks are accompanied by follow-up questions and program examples. The *Benchmarks* publication stresses that it was designed to stimulate further thinking and discussion. In this vein, several chapters in this book refer to these principles and have even adapted them to apply more directly to specific kinds of service-learning partnerships, including those with students.

Community-Campus Partnerships for Health: Principles of Good Community-Campus Partnerships

Community-Campus Partnerships for Health (CCPH) is a non-profit organization whose mission is "to foster partnerships between communities and educational institutions that build on each other's strengths and develop their roles as change agents for improving health professions education, civic responsibility, and the overall health of communities" (Community-Campus Partnerships for Health, 2001). The organization promotes service-learning as a core component of health professions education and as a means of developing partnerships. In addition, CCPH has intentionally established "a governing model and membership that reflect the full range of partners in community-campus partnerships" (S. Seifer, personal communication, June 2002). The CCPH partnership principles in Exhibit 1.2 were discussed at its 1998 conference and approved by the board of directors in October 1998.

The CCPH principles are easily generalizable to partnerships outside the area of health. Like the Campus Compact benchmarks, they emphasize the *process* of partnership—the development of mutual trust, respect, genuine commitment, and continuous feedback—through open and accessible communication. CCPH goes beyond the sharing of resources by clearly stating the need to balance power among partners as well. The CCPH website provides the full text of articles that explain in detail how to put each of the nine principles into practice (Community-Campus Partnerships for Health, 2001).

Judith A. Ramaley's Lessons Learned from Existing Partnerships

In *Civic Responsibility and Higher Education* (Ehrlich, 2000), Judith A. Ramaley examines what it means for a university to embrace its civic responsibility by linking learning to community life and serving as a center of community life. Although the Campus Compact benchmarks seek to weave partnerships into the philosophy and practices of higher education by transforming research, teaching, and service, Ramaley goes even further. Focusing on the comprehensive university, she proposes replacing the traditional concepts of

Exhibit 1.2. Principles of
Good Community-Campus Partnerships

1. Partners have agreed upon mission, goals, and measurable outcomes for the partnership.

2. The relationship between partners is characterized by mutual trust, respect, genuineness, and commitment.

3. The partnership builds upon identified strengths and assets, but also addresses areas that need improvement.

4. The partnership balances power among partners and enables resources among partners to be shared.

5. There is clear, open, and accessible communication between partners, making it an on-going priority to listen to each need, develop a common language, and validate/clarify the meaning of terms.

6. Roles, norms, and processes for the partnership are established with the input and agreement of all partners.

7. There is feedback to, among, and from all stakeholders in the partnership, with the goal of continuously improving the partnership and its outcomes.

8. Partners share the credit for the partnership's accomplishments.

9. Partnerships take time to develop and evolve over time.

Source: Community-Campus Partnerships for Health, 2001. Used with permission.

research, teaching, and service with "the richer and more multi-dimensional terms discovery, learning, and engagement" (Ramaley, 2000b, p. 233).

By broadening the definition of legitimate scholarly work to *discovery,* which involves a research agenda created in partnership with community members outside of academe, faculty and students can engage in new avenues of discovery, sharing, and application of knowledge. As the emphasis shifts from faculty as teachers and transmitters of knowledge to the centrality of *learning* and the role of students as co-creators of knowledge, many possibilities of learning *in* and *with* the community open up. *Engagement* differs from the customary definitions of outreach and professional or public service in that it involves a shared agenda that is beneficial to both the institution and the community, rather than the usual one-way transfer of knowledge and resources from the university to the community (Ramaley, 2000b).

Ramaley goes on to state that "collaborations and long-term partnerships are especially appropriate as a means for addressing the reform of large-scale systems, such as education, health care, public safety, economic development, and job creation, corrections and social services or workforce development" (p. 240). She offers nine lessons that can be learned from partnerships already in place (see Exhibit 1.3).

Following these lessons, drawn heavily from Holland and Gelmon (1998) and Holland and Ramaley (1998), Ramaley elucidates how institutions can create a receptive environment for the development of meaningful partnerships and for the practice of discovery, learning, and engagement. Ramaley's lessons learned from partnerships affirm the Campus Compact benchmarks and add to them both philosophical and practical dimensions.

On the philosophical level, Ramaley emphasizes the necessity for the institution as a whole to commit itself to engagement by embracing the broader concepts of discovery, learning, and engagement. Practically, she cautions us that partnerships must be firmly grounded in the institution's mission and strengths and that leaders must thoughtfully consider institutional limitations before making partnership commitments. She openly recognizes that university partners have a role in assisting community organizations that would like to partner with them but lack the infrastructure to do so. For both university and community partners, she stresses the importance of developing and sustaining broad-based capacity to engage in shared work.

Some of the chapters that follow refer specifically to one or more of these three partnership frameworks. In other chapters these principles are implicit, or similar principles are stated in the authors' own terms. In yet others, including Chapters Two, Three, and Nine, the authors propose their own frameworks for developing reciprocal service-learning partnerships.

Conclusion

In order to reap the tremendous potential benefits of servic-learning for students, institutions of higher education, and communities,

Exhibit 1.3. Ramaley's Lessons Learned
from Existing Partnerships

1. Each partnership has unique elements shaped by the history, capacity, cultures, missions, expectations, and challenges faced by each participating group or organization. What must remain as a constant, however, is that any partnership must be based on the academic strengths and philosophy of the university. The other constant feature must be the fact that the needs and capacities of the community must define the approach that the university should take to forming a partnership.

2. An ideal partnership matches up the academic strengths and goals of the university with the assets and interests of the community.

3. There is no such thing as a universal "community." It takes time to understand what elements make up a particular community and how people experience membership in the community. It is not easy to define who can speak for the community just as the university itself is not monolithic. Often, partnerships are fragmented by competing interests in the community itself.

4. Unless the institution as a whole embraces the value and validity of engagement as legitimate scholarly work and provides both moral support and concrete resources to sustain it, engagement will remain individually defined and sporadic. Such limited interventions cannot influence larger systems on a scale necessary to address community issues.

5. It is important to take time to think about what the university actually can bring to a partnership. Universities with limited research capacity and few graduate programs will find it difficult to provide the kinds of applied research and technical assistance that many communities need. Sometimes it is possible to make an alliance with a research university to broker and focus the research interests of faculty and graduate students on local problems. If sufficient research capability is not available, it is best to consider engagement as primarily a function of the curriculum.

6. A good collaboration will continue to evolve as a result of mutual learning. To be successful, collaboration should be built on new patterns of information gathering, communication, and reflection that allow all parties to participate in decision-making and learning. This requires time and face-to-face interactions.

7. Some communities are being partnered to the point of exhaustion. It is often necessary to identify ways to help community organizations and smaller agencies create the capacity to be an effective partner.

8. The early rush of enthusiasm can be replaced by fatigue and burn out unless the collaboration begins early on to identify and recruit additional talent to the

project or the collaboration. This is true both within the university community, where a few dedicated faculty cannot be expected to carry the entire engagement and civic responsibility agenda, and within the broader community, where a small number of community leaders and volunteers cannot be expected to handle a sustained effort over time. Both the university and its partners need to find ways to involve a truly representative cross-section of the talent in the community.

9. Like any other important effort, community partnerships must be accompanied by a strong commitment to a "culture of evidence." It is important to keep a running assessment of how well the partnership is working from the point of view of all participants.

Source: Ramaley, 2000b, pp. 240–242. Reproduced with permission of Greenwood Publishing Group, Inc.

service-learning must be grounded in solid, authentic, and reciprocal partnerships. Although there is no step-by-step plan for initiating, building, and sustaining partnerships, several sets of guidelines are available to inform our work. Although mutually beneficial democratic partnerships between colleges and communities are fundamental, a wide range of other partnerships is also essential. The remaining chapters of this book examine service-learning partnerships on campus, among institutions, in urban and rural settings, and involving relationships across social sectors and around the world. Although stunning in their variety, these partnerships share the goals of enhancing learning and bringing human and other resources to bear on addressing society's most pressing problems and meeting its greatest needs.

References

Astin, A. W. "Promoting Leadership, Service, and Democracy: What Higher Education Can Do." In R. G. Bringle, R. Games, and E. A. Malloy (eds.), *Colleges and Universities as Citizens.* Needham Heights, Mass.: Allyn & Bacon, 1999.

Bailis, L. N. *Taking Service-Learning to the Next Level: Emerging Lessons from the National Community Development Program.* Springfield, Va.: National Society for Experiential Education, 2000.

Boyer, E. L. *Scholarship Reconsidered: Priorities of the Professoriate.* Princeton, N.J.: Carnegie Foundation for the Advancement of Teaching, 1990.

Bringle, R. "Civic Engagement: Relationships and Service Learning." Presentation at the American Association for Higher Education National Conference, Mar. 2001.

Center for the Advancement of Collaborative Strategies in Health. *Partnership Self-Assessment Tool.* [http://www.cacsh.org]. June 2002.

Community-Campus Partnerships for Health. "Principles of Good Community-Campus Partnerships." [http://futurehealth.ucsf.edu/ccph/principles.html]. Apr. 2001.

Cone, R., Cooper, D. D., and Hollander, E. L. "Voting and Beyond: Engaging Students in Our Representative Democracy." *About Campus,* 2001, *6*(1), 2–8.

Ehrlich, T. *Civic Responsibility and Higher Education.* Phoenix: Oryx, 2000.

Grobe, T. *Synthesis of Existing Knowledge and Practice in the Field of Educational Partnerships.* Waltham, Mass.: Brandeis University Center for Human Resources, Heller Graduate School, 1990.

Holland, B. A., and Gelmon, S. "The State of the 'Engaged Campus.'" *AAHE Bulletin,* 1998, *51*(2), 3–6.

Holland, B. A., and Ramaley, J. A. *What Partnership Models Work to Link Education and Community Building?* Portland, Oreg.: Joint Forum of the U.S. Department of Education and U.S. Department of Housing and Urban Development, 1998.

Hollander, E., and Hartley, M. "Civic Renewal in Higher Education." In T. Ehrlich, *Civic Responsibility and Higher Education.* Phoenix: Oryx, 2000.

Hollander, E., Saltmarsh, J., and Zlotkowski, E. "Indicators of Engagement." In L. A. Simon, M. Kenny, K. Brabeck, and R. M. Lerner (eds.), *Learning to Serve: Promoting Civil Society Through Service-Learning.* Norwell, Mass.: Kluwer, 2001.

Jacoby, B. "Preface: Service-Learning in Today's Higher Education." In B. Jacoby (ed.), *Service-Learning in Higher Education: Concepts and Practices.* San Francisco: Jossey-Bass, 1996.

Jacoby, B. (ed.). *Service-Learning in Higher Education: Concepts and Practices.* San Francisco: Jossey-Bass, 1996.

Karasik, J. "Not Only Bowls of Delicious Soup: Youth Service Today." In S. Sagawa and S. Halperin (eds.), *Visions of Service: The Future of the National and Community Service Act.* Washington, D.C.: National Women's Law Center and American Youth Policy Forum, 1993.

Kendall, J. C. "Combining Service and Learning: An Introduction." In J. C. Kendall (ed.), *Combining Service and Learning: A Resource Book for Community and Public Service.* Vol. 1. Raleigh, N.C.: National Society for Experiential Education, 1990.

Kolb, D. *Experiential Learning: Experience as the Source of Learning and Development.* Englewood Cliffs, N.J.: Prentice Hall, 1984.

London, S. *Seminar on Higher Education and Public Life.* Washington, D.C.: Kettering Foundation, 2000.

London, S. *Higher Education and Public Life: Restoring the Bond.* Dayton, Ohio: Kettering Foundation, 2001.

London, S. *The Civic Mission of Higher Education: From Outreach to Engagement.* Dayton, Ohio: Kettering Foundation, 2002.

Mattessich, P. W., and Monsey, B. R. *Collaboration: What Makes It Work.* St. Paul, Minn.: Wilder Foundation, 1992.

Morton, K. "Issues Related to Integrating Service-Learning into the Curriculum." In B. Jacoby (ed.), *Service-Learning in Higher Education: Concepts and Practices.* San Francisco: Jossey-Bass, 1996.

Morton, K., and Battistoni, R. "Service and Citizenship: Are They Connected?" *Wingspread Journal,* 1995, *17,* 17–19.

Porter Honnet, E., and Poulson, S. J. *Principles of Good Practice for Combining Service and Learning.* Racine, Wis.: Johnson Foundation, 1989.

Ramaley, J. "Embracing Civic Responsibility." *Campus Compact Reader,* 2000a, *1*(2), 1–5.

Ramaley, J. A. "The Perspective of a Comprehensive University." In T. Ehrlich (ed.), *Civic Responsibility and Higher Education.* Phoenix: Oryx, 2000b.

Sax, L. J., Astin, A. W., Korn, W. S., and Mahoney, K. M. *The American Freshman: National Norms for Fall 1999.* Los Angeles: Higher Education Research Institute, University of California–Los Angeles, 1999.

Sigmon, R. "Service-Learning: Three Principles." *Synergist,* 1979, *8*(1).

Stanton, T. "Service-Learning: Groping Toward a Definition." In J. C. Kendall (ed.), *Combining Service and Learning: A Resource Book for Community and Public Service.* Vol. 1. Raleigh, N.C.: National Society for Experiential Education, 1990.

Torres, J. (ed.). *Benchmarks for Campus/Community Partnerships.* Providence, R.I.: Campus Compact, 2000.

Troppe, M. *Participatory Action Research: Merging the Community and Scholarly Agendas.* Providence, R.I.: Campus Compact, 1994.

Chapter Two

Developing a Theory and Practice of Campus-Community Partnerships

Sandra Enos and Keith Morton

In this chapter, we argue that colleges and universities that are deeply committed to service-learning should enter into authentic, sustained partnerships with the communities in which they are located. The decision to enter into such a partnership is critical, calling into question the very identity of both the institution and the community. In an authentic partnership, the complex dynamics of the relationship mean that the partners face the continuing possibility of being transformed through their relationship with one another in large and small ways.

Our argument asks institutions of higher education to rethink the traditional campus-community equation. As cultural geographer Lakshman Yappa has pointed out, colleges and universities engaged in community work typically "view the community as the domain of the problem, and the college as the domain of the solution" (Yappa, 1999). In our view, campus and community partners must come to understand that they are part of the same community, with common problems, common interests, common resources, and a common capacity to shape one another in profound ways.

We begin this chapter by presenting our case for creating and sustaining campus-community partnerships. We propose a framework for partnerships that distinguishes between transactional and transformational relationships, together with a suggestion of a typology for understanding the differing levels of depth and complexity of partnerships. We then discuss some of the challenges to developing authentic partnerships and how to address them.

A Case for Creating and Sustaining Campus-Community Partnerships

It is useful to approach service-learning, we think, by recognizing that it emerged out of a crisis of community experienced in industrializing societies in the late nineteenth and early twentieth centuries. Broadly understood, this crisis has led to a continuing perception that the social fabric is unraveling and that the lived experience of individual persons has become more privatized, compartmentalized, and fragmented over time. John Dewey (1927), a public philosopher and educational theorist at work in the first half of the twentieth century, captured this sense of isolation and fragmentation in an apt metaphor in *The Public and Its Problems*: "The planets in a constellation would form a community if they were aware of the connections of the activities of each with those of the others and could use this knowledge to direct behavior" (p. 54). Community service initially emerged as one experimental response to that crisis in the work of Dewey (1927, 1938), Jane Addams (1899), and Paul Hanna (1936), among others. It was the growing concern that young people were coming into adulthood unaware of what connected them to the public, unaware of what connected their individual activities to a community, that drove the concept of what Hanna called "education as community improvement" (p. 41).

In the intervening seventy years, "education for community improvement" has become "community service" and "community service" has become "service-learning," (Sigmon and Ramsey, 1967; Morton and Saltmarsh, 1997). The informing animus has consistently been the expectation that youth and community participants will learn from their joint activities how their interests and actions are connected, how their separate interests and actions indirectly affect one another, and how to increase their capacity to use this knowledge for the betterment of their shared physical and social space. The community emerges more clearly as a partner as we identify, describe, think about, and seek to respond to the direct and indirect impacts institutions of higher education and communities have on one another. This, we argue, is a useful way of describing the underlying philosophical and strategic objectives that drive service-learning and, thus, campus-community partnerships.

If you ask community leaders in the cities, towns, and neighborhoods that surround a campus whether the institution is a good neighbor, you will most likely hear equivocal responses. Residents will likely complain about excess noise and other disruptive behaviors of the students living among them. Families with lower incomes might resent the fact that student renters drive up housing costs. The parents of small children might complain about the expansion of the campus into areas previously occupied by public parks. Local elected officials often accuse institutions of receiving overly generous tax breaks while placing significant demands on local public resources, including water, sewage, waste, and fire and police protection. The owner of a local high-tech firm might lament that graduates applying for jobs lack the necessary skills. Leaders of social service organizations might tell of their relationships with faculty members who disappeared when the research funds dried up. Community residents might wonder what the university's researchers found out about their community after asking so many questions and conducting surveys over the years. In all of these responses, the community describes the university as if it were "in" the community but not "of" it.

Community residents and leaders generally believe that such institutions direct their interests and resources to matters far beyond the local community. They note, for example, that institutional participation in "urban revitalization" is often a thin veneer for the "gentrification" of a neighborhood, displacing long-time residents rather than improving their lot. And they wonder why institutions are not more broadly and deeply engaged in enhancement of public education, assistance to immigrants settling in their shadows, or building healthy communities.

It can be hard for academic leaders to reconcile such criticism with the often considerable efforts their institution devotes to community outreach. These efforts may include credit-bearing and noncredit academic programs designed to meet community needs, extension services, faculty membership on community boards, public invitations to events, and support of student community service and service-learning.

The differing ways in which campus and community perceive their relationship goes to the heart of higher education's construction of itself, in Yappa's terms, as the "domain of the solution" and the community as "the domain of the problem" (1999). Walzer (1984) proffers that members of a community have a right to make claims on the goods and services of that community and that balancing these claims is called justice. A community is arguably under no obligation to share its resources with others outside it. When nonmembers make claims on those goods and services, a community's decision about whether to share them is a decision about charity, a sharing of its surplus. The essential question, then, is where one draws the boundaries of membership. The neighbors of colleges and universities, we believe, are asking for justice and receiving charity (Morton, 1997). That is, they perceive colleges and universities as being in, rather than apart from, their communities, even as the institutions view themselves as separate and distinct from the community. From the community perspective, campus and community are one domain, and this shared identity gives the community a right to influence the allocation of higher education's goods and resources, particularly those that directly affect their quality of life. Institutions must not enjoy the community's resources while holding back on their own.

Toward a Theory of Partnership Development

Much has been written of late proposing standards or benchmarks of good partnerships between higher education and the community (see Chapter One). To address the myriad issues and considerations that surface in campus-community partnerships, we offer a theoretical perspective as a lens through which to examine the developmental practice of relationship building. What we provide here is a way of examining partnerships as they move from transactional to transformative relationships. Adapting theories that have been used to examine leadership (Burns, 1978), we will show how partnerships have the ability not to just get things done but to transform individuals, organizations, institutions, and communities.

The differences between transactional and transformative relationships are shown in Exhibit 2.1. Transactional relationships are those that are instrumental, designed to complete a task with no greater plan or promise. The parties engage together because each has something the other finds useful. The relationship works within existing structures. No change is expected, and little disruption occurs in the normal work of the organization and its players. Individuals leave the transaction satisfied with the outcome but not much changed. Commitments are limited and, perhaps, project-based. On the other hand, transformative relationships proceed with less definition, with an openness to unanticipated developments, with a deeper and more sustained commitment. Individuals question or reflect deeply on their institutions and organizations and examine how they do business, how they define and understand problems. Here, there is an expectation that things may change, that the order may be disturbed, and that new relationships, identities, and values may emerge.

Using this framework, we suggest that most of our service-learning and community service efforts can be characterized as transactional. Our commitments are limited, and we work within existing frameworks. Partners bring needs to the table and engage in mutually rewarding exchanges, although some would suggest that students benefit more from service than do community agencies or clients (Gelmon, Holland, Seifer, Shinnamon, and Connors, 1998; Ferrari and Worrall, 2000). Our identities as members of institutions survive intact. For example, although our students have been involved in after-school programming in a nearby school, our interest in that community terminates with the end of the semester. We may not feel that we are members of that community, nor will that community claim us as a member. Our community service and service-learning projects may be well managed, we can track and document service hours, and we can guarantee agencies that students will appear semester after semester for assignments. This is not to say that these transactional relationships are not important, but we can expect that little or nothing will be changed by them over time.

Too often, then, we think of campus-community partnerships as linear, transactional relationships between or among represen-

Exhibit 2.1. Transactional and Transformative Relationships

Criteria	Transactional	Transformative
Basis of relationship	Exchange-based and utilitarian	Focus on ends beyond utilitarian
End goal	Satisfaction with exchange	Mutual increase in aspirations
Purpose	Satisfaction of immediate needs	Arouses needs to create larger meaning
Roles played by partners	Managers	Leaders
Support of existing institutional goals	Accepts institutional goals	Examines institutional goals
Boundaries	Works within systems to satisfy interests of partners	Transcends self-interests to create larger meaning
Partner identity	Maintains institutional identity	Changes group identity in larger definition of community
Scope of commitment	Limited time, resources, personnel to specific exchanges	Engages whole institutions in potentially unlimited exchanges

tatives of institutional interests. Community partners are interested in serving their clients and advocating for their cause; higher education institutions are interested in learning. From our experience, we know that campus-community partnerships have the potential to be far more. They can be dynamic, joint creations in which all the people involved create knowledge, transact power, mix personal and institutional interests, and make meaning. We also know from experience and observation that it is difficult to predict how partnerships will develop. When viewed as transformational relationships, however, this unpredictability is perceived as exciting, full of promise, and worthy of nurturing. In this sense, relationships have the potential and complexity of human beings.

A Preliminary Typology

With this framework in mind, we think it useful to advance a concept of partnership development, and so propose the following as a point of departure for further conversation about campus-community partnerships. We offer this concept tentatively, as the literature of service-learning has paid little explicit attention to the development of campus-community partnerships over time or to how the relationships of the partners change and why. Although this typology does represent our experience, we believe that it needs to be tested against the experience of many partnerships, described in more robust ways, and likely modified before it can be accepted as generally accurate or used for long-term planning.

Figure 2.1 indicates that campus-community partnerships can be sustained over time (the horizontal axis) and described by their complexity and integrity (the vertical axis). It suggests, too, that campus-community partnerships are not developmental in any linear way, but are perhaps better understood as accretions that are layered over time. In addition, it implies that the increasing depth and complexity of a partnership does not bring a halt to simpler, less complex service activities. Instead, this figure calls us to critically differentiate the types of service we are doing, to accurately project and assess their learning potential and outcomes, and to make deliberate choices as we move from transactional to transformational relationships, whether at the individual or institutional levels.

One-time events and projects, such as cleanups, painting, and fundraisers, are sometimes useful to community partners. In the short run, one-time events are typically a drain on an organization's resources, requiring more effort in planning and coordinating than is generated in return. On the other hand, they can also serve as a way of discovering potential for continuing to work together: identifying one another's strengths, weaknesses, opportunities, and threats; highlighting potential leaders; and learning how missions and interests align. Before embarking on one-time events, it is important to discuss with the community agency whether the objectives are only short-term or if the possibility exists to create momentum for other, more sustained, work. It is unusual for one-time events to have any transformative element. They require part-

Figure 2.1. A Framework for Development of Campus-Community Partnerships

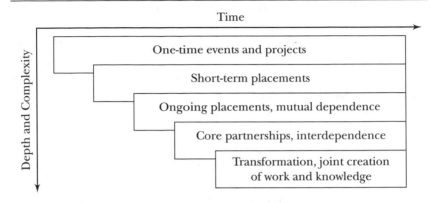

ners to reveal relatively little about themselves, the definition of the work to be done is seldom contested, and there is rarely any opportunity for the creation of new knowledge. Conflict and discord with "powerful others" is generally absent or minimized. As a result, the public dimensions of such events are typically celebratory and affirming of a common perspective rather than open, diverse, and contested. Accountability is circumscribed, and risks are kept to a minimum.

Service-learning programs based on *short-term placements,* typically of a semester's duration, generally provide direct labor to a community partner sustained over a long enough period to justify the efforts associated with training and supporting volunteers. In addition, this type of partnership is likely to generate simple problems for the partners to solve, such as what to do when a volunteer fails to show up or how to handle the transition of a supervisory staff person. Much can be learned from how these problems are handled. However, it is important to note that managing placements of relatively short duration puts significant stress on the resources of both campus and community partners. Preparing and training students, designing and facilitating reflection on experience, supporting them, and developing and assessing the results of placement require time and resources. A one-semester commitment is generally just long enough to make use of these resources worthwhile. Thus, the cost-benefit ratio of such relationships may enable the partners to sustain them, but it is unlikely that they will generate new resources or knowledge. Like one-time events, short-term placements make relatively few demands on the status quo of institutions. In this type of arrangement, faculty more often use the service experience to illustrate or affirm existing academic knowledge. Quite often, short-term placements position the faculty member and students as sympathetic but politically neutral observers of the public issues that affect the service site. Although there is some indication that students who serve at a site for two to five hours per week or for a total of thirty or more hours in a semester may reap educational benefits, such learning is not likely to be transformative (Eyler and Giles, 1999). At least the potential exists that the students' curiosity to inquire further will be stimulated (Dewey, 1938). Accountability is limited by time, formally concluded with the end of each semester.

Ongoing placements and *mutual dependence* describe what happens when short-term placements are sustained over time, so that the costs of maintaining the campus-community partnership decrease without loss of benefit to the parties involved. Dependable resource commitments are made by both sides, a depth of understanding of the missions and interests of all parties is established, and the continuity of partnership often leads to deepening personal relationships between the principals responsible for brokering the relationship. It is likely that partners will begin to gain some understanding of how their respective institutions function around issues as mundane as calendars or as complex as priority setting or funding. Expectations for accountability begin to increase incrementally. The partners contend with the ways in which their interests and their perceptions of the "situation" that led to the partnership are similar and different, setting the stage for mutual learning and the creation of a shared definition of the work they are doing. And it is in this type of partnership that the partners will likely begin to appreciate the powerful others with whom they each contend, the various constituencies they each serve, and the ethical and existential dilemmas with which each of them grapples. All of this creates the potential for significant learning, as the partners describe their common experiences to one another, discuss what their experience means, and arrive at provisional conclusions that allow them to strategize, plan next steps, and develop their capacity to carry out those steps.

Faculty, students, and community partners join together in learning about their relationship so that the situation is experienced and interpreted with sufficient complexity to be engaging in its particulars and also representative of broader issues or arguments. As these relationships progress over time, claims of academic expertise may be challenged by the collective experience of students or community partners. Academic neutrality may be a more difficult stance to maintain as the partners learn to empathize with one another. Transformation becomes a possible, if not sought-after, outcome as the partners begin to challenge their initial assumption that the community is the domain of the problem and the campus the domain of the solution, and to examine the possibility that they share a common domain. This is a critical stage in the development of a partnership, as the partners may also retreat from this new understanding, choose to remain within conventional definitions of their roles, and resist changing the institutions of which they are a part. For example, partners working together on low-income housing may begin with the belief that the core problem is poverty: the absence of resources in a category of persons known collectively as the poor. Over time, they may come to understand that it is not a problem of poverty at all but rather a problem of wealth. A focus on fund-raising and "sweat equity" as ways to build houses (transferring economic resources from the domain of the solution to the domain of the problem) may expand to the consideration of ways in which powerful institutions (including colleges and community-based organizations) gather, secure, and control access to economic resources. In another, perhaps more common, example, a tutoring program that is organized by a partnership between a college and a middle or high school to improve literacy among adolescents may initially define success as improved test scores, a drop in absenteeism, and improved rates of graduation. Gradually, it may expand its perspective to ask how many of these students are applying to and being accepted at the college, or how many of these students are offered and accept meaningful opportunities to stay in or return to their community, slowing the steady drain of talent created by "up and out" strategies.

Core partnerships extend and deepen the energy and synergy of ongoing placements. The partners are able to empathize and accurately represent one another's interests. Their interests are likely to extend to understanding the extensive context in which each of them operates, and interpersonal relationships are often deepened. Significant risks can be taken as institutional relationships are tested. The objective of this type of partnership is mutual learning. This is what Freire (1981) described as learning that enables "people [to] develop their power to perceive critically the way they exist in the world with which and in which they find themselves; [and] come to see the world not as a static reality but as a reality in process, in transformation" (p. 64). What distinguishes core partnerships is that this type of learning is one of the implicit or explicit objectives of the partnership.

As the partners come to believe that they share a common domain, that each contributes experience and knowledge, their relationship becomes based on *interdependence* rather than mutual dependence. The true test of their common learning is the capacity for action based on the learning. Knowledge is held to the test of whether it works in both campus and community arenas. Will the people who matter to our organizations believe and trust what we are telling them? Will they be willing to act on the knowledge generated? If not, how is it useful knowledge? What will compel them to action?

Transformative partnerships do not necessarily evolve naturally from any of the other types of partnerships. Rather, they are a matter of campus and community partners recognizing and inviting the possibility that their *joint work is likely to transform them both.* There is a mutual redefinition of the issues on which they are joining energy to work, an understanding that they are working out of a shared context and that they are interested in what transformation means for both individuals and institutions. Institutional power is engaged in their joint work, as a resource and as a challenge. At this level, institutional change is an explicit possibility, and as a result, the nature of the organizations emerges as a matter of significance.

We believe that truly transformative partnerships would not only transform individuals involved in that relationship but also extend their influence into other parts of the organizations and the community at large. For faculty members, we envision the development of expanded roles and the weakening of disciplinary boundaries as the campus confronts complex social issues that do not lend themselves to specialization. We see teaching transformed in a manner that moves from teacher-controlled content units to those enriched with problem-centered and student-focused learning. For students, college would no longer be a place where they were filled up with facts forgotten as soon as the blue books were handed in, but rather a series of rich, active learning opportunities— experiences in service, citizenship, knowledge construction, and community building. Community members would increasingly look to higher education to mobilize resources, create social capital, and engage in work currently referred to as civic renewal. Although some may suggest that this vision flies in the face of economic realities and market pressures, we suggest that it reflects significant changes already in progress on many campuses that are transforming the ways students learn, the ways campuses engage with communities, and the ways in which faculty do their work.

Challenges to Developing Campus-Community Partnerships

As the previous sections show, our theory and typology of campus-community partnerships are based on learning about and from relationships and acting upon what is learned to improve the relationships and the shared public world in which they exist. However, although service-learning is fundamentally about relationships, even the use of the terms *campus* and *community* creates a dichotomy that suggests isolation. In fact, the very nature of higher education presents significant challenges to the development of campus-community partnerships and to their evolution toward the depths and complexity of transformative relationships.

The Loosely Coupled Nature of Colleges and Universities

It has been argued that it is very possible, and indeed very likely, that some domains of the university may be involved in excellent partnerships with the community while other relationships are foundering or nonexistent (Singleton, Hirsch, and Burack, 1999).

This is not simply a management deficit, a lack of planning, or a result of limited vision. More often, it is the result of the "loosely coupled" nature of higher education. A loosely coupled organization is one in which units are relatively autonomous and not dependent upon other parts of the organization to accomplish their work. A failure or lack of performance in one unit does not mean that other units will suffer the same fate. Loosely coupled organizations, in fact, have the advantage of being very adaptable to their environments. Members of the organization may be connected to multiple and divergent sources of information, stimulation, and networks and can adapt programs and resources to changes in these disparate environments.

A disadvantage of this design is that there may be little communication and coordination among the units; a lack of common understanding about mission, direction, and goals; and competition for resources that does not address the key issues facing the organization. Loosely coupled organizations are difficult to transform or change deeply because separate units have maintained independence for so long and because there are multiple sources of leadership and vision (Weick, 1976; Orton and Weick, 1990).

This loosely coupled nature complicates partnering and engagement between and among campuses and communities. Some campuses that would not be characterized as highly engaged by any measure take pride in faculty deeply committed to community, yet do not reward them in any significant way. Community involvement is often considered an individual faculty member's personal interest or pet project. Although this work may be recognized, there are no plans to deepen or broaden it across campus. In other instances, programs, institutes, or centers engage with communities as the central feature of their work. While these units may be respected on campus, they also may face considerable competition from other units for funding and support. They may become isolated and fragmented as the balance of the campus considers this work secondary—"nice to do," perhaps, but not essential to the campus mission and not integral to faculty reward structures.

Individuals in higher education who are interested in significant partnerships with the community must become organizationally literate, which is to say that they must understand how their

institution works, how it makes decisions, how resources are allo- ✓
cated, what problems and issues are important to leaders, and what
opportunities exist for innovation and change. As noted above,
one advantage to the loosely coupled organizational form is that
it has the ability to respond quickly to issues that arise in the surrounding environment. A faculty member needs few resources or
approvals "from the top" when she first experiments with this pedagogy. A historian who sits on the board of a local arts organization
can mobilize the students in his seminar course to assist the agency
in developing an organizational history. Members of an academic
department can work on a service-learning project with a newly ap-
pointed commission studying race and police-community relations
without a mandate from the institution. Individuals who learn to
navigate loosely coupled institutions can enhance their capacity
for building rewarding partnerships by recognizing and using the
advantages of such organizations.

Risk and Trust

Service-learning partnerships exist along a continuum of risk and
benefit from what can be characterized as low-risk, lower benefit
to higher risk and higher benefit. Low-risk might be exemplified
by service work in soup kitchens that may teach students about
homelessness while also serving the hungry, but that fails to get at
the political and social issues that are the root causes of hunger or
potential solutions to the problem of homelessness. In the mid-
range, a service-learning program may begin working with a local
community development organization by participating in the
cleanup of a vacant lot and, over time, add the shared responsibility for a full home renovation, development of a community garden, and research on the social, political, and economic interests
that shape the choices of those served by the organization. At the
other end of the continuum are partnerships that have potentially
great benefit but pose higher risks, such as investigating local patterns of land use, home ownership, absentee landlords, and economic discrimination.

Without doubt, such partnerships entail considerable risks to
all parties involved. The creation of a new partnership, the en-
trance of a new partner, or an old partner taking on a new role can

shift the social and political ecology of the partners' respective interests, often with unintended consequences. For example, the university's involvement in land use, housing, and economic issues could lead to transformation that changes the institution's political stance regarding these issues in ways that may benefit the community but that may inadvertently lead to loss of political support for the university by state or local officials who oppose the direction of the transformation. On the other hand, there is the potential that disturbances in the existing social and political ecology could unfairly affect the community. If, for example, the partnership leads to increased dependency by the community rather than mutuality, the risks to the community may be greater than intended.

It is because of these risks to both parties that trust is required. In the context of campus-community partnerships, trust can be understood as a mutual understanding of the interests of the partners, together with some faith that the partners will stay with the relationship despite obstacles or difficulties that will surely arise. Nyden, Figert, Shibley, and Burrows (1997) emphasize that trust cannot be "signed off on" in a contract, that it emerges gradually as a working relationship develops: "Collaborative relationships are not created from the top down. They usually involve a number of steps that start with smaller, limited projects to test the waters and then build into larger projects" (p. 5). Torres (2000) agrees, stating that "partnerships may be seen as a series of interpersonal relationships built one on top of the other to create a bond between institutions" (p. 14).

Neutrality of Scholarship and Expertise

As described in Chapter Nine, the purpose of most faculty research is to contribute to the knowledge base of the faculty member's discipline. Using the terminology proposed by Boyer in *Scholarship Reconsidered* (1990), the "scholarship of discovery" is the most highly respected and rewarded by the academy as far as promotion and tenure and the likelihood of receiving research grants and prestigious awards. Traditional, discipline-based research is more likely to appear in refereed journals and in books from the most widely regarded top publishers. Such research is generally characterized as "pure" research rather than "applied" in the sense of the "scholarship of application" promoted by Boyer (1990). Traditionally, pure research is also likely to be more neutral than research designed to meet community needs.

Academic neutrality is easily maintained when scholars and academics are at political arms length from a thorny problem. Substantial challenges arise when faculty and others engaged on the scene face situations where conversations, discussions, and actions reveal issues that are public and political. In our classes, for example, our students have seen fourth graders summarily neglected during school hours and placed in classrooms where some supervision but very little teaching is occurring. We have had students working in court settings where individuals charged with child sexual abuse are seated in the same waiting areas as families and children victimized by such defendants. In cases like these, we can place the burden on students to examine these situations critically. We can also suggest ways for them to address the problem by taking some action, but our knowledge of these conditions poses a more difficult question. How should *we* be involved? As faculty members with an aim to educate, we could simply leave the situation as is and make a note to consider this when thinking about next semester's assignment. Or we could contact the program administrators, write a letter, or request a meeting. It is just these kinds of situations that make some colleges wary of community involvement. These instances become conflicted, as well, when as individual actors we are uncertain about, or in disagreement with, the stances of our institutions on controversial issues.

Expertise is easier to maintain when it is not challenged by application. Increasingly, advocates of service-learning, community-based research, and participatory action research are arguing for recognition, support, and reward of research that meets community needs and that results in shared production of knowledge. Here, investigators move from positions of experts to those of organizers and facilitators of research. Too often, higher education faculty and students reserve for themselves the authority to name an experience or situation and to determine what is or is not meaningful. That is, they get to tell the story about what happened without the community playing a lead, or even an active, role in the telling. In such cases, the campus "experts" determine how the community is to be interpreted and understood by defining the community's problems, the likely strategies for response, what resources exist, and the ways in which those resources will be allocated.

We believe that campus-community partnerships are about the democratic process of arriving at an agreed-upon description of a situation, a description in which both partners are actors and both are changed, dramatically or subtly, by their inclusion in the story. As a result, they challenge and transform traditional roles.

Many institutions are not comfortable renegotiating faculty roles to support campus-community partnerships. Similarly, faculty members deeply engaged in service-learning are likely to experience a changing self-definition, moving from a core identity of pedagogue to that of community member or citizen or servant. There may be false starts, confusion about objectives, battles over research protocols, conflicts over time frames, and other issues with which to contend. Academic researchers and teachers accustomed to maintaining center stage in their work open themselves to untold risks in subjecting their work and views to nonacademic community-based audiences.

Institutions can support faculty moving out of traditional roles and into community-focused work in a variety of ways related to faculty recruitment, development, and assessment (Bringle, Hatcher, and Games, 1997). Redefining the criteria that determine how funds and release time for research are allocated to include community-based research is a critical first step. Similarly, institutional recognition and awards processes can be broadened to showcase outstanding community work by faculty and students. However, the most important and most difficult means for institutions to support community-based research, as well as teaching and faculty service, are embedded in the promotion and tenure process. Changing or expanding the faculty reward system requires a fundamental shift in campus culture and so is, by definition, a difficult and incremental journey. It is encouraging that the American Association for Higher Education, the New England Resource Center for Higher Education, and other national organizations—including disciplinary associations—are addressing this challenge.

The Problems of Accountability

As a result of higher education's view of itself as the "expert," accountability in service-learning, together with what defines success, is all too often stated in terms of students and institutions. Consider this example. One of the authors of this chapter previously worked as executive director of a community organization whose programs included a buddy program for fourth- to sixth-grade students from an economically poor, urban school system. Over a four-year period, two directors built the program into what was considered a clearly successful model. It matched 140 college student volunteers with a like number of younger students, it had a retention rate of volunteers over three years of 98 percent, its student volunteer staff of ten was in demand by other youth-serving organizations in the area, and its reflection process was considered exemplary. However, at a year-end picnic, the mother of one of the children in the program approached the director and told her that she had some concerns. "I don't like it," she said, "that a school social worker selected my child for this program. It meant I couldn't say no without having her and the teachers think I'm a bad parent, and as a black, single mother who is out of work, they already think that about me. Don't get me wrong. My son likes his buddy. But the problem is that I have three children, and you have given one of them something the other two can't have. So my other two children think it's unfair and they fight all the time. It hurts our family. If you want to help, why can't you do something to help our family, rather than one child? Why didn't you ask me what I wanted?" (K. Johnstad, personal communication, May 1991).

Like all organizational forms, higher education seeks to place some boundaries around itself to minimize and control demands from the environment. Its self-proclaimed neutrality can, in this regard, be used to reserve its expertise and to define the scope of its accountability. In our arguments to engage with community, we suggest that the high walls between campus and community be broken down or at least that some doors be opened and partners be invited in. Accountability should be made a topic of broader public dialogue, including accountability for telling the story from the community's perspective. This "dialogical process," to borrow a phrase from Freire (1981, pp. 68–73), seems to us a fundamental dimension of accountability. This invitation should include ongoing assessment of the community's assets and issues, careful assessment of how the community benefits (or does not benefit) from the partnership, assessment of what the community can teach, evaluation of what can be offered and exchanged, and an agreement about what the partners are accountable for. We have discussed how faculty members of higher education institutions are typically accountable to professional disciplines and to a lesser degree to departments and programs. Accountability in the academy most often does not focus on the tangible and local impact of our work.

Even in service-learning, the research focus has been on assessing learning and to a lesser degree on institutional and organizational change. As difficult as these dimensions are to measure and evaluate, determining community impact and the quality of partnerships is even more elusive. The problem of accountability is thorny enough that it can drive faculty and students away from service-learning. For example, we have just achieved our semester-long goal of cleaning up a park and creating a garden. What are we accountable for here? If we publish an article about the experience, are we accountable to report our research back to the community? If the community requires additional assistance in maintaining the garden after students have completed the course, are we accountable for organizing follow-up work? Are we willing to expand our circles of accountability as partners? To what extent can this challenge traditional ways and means of measuring and evaluating the quality of our work?

The issue of accountability also calls particular attention to the networks of which the partners are a part and asks the partners to understand more deliberately the significance of those networks. A community partner might want, for example, to learn about the accreditation process that colleges and universities undergo, or how the promotion and tenure process works. Likewise, a campus partner might want to know who is on the board of a nonprofit organization or who are the official and unofficial neighborhood leaders. These networks can be viewed as forces that hold the partners accountable, influences that shape their perspective and potential. Such networks may be invaluable as we seek to broaden the scope of our work—from the faculty member's perspective to other colleagues or disciplines and from the community partner's perspective to other agencies or neighborhoods.

Conclusion

Service-learning has provided an important opportunity for colleges and universities to reimagine their roles and missions in communities. In some instances, this has happened "through the back door," almost by accident. We have made an argument for the value of campus-community partnerships grounded in what we believe to be a crisis of community on the part of higher education. As we have discussed, there are multiple challenges to extending and deepening our current practices. These challenges cannot be adequately addressed without considering profound changes in how colleges perceive themselves and the concept and practice of service-learning.

Our hope is that service-learning will not become something educational researchers document in a historical review published in 2030 as a passing fad, an innovative pedagogy, that disappeared as corporate influences remade the modern university into an efficient vehicle for delivering standardized education in a low-cost, but highly profitable, fashion. When we speak of campus-community partnerships and transformation, we mean significant changes in how universities understand the world. Disciplinary specialization is not well suited to dealing with the complex social problems we may encounter in partnerships. Is inner city poverty an economic problem, a sociological one, a psychological one, or, perhaps, a political one? For which academic department is the problem of failing schools the appropriate domain: education, public affairs, urban studies, government and politics, or business? The problem of disciplinary fragmentation surfaces quickly in the real world, and it is here that transformation becomes critical. Transformation promises a more holistic and coherent understanding of our common situations. This requires a more interdisciplinary view of the world than is customary in higher education. There is a danger that we may lose some of our core identities as political scientists or sociologists, for example, but there is also a potential that our disciplinary affiliations will be enriched by revitalizing our sense of why we chose our fields in the first place.

There is an important role for higher education in the global society, but the exact nature of that engagement is contested. Higher education's future and best self, we would argue, can be found by engaging community partners in mutually transformative work that allows us to reimagine, in ways both creative and practical, sustainable communities. Our choice of partners and our visions of what may be accomplished together create opportunities for us to become members of communities and of a world of which we would like to be part.

References

Addams, J. "The Subtle Problems of Charity." *Atlantic Monthly,* 1899, *83*(496), 163–178.

Boyer, E. L. *Scholarship Reconsidered: Priorities of the Professoriate.* Princeton, N.J.: Carnegie Foundation for the Advancement of Teaching, 1990.

Bringle, R. G., Hatcher, J. A., and Games, R. "Engaging and Supporting Faculty in Service-Learning." *Journal of Public Service and Outreach,* 1997, *2*(1), 43–51.

Burns, J. M. *Leadership.* New York: HarperCollins, 1978.

Dewey, J. *The Public and Its Problems.* Athens, Ohio: Swallow Press, 1927.

Dewey, J. *Experience and Education.* New York: MacMillan, 1938.

Eyler, J., and Giles, D. E., Jr. *Where's the Learning in Service-Learning?* San Francisco: Jossey-Bass, 1999.

Ferrari, J. R., and Worrall, L. "Assessments by Community Agencies: How "the Other Side" Sees Service-Learning." *Michigan Journal of Community Service Learning,* 2000, *7,* 35–40.

Freire, P. *Pedagogy of the Oppressed.* New York: Continuum, 1981.

Gelmon, S. B., Holland, B. A., Seiffer, S. D., Shinnamon, A., and Connors, K. "Community-University Partnerships for Mutual Learning." *Michigan Journal of Community Service Learning,* 1998, *5,* 97–106.

Hanna, P. R. *Youth Serves the Community.* Englewood Cliffs, N.J.: Appleton-Century-Crofts, 1936.

Morton, K. "Campus and Community at Providence College." *Expanding Boundaries: Building Civic Responsibility Within Higher Education,* 1997, *2,* 8–11.

Morton, K., and Saltmarsh, J. "Addams, Day, and Dewey: The Emergence of Community Service in American Culture." *Michigan Journal of Community Service Learning,* 1997, *4,* 137–149.

Nyden, P., Figert, A., Shibley, M., and Burrows, D. "University-Community Collaborative Research: Adding Chairs at the Research Table." In P. Nyden, A. Figert, M. Shibley, and D. Burrows (eds.), *Building Community: Social Science in Action.* Thousand Oaks, Calif.: Pine Forge Press, 1997.

Orton, J. D., and Weick, K. E. "Loosely Coupled Organizations: A Reconceptualization." *Academy of Management Review,* 1990, *15*(2), 203–223.

Sigmon, B., and Ramsey, W. *Manpower for Development: A Report of Student Internships in Resource Development, Economic Development and Legal Services Development.* Oak Ridge, Tenn.: Resource Development Office, Oak Ridge Associated Universities, Inc., Jan. 13, 1967.

Singleton, S., Hirsch, D., and Burack, C. "Organizational Structure for Community Engagement." In R. G. Bringle, R. Games, and E. A. Malloy (eds.), *Colleges and Universities as Citizens.* Needham Heights, Mass.: Allyn & Bacon, 1999.

Torres, J. *Benchmarks for Campus/Community Partnerships.* Providence, R.I.: Campus Compact, 2000.

Walzer, M. *Spheres of Justice: A Defense of Pluralism and Equality.* New York: Basic Books, 1984.

Weick, K. E. "Educational Organizations as Loosely Coupled Systems." *Administrative Science Quarterly,* 1976, *21*(1), 1–21.

Yappa, L. Comments made at the National Society for Experiential Education Pre-conference Workshop, "Service Learning and Social Justice," Oct. 20, 1999, San Diego.

Chapter Three

Assessment as a Means of Building Service-Learning Partnerships

Sherril B. Gelmon

This chapter addresses assessment as a critical component of building and sustaining service-learning partnerships. It begins with a discussion of the concepts of community and partnerships, as the context of assessment. It presents alternative approaches to assessing the process and impacts of partnerships. These approaches are then synthesized into a community-level assessment matrix. The chapter concludes with strategies for overcoming barriers to assessment of partnerships and a view toward the future.

Assessment offers a structured framework for self-appraisal, legitimizes inquiry, demands the collection and analysis of data, and provides the evidence for planning and decision making. It can contribute to improved student learning, program design processes, faculty performance, and community organization effectiveness. Faculty, students, community partners, and other institutional participants all come to partnerships with different concerns and expectations, thus demanding an intentional assessment strategy (Holland, 2001). In beginning any assessment, one should ask a series of key questions. The answers to these questions will frame the design of the assessment.

- What is the aim of the assessment?
- Who wants or needs the assessment information?

- What resources are available to support the assessment?
- Who will conduct and be involved in the assessment?
- What will we measure?
- How will we gather the evidence to demonstrate what we want to know?
- What are the common themes and concerns that can be anticipated?
- How can we ensure that results are used in ways that promote improvement?

Further detail on the use of these questions to frame assessment design may be found in Gelmon and others (2001).

The Assessment Context: Defining Community and Partnerships

Effective and sustainable service-learning depends upon a number of mutually beneficial partnerships, at the heart of which are partnerships between campus and community (Holland and Gelmon, 1998). Until the mid-1990s, most assessments of service-learning focused almost exclusively on assessment of impact on students. It has become increasingly clear that it is essential to assess "community" as another distinct constituency (Driscoll, Holland, Gelmon, and Kerrigan, 1996). But how does one define community? There is no one community, and we have learned that faculty and students have a wide range of perceptions of who the community is (Gelmon and others, 2001). Developing an understanding of what "community" means to students, faculty, and the institution, let alone the community partners, is therefore essential.

One of the challenges faced by universities when working with communities is that there is often a chasm between the (unrealized) expectations and (mis)understandings of the community partners and the services and resources the university can provide (Wealthall, Graham, and Turner, 1998). The university must pay special attention to clarifying expectations and abilities. It is critical that students and faculty work closely with community liaisons to develop genuine understandings of one another's assets and needs. Inevitably, community need is far greater than the capacity of the campus service-learning effort to respond (Gelmon and others, 1998). The assessment challenge lies in determining what is reasonable to expect and accomplish within the service-learning activity, to what extent expectations have been met, and what factors have been barriers and facilitators of the accomplishments of service-learning.

As is the case with the term *community*, one must also have a clear idea of what is meant by the term *partnerships* in order to assess them. The definition will have implications for the design and content of the assessment. Community-university partnerships are "organic, complex and interdependent systems" (Sigmon, 1996). They are subject to frequent evolution and change as a result of changes in clients or personnel; increasing, decreasing, or reallocated resources; or environmental circumstances. It is useful to view partnerships from a systems perspective, recognizing that a change affecting any partner is likely to have an impact on multiple aspects of the partnership (Gelmon, 1997). Service-learning partnerships not only comprise educational institutions and community organizations but involve the many constituents of these organizations—students, clients, faculty, service providers, administrators, formal and informal community leaders, and others. As a result, assessment must include the partnership relationship itself, as well its products and processes (Gelmon and others, 2001).

The formation of community-university partnerships enables the university to realize its goals with respect to community-based teaching and learning, and enables the community organization to access university resources and expertise in support of its activities. An alternative approach to conceptualizing partnerships is currently being developed and tested through an eight-university demonstration program in South Africa funded in large part by the Ford Foundation. In the Community-Higher Education-Service Partnerships program (CHESP), the partnership is viewed as the unit of transformation and consists of a *three-way interaction* among historically disadvantaged communities, higher education institutions, and service providers including nonprofit organizations and government agencies. The CHESP program (see Figure 3.1) is based on a conceptual map using a Venn diagram of the three interacting domains, which yields four "interface" zones of potential partnership: between the community and higher education, between higher education and service providers, between service providers and the community, and in the central zone where the three circles overlap (Lazarus, 2001). It is this fourth zone where the three sectors interact, work together, and collectively accomplish their goals that represents CHESP's unique conceptualization of the term *partnership*.

This model is appealing in that it gives explicit voice to the community and engages the community as an equal partner in the planning, implementation, and delivery of community-based academic experiences for students. Our model in the United States often involves faculty selecting a community-based service provider as a partner and relying upon the partner to ensure that there is appropriate representation of the target community. Frequently, however, this results in a potentially paternalistic approach, in which the service provider identifies selected token community representatives to participate in planning but the community at large is not necessarily actively involved in the identification of needs and assets or in priority setting for the areas of emphasis for the academic work. Despite good intentions, we often leave the "true" community out of our work in community-based learning.

In contrast, the CHESP approach requires that any academic community-based work begin with a comprehensive community situation analysis that fully involves representatives from all three sectors. It avoids the common pitfall of viewing the community as

Figure 3.1. The CHESP Domains

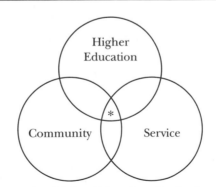

* = Community–Higher Education–Service Partnership

Source: Lazarus (2001a)

a single, monolithic entity. A matching of community needs with potential academic learning experiences is then conducted, and triads consisting of a representative from each of the three constituencies work together to develop the academic experience in the context of a course.

Assessment of these partnerships is now under way and emphasizes learning about process and progress, as well as outcomes (Gelmon and Lazarus, 2001). This emphasis on process and progress is particularly important because true community impact may not be demonstrable for a long period of time. In addition to community impact, the CHESP assessment seeks to generate evidence for use in facilitating program development and influencing institutional and national higher education policy.

Assessing the Process and Impact of Partnerships

A partnership is not only an entity; it is also a process. A process that supports collaboration, provides a basis for mutual participation of the partners in defining partnership objectives, and documents results is essential for successful partnerships (Messer, 1996). To ensure that partnerships are effective, assessors should seek evidence of the procedures in place to support and validate all aspects of the partnership process. Process components to be assessed might include definition of partnership goals, activities, and learning opportunities; delineation of university and community organization responsibilities; roles of key individuals for each academic and community partner; and mechanisms to report progress and to use past experience to improve existing and new partnerships. Experience in service-learning partnerships clearly points to the importance of the processes of creating, building, and sustaining relationships. Assessment of impact—what is transformed, strengthened, and accomplished as a result of the partnership—is also crucial. What difference do partnerships make, and to whom? What specifically does *impact* mean? It is essential to be clear that impact does not only equate with product, or even necessarily with outcome if the latter is defined as a single tangible end product. Rather, impact can be viewed as a process outcome, as well as a summative outcome. Thus assessment of impact must take into account not only the final product but also the work conducted, insights gained, and intermediate outcomes identified throughout the process that leads to a final impact. In the case of partnerships for service-learning, assessment should be designed to help the partners understand the impacts on a variety of constituencies, including students, faculty, community agencies, community members, and higher education institutions (Driscoll, Holland, Gelmon, and Kerrigan, 1996). Impact can be assessed both from the perspective of an individual constituency and through triangulation of multiple perspectives.

The Fact-Finding Approach to Assessing Process

A fact-finding approach to assessment of the partnership process that focuses on the level of collaboration in the partnership has been proposed by Bergstrom (1996). They present a matrix that defines five levels of relationships: networking, cooperation or alliance, coordination or partnership, coalition, and collaboration. Each level is then characterized in terms of process factors that have the potential to be useful for universities and their community partners in exploring and defining the specific components necessary to build effective working relationships.

- *Understanding the community.* Provides the foundation for partnerships by identifying vision; key individuals; sources of power; assets; audiences; and potential challenges.
- *Community development.* Refers to the process of mobilizing communities to address important issues and build upon their strengths. Involves communication, mission, and goals definition; creation of teams; mobilization of resources; and development of trust.
- *Leadership.* Facilitates communication, team building, and development of partnership strength; ensures that appropriate members from each partner organization participate in the collaboration.
- *Communication.* Demands open interaction using language that enables all participants to understand partnership processes and activities; formal and informal communication channels are necessary.
- *Research and evaluation.* Enable participants to know if they are successful or to understand what occurred to get in the way of

that success; efforts can focus on structure, process, or outcomes.

• *Sustainability.* Requires sufficient commitments, resources, membership, and accepted modes of practice to enable planning and activity; partnerships identify emerging trends and issues and develop strategies for responding to them (Bergstrom, 1996).

Together, these factors offer a framework for understanding the process of collaboration and for assessing the level of partnership. The evidence of each of the process factors will vary depending on the level of collaboration, as will the way partnerships at the various levels operate in terms of each of the factors.

A similar and readily accessible set of tools for understanding the process of partnerships is offered by Fawcett and others (2000). This framework takes into account the various steps involved in the partnership process and concentrates the assessment on the component parts of each of the steps. Fawcett and his associates have designed "The Community Toolbox," a web-based resource for building healthier communities that is built upon a competency framework that addresses the skills and activities necessary in effective partnerships (Fawcett and others, 2000). This model can be used to build an approach for focused assessment of specific actions or processes or for a broad-based assessment of the partnership process. "The Community Toolbox" can be accessed at [http://ctb.ukans.edu].

A Performance Improvement Framework

Assessment of community-university partnerships can also be viewed from the perspective of performance. As such, assessment can be a strategy for improvement and can provide the evidence that will serve as the basis for future program planning and enhancements (Gelmon, 2000). It can also be used for the purpose of internal review, external assessment, professional or institutional accreditation, or demonstration of accomplishment of project outcomes.

In thinking of assessment as an improvement effort, one can focus on such areas as:

- *Baseline information.* Description of the partners and the partnership, governance policies, partnership activities.
- *Significance of the partnership.* Extent to which the partnership addresses areas of importance and consequence as identified by university and community organization partners; extent to which participants in the partnership—faculty, students, community partners, academic administrators, community stakeholders—participate in the planning, activities, and assessment of the partnership.
- *Resources for supporting partnership activities.* How resources, including human, fiscal, and in-kind, are identified and provided; scope and extent of resources; additional university support; how skills and knowledge of community members are involved in the partnership.
- *Scholarship.* Extent to which the partnership enriches practice and disciplinary knowledge; how students are exposed to knowledge that resides in the community and the academy; extent to which community partners participate in academic programs connected with the partnership.
- *Results achieved.* Extent to which partners' expectations are met by the partnership activities; participation of partners in the assessment of student performance, of project outcomes, and of partnership effectiveness.
- *Anticipated benefits, products, results.* Ongoing value of the partnership to the community partners; how all partners use the results over time; opportunities for continued collaborative teaching, research, and service; how students apply knowledge and skills acquired or enhanced through partnership activities to their personal, social, and professional lives beyond their immediate involvement (Gelmon, 1997).

This approach emphasizes the integration of the various activities that take place in and around community-university partnerships and offers a framework for creating a comprehensive strategy for performance improvement. The identification of opportunities for improvement in any combination of the six points identified above can serve as the basis for making improvements to strengthen partnerships.

A Multiconstituency Approach

Over the past seven years, a multiconstituency approach to assessment has been developed, initially for use in the assessment of service-learning and now applied more broadly to a range of community-based learning. This approach began at Portland State University (PSU) as part of an effort to assess the impact of service-learning on students, faculty, the institution, and the community (Driscoll, Holland, Gelmon, and Kerrigan, 1996). The model was greatly expanded and revised for the assessment of the impact of service-learning in health professions education for the Health Professions Schools in Service to the Nation (HPSISN) program, a national service-learning demonstration program (Gelmon, Holland, and Shinnamon, 1998). This evaluation added the component of community partnerships as a fifth area of focus for assessment. In both the PSU and HPSISN cases, the goal of the assessment was to explore the implementation of service-learning and its differential impact on various constituencies, then to identify lessons learned for future service-learning efforts.

Subsequently, the model has been applied in other assessments of the impact of learning in the community. These include projects on community-based health improvement by interdisciplinary teams of health professions students (Gelmon, White, Carlson, and Norman, 2000); cross-sectoral community development to build collaborations addressing specific community health problems (Gelmon and others, 1998); a new master's in public administration degree with a concentration in tribal administration, delivered via distance-learning technology (Holland, 2000); and small, private colleges enhancing civic engagement programs with attention to institutional change, partnership characteristics, and impacts on community and students (Holland, 2001).

In each of these applications, a key issue has been to account for multiple voices in assessing impact on a particular population. For example, if one wishes to understand the impact of a service-learning experience on students, it is essential to seek the students' voices, but also to invite faculty perspectives on the students' learning, community agency perspectives on student performance and behaviors, and institutional perspectives on how students are supported and encouraged in their community experiences. This approach enables one to develop a sort of 360-degree view of service-learning and to better understand each perspective because of the additional insights gained through multiple voices.

A Community-Level Assessment Matrix

Several frameworks and methodologies have been used to assess service-learning partnerships from the perspective of higher education institutions (Furco, 2000; Holland, 1997; Bringle and Hatcher, 1996; Pigza and Troppe, this volume). Factors common to most of these models include relevance of service-learning to institutional mission; faculty support for, and involvement in, service-learning; level of student participation; number and quality of community partnerships; and extent of funding and other forms of institutional support. Although these approaches serve the purpose of institutional self-assessment well, they clearly and intentionally focus on colleges and universities rather than on partnerships. As a result, they are the subject of Chapter Six rather than this chapter.

Assessment of the multiple impacts of service-learning on students and the processes that engender them increased substantially in the 1990s. Several national studies addressed the impact of service-learning on students (Eyler and Giles, 1999; Gray and others, 1999). Dozens of smaller-scale studies were also conducted and published (Eyler, Giles, and Gray, 1999).

Despite the proliferation of service-learning assessment models and reports regarding institutions and students, there is widespread agreement among service-learning practitioners and advocates that there remains a dearth of assessment of community-university partnerships and of community impacts (Cruz and Giles, 2000). As a result, this chapter offers a synthesis of the assessment approaches presented earlier into a conceptual framework that forms the foundation for assessment of community-university partnerships *at the community level*. The components of such a framework will, by necessity, be driven by the goals and contexts of individual situations. Each project and partnership will dictate specific variables as the focus for assessment. In order to illustrate how an assessment team might take these various frameworks and develop its own approach to assessment, an example of an assessment matrix for understanding impact on the community is presented in Exhibit 3.1. The concepts, or variables, are presented in two sections: those most applicable to the community partner organization and those related to the community-university partnership. A more detailed description of this matrix may be found elsewhere (Gelmon and others, 2001), but an overview of the core concepts is presented here.

- *Capacity to fulfill organizational mission.* How does involvement in the service-learning partnership affect the organization's capacity to fulfill its mission? Participation may affect the types and frequency of services offered and the number of clients served. The number of students who can be accommodated by the organization might also change as the organization develops internal capacity to work with, and integrate students into, daily work and routines. Agencies that rely primarily on volunteers are able to increase their organizational capacity significantly through service-learning partnerships. The organization may also gain access to assets (its own, its clients, or the university's) that affect its capacity or program strategies.
- *Economic benefits.* Does the participation of faculty and students in the service-learning interaction help the organization to derive economic benefits in terms of human, fiscal, information, or physical resources? Sometimes organizations identify new staff from among the student participants and thus save the time and expense of a search process. The collaboration may also facilitate identification of new funding opportunities for which the community agency may apply, with or without the participation of the university. Another potential benefit is the timely or advanced completion of projects with the addition of new expertise that the organization might not normally have readily available, such as graphic design, computer training, or development of marketing materials. Such benefits are often key motivators for community organizations to partner with academic institutions.
- *Social benefits.* What new connections or networks with individuals or other community organizations are identified through the partnership? These may occur, for example, if the partnership brings together multiple community partners who had

not collaborated before. These connections can lead to future collaboration to address issues of mutual concern without the involvement of university partners.

- *Nature of community-university partnership.* What is the nature of the partnership? How is it established, organized, and managed? This may be illustrated by soliciting the partners' perspectives on the kinds of activities conducted and of the barriers and facilitators to both establishing the partnership and engaging in these activities. Important insights about mutual respect and common goals may result.

- *Nature of community-university interaction.* What are the nature and extent of the interactions between the partners? How do these take place? In addition to students' service activities at the community agency, other interactions can include campus representatives' visits to the organization to engage in service, attend community group advisory meetings, or participate in community activities. Interactions might also occur when community partners go to the campus to participate in classroom-based reflection sessions or program planning activities. In addition, partnership interactions might also focus on very specific work to support the community organization, such as web design, multimedia presentation development, or brochure production. Communication is another essential element to be examined in terms of methods, patterns, and partners' levels of awareness about one another's activities.

- *Satisfaction with partnership.* What are the perceptions of the partners regarding mutuality of effort and reciprocity in activity? What is the level of responsiveness to concerns? Satisfaction by both parties is essential to the development, implementation, and maintenance of a partnership. The assessment of this concept requires the creation of a safe environment in which partners can offer praise as well as express concerns without fear of reprisal. Cultural norms regarding expressions of satisfaction must be taken into account when attempting to collect data.

- *Sustainability of partnership.* What key events have created barriers to collaboration or accelerated collaborative efforts? Identification of these events can provide useful insights into the strengths and challenges of the partnership. Significant effort

Exhibit 3.1. A Community-Level Assessment Matrix

What do we want to know? (Concepts)	How will we know it? (Indicators)	How will we measure it? (Methods)	Who or what will provide the data? (Sources)
Variables about community partner organization			
Capacity to fulfill organizational mission	Types of services provided Number of clients served Number of students involved Variety of activities offered Insights into assets and needs	Survey Interview Focus groups Documentation review Critical-incident review	Community partner Students Faculty Advisory committees Governing board
Economic benefits	Identification of new staff Impact on resource utilization through services provided by faculty/students Identification of funding opportunities	Interview Focus groups Documentation review	Community partner Students Faculty Governing board
Social benefits	New connections or networks Number of volunteers Impact on community issues	Interview Focus groups Documentation review	Community partner Students Faculty Governing board

Variables about community-university partnership

Nature of community-university partnership	Creation of partnerships Kinds of activities conducted Barriers/facilitators	Interview Critical-incident review Documentation review	Community partner Faculty Governing board
Nature of community-university interaction	Involvement of partners in campus activities Involvement of campus representatives in community activities Communication patterns Community awareness of university programs and activities University awareness of community programs and activities	Interview Focus groups Documentation review	Community partner Faculty Students Governing board Advisory committees
Satisfaction with partnership	Perception of mutuality and reciprocity Responsiveness to concerns Willingness to provide feedback	Interview Survey Focus groups	Community partner Faculty Advisory committees
Sustainability of partnership	Duration Evolution	Interview Survey Critical-incident review	Community partner Faculty Governing board

Source: Gelmon and others, 2001, p. 92. Used with permission.

is invested in creating partnerships; if they are successful, the partners usually desire to sustain them. Sustainability can be understood through gaining insights into the duration of partnerships and processes related to their evolution. It is essential to examine the partners' intentions for sustaining the relationship and to investigate the time invested in the partnership in relation to its value to the partners (Gelmon and others, 2001).

The assessment methods listed in column 3 of the matrix in Exhibit 3.1 are the methods for measurement or observation that are used most often in service-learning assessments. One can think of these methods as falling into one of three categories: interactive methods, in which an evaluator interacts with individual respondents through interviews or with groups of respondents through focused discussions (focus groups); independent responses, to a predefined set of questions in a survey or through a more reflective, critical-incident review highlighting key events in a process; and documentation, which includes review of records, reports, minutes, policies, and similar existing documents. Details on assessment design, administration, and analysis of data collected can be found in Gelmon and Connell (2001) and Gelmon and others (2001).

Individuals designing and conducting the assessment must be cautious to avoid criteria that might be interpreted as a performance review of the community organization. Such a review must not be the focus of assessment of service-learning partnerships, because it could easily be viewed as threatening or intrusive by the community partner. Thus, the assessment should focus explicitly on the impacts on the partner organization that result from participation in the service-learning activities.

As this chapter is being written, a framework is being developed and tested to assess the CHESP program in South Africa that is described on pages 44 to 46. In framing the assessment of this program, one of the research questions focuses on partnerships and asks, "What are the key characteristics of successful community-higher education-service partnerships and what factors may promote or prohibit these?" (Gelmon and Lazarus, 2001). The key concepts and indicators that were proposed as a framework for exploring this question, outlined in Exhibit 3.2, are slightly different from those in Exhibit 3.1.

This approach incorporates the three perspectives integral to the CHESP partnership model (Figure 3.1) and places the emphasis on key concepts that cross all three sectors participating in the partnerships. Measurement methods and sources of data will be added to produce a more complete guide for assessment implementation; however, what is valuable to note here are the similarities to the "two-way partnership" matrix in Exhibit 3.1 (such as attention to benefits and to sustainability), and the differences, such as the CHESP emphasis on the scholarship of engagement. It is hoped that the insights gained through the CHESP assessment will advance our knowledge about the conceptualization of partnerships and also about methods and strategies for partnership assessment.

Exhibit 3.2. The CHESP Assessment Framework

What do we want to know? (Concepts)	How will we know it? (Examples of Indicators)
Benefits of partnerships	Community perspective Higher education perspective Service sector perspective
Participation and collaboration	Planning Decision making Implementation Management
Communication	Within individual partnerships Between partnerships
Sustainability	Organizational structures Resource allocation
Scholarship of engagement	Discovery Integration Application Teaching and learning

Strategies for Successful Partnership Assessment

In order to effectively use assessment as one of the building blocks of service-learning partnerships, the assessment team should pay close attention to several strategies that can help to ensure success. These include involving partners in assessment, overcoming common barriers to assessment, and sharing assessment results.

Involving Partners in Assessment

A key issue in engaging community partners in assessment is to be respectful of their time, obligations, and resources. Students can be required to spend substantial time writing a reflective journal, but one cannot necessarily expect the same commitment from community partners. Similarly, faculty can be expected to convene at the researcher's convenience for interviews or focus groups, but the researcher must go to the community partner at the partner's convenience. Researchers must also make it clear to community partners what they stand to learn and gain from, for example, meeting at a central location during peak working hours for a focus group. Care must be given to selecting methods for assessment of community impact that create the least burden of evaluation and provide the most benefit for both the university and the community partner. This may result in some compromises in terms of the kinds of data can be collected, but any losses will likely be offset by the increased response rate and enhanced quality of the data (Gelmon and others, 2001).

Community partners value the opportunity to provide feedback and often report that invitations to participate in assessment activities help them to feel that their role in the university's activities is valued (Gelmon and others, 1998). They are sometimes intimidated, however, by participating in university-led discussions if they lack the academic credentials of faculty and institutional administrators. It is important to make community partners feel welcome and appreciated.

Another distinct challenge is creating the appropriate environment for candid communication where community partners feel able to share honest, critical observations. Community partners are usually eager to praise, because they are often grateful for the services provided and the benefits they derive from the partnership. As a result, they may be reluctant to be critical for fear of potentially losing the partnership or jeopardizing their relationship with the university. There may also be cultural norms about not criticizing someone who is helping you. Researchers should seek information about such norms and provide assurances that criticism will not lead to any negative actions.

Overcoming Typical Barriers to Assessment

Several common problems arise when contemplating and implementing assessment in the context of partnerships for service-learning. As mentioned above, assessment can be viewed as an unreasonable and unnecessary burden unless it is carefully explained to community partners. Even for university partners who believe in the importance of assessment as a key element of the partnership, the prospect of finding the time to do it can be daunting in the midst of service-learning activities and other work. Coupled with lack of intellectual investment in assessment by partners who are more focused on getting things done, the perceived burden of assessment can result in relegating it to a low priority. By emphasizing the direct linkage of assessment to program improvement, university and community partners can work together to create a culture of assessment within the partnership that values both the roles and outcomes of assessment. Assessment will only be successful if it becomes an integral part of daily work. A crucial step is to clearly establish the linkage of assessment to the routine work of the partnership and to integrate assessment strategies and methodologies as seamlessly as possible to minimize the perception of the additional burden of assessment. This requires a committed advocate for assessment who spends considerable time describing and reinforcing its importance. Participants must derive immediate value and benefit from the assessment and be able to readily access assessment data to use for their own improvement purposes, rather than wait a long time for the results of a complex, and often academic, assessment.

Another assessment challenge common to service-learning partnerships is a lack of expertise and resources for assessment. Colleges and universities are rich in both of these. Faculty with interest and expertise in program evaluation and assessment methodologies may be willing to integrate partnership assessment into their own work, identify graduate students seeking research projects for master theses or doctoral dissertations, or make the assessment a course-based project. Academic departments in which such faculty reside include sociology, psychology, anthropology, education, public affairs, health administration, social work, government and politics, public health, and urban studies.

In order to keep assessment manageable, partners should use a matrix like the one proposed in Exhibit 3.1 to limit the scope of assessment concepts and the number and complexity of methods. It is important to select assessment concepts, measures, and sources based on what is most relevant to the goals of the program. Although this matrix may be useful across a number of partnership contexts, it is a suggestion only and should not be interpreted as an all-purpose set of indicators, measures, and sources. A faculty expert can assist the partners to select appropriate methods based on the kinds of data desired and advise partners regarding the level of difficulty, time, and cost of data collection and analysis.

Sharing the Results of Assessment

Assessment results should be reported regularly and widely to demonstrate the learning achieved through the assessment and to stimulate use of the results to enhance the partnership and its activities. A fairly typical method is to write a report that describes project goals, what was measured, what was accomplished, and the results. The concepts and indicators in the matrix should be used to guide the synthesis of findings and their presentation in the report. Assessment results also form the basis for scholarly presentations and publications. Consideration should also be given to alternative forms of reporting to ensure wider and more rapid dissemination, such as presenting findings in poster format displayed in a campus cafeteria or at the library or posting selected results and participants' stories on a university website.

Community partners are usually eager to learn the results of the assessment and to use relevant information for their own purposes. One way to ensure rapid dissemination is to engage community representatives throughout the project activity, as is illustrated in the design of the CHESP project. Other mechanisms of communication can be through community forums, where findings are presented and implications discussed; through reports to advisory councils, which in turn can determine how the information can best be used; and through linkages with community groups that span a number of organizations, such as neighborhood associations, healthy cities–healthy communities councils, and local community trusts. Higher education partners must always be cognizant of presenting data in a community-friendly way. Presentation content and styles that may be well suited for an academic disciplinary meeting may be rebuffed by community groups as being too theoretical (having too much "fluff") and not containing enough useful material.

Conclusion

Assessment of both the processes and impacts of community-university partnerships for service-learning is essential to determine the extent to which benefits are derived for both partners. Without ongoing assessment, it is all too easy for partnerships to veer off track and to become unfocused and unproductive. Partnership assessment presents significant challenges, both conceptual and practical. This chapter describes approaches and methods that enable partners to craft assessments that meet their specific needs. It is heartening that significant work is under way in the area of assessment of service-learning partnerships.

Cruz and Giles (2000) propose a four-part model for service-learning assessment from the community perspective that holds much promise for the future. Their model, like this chapter, proposes that the university-community partnership itself be a unit of analysis. It also extends the principles of good practice for service-learning (Sigmon, 1979; Porter Honnet and Poulsen, 1989) to the process of evaluation and research. As far as methodology, Cruz and Giles propose the use of participatory action research, which emphasizes engagement with the community in defining assessment needs and strategies; conducting the research; and analysis, dissemination, and use of the results. The fourth aspect of the Cruz and Giles model is the asset-based approach promulgated by Kretzman and McKnight (1993). This approach is based on the premise that the first step is to map the assets of a community rather than its needs or deficits. Cruz and Giles (2000) extend this asset-identification focus to the community-university partnership itself and highlight mutual exchange and net gain in assets.

In conclusion, partnerships must be assessed as part of the overall assessment of the impacts of service-learning. The components of the partnership must be understood, and the goals of the partnership must be the foundation for assessment activity. Insights about the purpose and impacts of community-university partnerships will enable partners to better understand the multiple factors contributing to the success of service-learning.

References

Bergstrom, A. (ed.). *Collaboration Framework: Addressing Community Capacity.* Fargo, N.D.: National Network for Collaboration, 1996.

Bringle, R., and Hatcher, J. "Implementing Service Learning in Higher Education." *Journal of Higher Education,* 1996, *67*(2), 221–239.

Cruz, N. I., and Giles, D. E. "Where's the Community in Service-Learning Research?" *Michigan Journal of Community Service Learning,* Special Issue, Fall 2000, 28–34.

Driscoll, A., Holland, B., Gelmon, S., and Kerrigan, S. "An Assessment Model for Service Learning: Comprehensive Case Studies of Impact on Faculty, Students, Community and Institution." *Michigan Journal of Community Service Learning,* 1996, 3, *66–71.*

Eyler, J., and Giles, D. E., Jr. *Where's the Learning in Service-Learning?* San Francisco: Jossey-Bass, 1999.

Eyler, J., Giles, D. E., Jr., and Gray, C. *At a Glance: Summary and Annotated Bibliography of Recent Service-Learning Research in Higher Education.* Minneapolis: Learn and Serve America National Service-Learning Clearinghouse, 1999.

Fawcett, S., and others. "The Community Tool Box: A Web-based Resource for Building Healthier Communities." *Public Health Reports,* 2000, *115,* 274–278.

Furco, A. *Self-Assessment Rubric for the Institutionalization of Service-Learning in Higher Education.* Berkeley: University of California–Berkeley, 2000.

Gelmon, S. B. *Facilitating Academic-Community Partnerships Through Educational Accreditation: Overcoming a Tradition of Barriers and Obstacles.* Rockville, Md.: Bureau of Health Professions, Health Resources and Services Administration, U.S. Public Health Service, 1997.

Gelmon, S. B. "How Do We Know That Our Work Makes a Difference? Assessment Strategies for Service-Learning and Civic Engagement." *Metropolitan Universities*, 2000, *11*, 28–39.

Gelmon, S. B., and Connell, A. *Program Evaluation Principles and Practices.* Portland, Oreg.: Northwest Health Foundation, 2001.

Gelmon, S. B., Holland, B. A., and Shinnamon, A. F. *Health Professions Schools in Service to the Nation: 1996–1998 Final Evaluation Report.* San Francisco: Community-Campus Partnerships for Health, UCSF Center for the Health Professions, 1998.

Gelmon, S. B., and Lazarus, J. "Research and Evaluation Programme: Implications for Exemplars." Cape Town, S.A.: Joint Education Trust/CHESP, 2001.

Gelmon, S. B., White, A. W., Carlson, L., and Norman, L. "Making Organizational Change to Achieve Improvement and Interprofessional Learning: Perspectives from Health Professions Educators." *Journal of Interprofessional Care*, 2000, *14*(2), 131–146.

Gelmon, S. B., and others. "Community-University Partnerships for Mutual Learning." *Michigan Journal of Community Service Learning, 1998, 5*, 97–107.

Gelmon, S. B., and others. *Evaluation of the Portland Health Communities Initiative 1996–1998.* Portland, Oreg.: Healthy Communities and Portland State University, 1998.

Gelmon, S. B., and others. *Assessing the Impact of Service-Learning and Civic Engagement: Principles and Techniques.* Providence, R.I.: Campus Compact, 2001.

Gray, M. J., and others. *Combining Service and Learning in Higher Education.* Santa Monica, Calif.: Rand, 1999.

Holland, B. A. "Analyzing Institutional Commitment to Service: A Model of Key Organizational Factors." *Michigan Journal of Community Service Learning*, 1997, *4*, 30–41.

Holland, B. A. "Evaluation Plan for the PSU Masters in Tribal Administration Program." Unpublished report, Portland (Oreg.) State University, 2000.

Holland, B. A. "A Comprehensive Model for Assessing Service-Learning and Community-University Partnerships." In M. Canada and B. W. Speck (eds.), *Developing and Implementing Service-Learning Programs.* New Directions for Higher Education, no. 114. San Francisco: Jossey-Bass, 2001.

Holland, B. A., and Gelmon, S. B. "The State of the 'Engaged Campus': What Have We Learned About Building and Sustaining University-Community Partnerships?" *AAHE Bulletin*, 1998, *51*(2), 3–6.

Kretzman, J., and McKnight, J. *Building Communities from the Inside Out: A Path Toward Finding and Mobilizing a Community's Assets.* Chicago: ACTA, 1993.

Lazarus, J. *The CHESP Program: Progress Update and Implementation Strategy.* Cape Town, S.A.: CHESP and Joint Education Trust, 2001.

Messer, B. (ed.). *Handbook: The Formation, Planning and Reporting of Community/University Partnerships Projects.* Portland, Oreg.: Center for Academic Excellence, Portland State University, 1996.

Porter Honnet, E., and Poulsen, S. J. *Principles of Good Practice in Combining Service and Learning.* Racine, Wis.: Johnson Foundation, 1989.

Sigmon, R. "Service-Learning: Three Principles." *Synergist,* 1979, *8*(1).

Sigmon, R. "Anatomy of a University-Community Partnership." Presented at Community Partnerships in Health Professions Education: A National Conference on Service Learning. Boston, Mar. 1996.

Wealthall, S., Graham, J., and Turner, C. "Building, Maintaining and Repairing the Community-Campus Bridge: Five Years' Experience of Community Groups Educating Medical Students." *Journal of Interprofessional Care,* 1998, *12* (August), 289–302.

Chapter Four

Developing Collaborative Student Affairs–Academic Affairs Partnerships for Service-Learning

Cathy McHugh Engstrom

Although it is undesirable and unwise to propose a single model for the development of service-learning programs, the literature suggests that the most effective programs are based on partnerships between faculty and student affairs professionals (Robinson and Barnett, 1997; Engstrom and Tinto, 1997, 2000; Jacoby, 1999). Whatever the institutional location or reporting structure of service-learning programs, student learning experiences are enhanced when the expertise of both academic affairs and student affairs is tapped. The purpose of this chapter is to critically examine the complex, multidimensional nature of partnerships for service-learning between faculty and student affairs. It then explores the implications of these relationships for engaging students (and other service-learning partners) in more integrated learning experiences, advocating for a scholarship of engagement, pushing reform of organizational structures that hinder individual and organizational learning, and institutionalizing service-learning.

First, I provide a brief overview of the context for student affairs–academic affairs partnerships. Second, I propose a partnership framework for carefully examining how faculty and student affairs professionals work together. I identify dimensions that are valuable to consider in analyzing the potential sustainability of a partnership and in promoting deeper student learning (Kuh, 1996). Third, I describe three types of service-learning partnerships between student affairs and faculty. I contend that these different partnership models—clearinghouse, cooperative, and collaborative—have varying degrees of influence in promoting holistic learning experiences and institutionalizing a spirit and scholarship of engagement.

Fourth, I argue that only partnerships that demonstrate characteristics of collaboration have the power to transform our institutions into learning-centered organizations (Engstrom and Tinto, 2000) that promote civic responsibility. I offer descriptions of programs that have incorporated dimensions of collaborative relationships between faculty and student affairs professionals. Finally, I conclude by proposing strategies to help student affairs and academic affairs work toward developing partnerships that minimally challenge—and optimally begin to dismantle—organizational barriers hindering service-learning and other learning-centered work. Please note that I use the terms *faculty* and *academic affairs* interchangeably in this chapter, although I acknowledge that the latter is a broader term that includes academic administrators and others.

Setting the Context for Student Affairs– Academic Affairs Partnerships

Strong forces in the history of American higher education have acted as barriers to developing meaningful, enduring partnerships between faculty and student affairs. Our system of higher education has been built upon notions of separatism, specialization, and competition (Engstrom and Tinto, 2000). With the emergence of the German research model in the mid-1800s, the primary focus of faculty at many institutions became research and the production of knowledge. Faculty were rewarded for their research and expertise in their academic disciplines. Student affairs professionals, on the other hand, were viewed primarily as responsible for the psychosocial and emotional well-being of students. Throughout most of the twentieth century, student affairs units and academic departments became increasingly autonomous and specialized.

Concerns about limited resources in the 1980s and early 1990s intensified territorialism and engendered mistrust (Engstrom and Tinto, 2000).

As student affairs functions and academic departments became more specialized and discrete over the years, each developed its own culture, including unique value systems, ways of knowing, norms of behavior, roles and responsibilities, customs, language, and work habits. These different cultures translated into different organizational structures, professional preparation, goals, priorities, and reward systems. The strength and sustainability of these cultures have resulted in "an inability on the part of institutions to change quickly in response to changing needs of students" (Love and Goodsell Love, 1995, p. 21) and led to relationships often characterized by misunderstanding, disrespect, conflict, and antagonism (Blake, 1979; Schroeder, 1998). For a comprehensive overview of the literature on the real and perceived differences between student affairs and faculty, see Engstrom and Tinto (2000).

Over the past decade and a half, national reports have called for major reform in higher education to address increasing internal and external criticism and decreasing public trust. Educators have identified a critical need to refocus on the primary purpose of higher education, namely to increase the relevance and importance of the undergraduate experience and student learning (National Association of State Universities and Land-Grant Colleges, 1997; Boyer Commission, 1998; Wingspread Group, 1993). However, for the most part, prevailing organizational structures in higher education institutions often define and create individual, isolated, disconnected experiences within the narrow boundaries of separate disciplines and administrative, bureaucratic units (Engstrom and Tinto, 1997; Kezar and Rhoads, 2001). A student-learning paradigm requires a new way of thinking and acting at both institutional and individual levels (Barr, 1998). Pascarella stressed that "faculty members, joined by academic and student affairs administrators, must devise ways to deliver undergraduate education that are as comprehensive and integrated as the ways students actually learn" (Terenzini and Pascarella, 1994, p. 32). Educators have challenged institutions to seriously consider how to design integrated learning experiences and to confront the seemingly insurmountable divide between classroom and out-of-class learning (American College Personnel Association, 1994; Kuh, 1996; Love and Goodsell Love, 1995). Kezar and Rhoads recommend that we focus on freeing ourselves from "the philosophical boxes" (2001, p. 162) that have hindered the ability of student affairs and faculty to learn new ways of thinking about how institutions might be organized to promote more holistic learning approaches.

Barr also pointed out that the most effective way to institutionalize a student-learning paradigm is to transform the workplace of faculty and administrators into "learning organizations" (Senge, 1990). In learning organizations, cross-disciplinary, cross-functional, collaborative work habits and attitudes are paramount. Institutions exhibit the following norms, values, and behaviors when a student-learning imperative is reinterpreted into a learning imperative for everyone: a discourse for promoting shared-learning experiences is fostered and rewarded; faculty and student affairs learn to appreciate and learn from the perspectives and experiences of one another; individuals are open to surfacing and reflecting upon their own assumptions and attitudes and possible transformation of those views; and conflict is expected and valued for its learning power and contribution to building communities based on difference, care, and authenticity (Engstrom and Tinto, 2000).

A student-learning paradigm suggests a "whole new mindset" (Terenzini and Pascarella, 1994, p. 32), different roles and responsibilities for faculty, student affairs, and college and university structures (Engstrom and Tinto, 2000; Love and Goodsell Love, 1995; Kuh, 1996). In order to move toward structural reform that values relational ways of knowing and related pedagogies, faculty and student affairs professionals must develop strong partnerships (American Association for Higher Education, American College Personnel Association, and National Association of Student Personnel Administrators, 1998; American College Personnel Association, 1994; Schroeder, 2000) to "capitalize on the interrelatedness of the in- and out-of-class influences on student learning" (Terenzini and Pascarella, 1994, p. 32).

Clearly, the building of partnerships among faculty, student affairs professionals, community representatives, and students is critical to creating service-learning experiences that result in transformative learning for all participants. Bringle and Hatcher (2000) contended that the institutionalization of service-learning is grounded in the development of partnerships that are reciprocal, sustainable, and meaningful to all stakeholders. But what types of partnerships currently exist? What are the dimensions of how we do our work together? What are the implications of transforming our institutions into learning-centered institutions that recognize their interconnections with, and responsibilities to, their neighbors and society?

A Framework for Analyzing Faculty–Student Affairs Partnerships

Over the past two decades, academic affairs and student affairs have come together to offer service-learning experiences in a multitude of ways. How might these various partnerships be characterized? What dimensions can we identify that relate to the power and sustainability of service-learning? I propose that a close examination of the nuances, unspoken assumptions, and behaviors embedded in student affairs–faculty partnerships can provide invaluable insights into how institutions implement service-learning initiatives that successfully challenge traditional organizational structures and contribute to the institutionalization of service-learning on campuses.

I have identified the following interrelated questions that are useful for framing and carefully examining the array of current and evolving student affairs–academic affairs relationships on behalf of service-learning. They can assist us in exploring the nature of the partnerships at our institutions.

In what ways do faculty and student affairs professionals work together through service-learning activities to

- Develop shared, mutually agreed-upon vision and goals to ground service-learning initiatives?
- Forge a heightened understanding and appreciation about one another's work?
- Challenge their "mental maps" and consider cross-divisional and interdisciplinary perspectives based on shared learning goals?
- Invest the time and energy necessary to engage in ongoing, regular communication?

- Value, solicit, and learn from the diverse expertise, perspectives, and knowledge of individual partners?
- Develop a "seamless curriculum" and support pedagogies that integrate social, intellectual, and affective domains of learning and view in- and out-of-class distinctions as artificial and permeable?
- Create and implement shared, inclusive, facilitative decision-making structures that promote work toward the shared vision?
- Feel comfortable with and value the increasing ambiguity and fluidity in each other's roles and responsibilities?
- Support each other's personal growth and development and create structures that promote reciprocal learning?
- Reinforce the fact that they are working together over time rather than for a one-time experience?
- Create relationships based on respect, trust, and mutual understanding?
- Recognize conflict as a source of learning and resolve difficult issues through conversations based on candor, honesty, and empathy?
- Create a safe environment to take risks, make mistakes, and share vulnerabilities?
- Develop a belief that each participant's involvement makes a significant, positive difference in the lives of students, the institution, and the community?
- Stimulate creativity and entrepreneurialism in each other's work?
- Share resources such as staff, funds, and facilities?
- Engage in joint scholarship, assessment, and evaluation regarding service-learning?
- Celebrate shared accomplishments together?
- Demonstrate courageous leadership by consistently advocating for one another and communicating publicly about the contributions each partner makes to student learning?
- Identify and challenge organizational structures and systems that hinder efforts between faculty and student affairs to work toward designing innovative, seamless learning experiences?
- Work to eradicate inequitable power dynamics in the institution and the community?

Responses to these questions can provide substantial insight into the degree to which partnerships are, and can be, built upon a foundation of mutual learning and trust.

I recognize that this focus on deconstructing the nature of student affairs–faculty partnerships is somewhat artificial and potentially misleading because partnerships for service-learning should never be developed in isolation from the development of relationships with students and the community. However, it is my hope that a critical examination of the dimensions of student affairs–academic affairs partnerships can become a model for understanding and developing sustainable relationships with other key stakeholders.

Moving from Clearinghouse to Collaboration: A Partnership Development Scheme

In this section, I present a scheme, or series of models, for the development of collaborative service-learning partnerships between student affairs and academic affairs based on the questions enumerated on pages 69 and 70. In this scheme, I contend that an institution that operates service-learning as a clearinghouse model in which an office based in student affairs merely provides information and services to faculty would be able to offer minimal responses to the questions I have posed. Relationship building is not an essential component of this model, which is based on furnishing resources to faculty, students, and community agencies in a one-dimensional way. The interactions between faculty and student affairs staff are likely to be superficial, one-time, and a means to an end.

Cooperative partnerships require more engagement by faculty and student affairs in developing and implementing service-learning initiatives. However, faculty members and student affairs staff still work rather independently. The strengths and expertise of each partner typically merge to enable the performance of distinct, well-defined roles and responsibilities. Both faculty and student affairs professionals may be actively engaged in the student learning process, but not in learning from one another.

Collaborative relationships are characterized by higher levels of consensus about the purpose of service-learning and shared learning goals; interdependence between partners; degree to which an integrated notion of curricular and cocurricular learning is designed into the service-learning experience; comfort level in working across the many subcultures embedded in both student affairs and academic affairs; frequent, ongoing communication; and working together as co-learners (Engstrom and Tinto, 2000). These relationships tend to be complex and time consuming.

Ultimately, collaborative partnerships between student affairs and academic affairs would involve students and community members as full, active partners. The development of this highest level of partnership would result in a dismantling of current organizational structures to become more fluid, permeable, nonhierarchical, and equitable; significant changes in how partners think about and engage in their work; and a shift to teacher-learner roles that are in constant flux based on the partners' knowledge and experiences in particular areas (Engstrom and Tinto, 2000). Because the principles and pedagogies that undergird service-learning consistently embrace working collaboratively, it is worth striving toward the collaborative model with passion and vigor. The examples that follow will provide insight into strategies critical to moving institutions of higher education to systematically and intentionally create holistic learning experiences for students; become "learning organizations" (Senge, 1990) in which students, faculty, student affairs, and community partners come together as co-learners and co-teachers; and institutionalize a spirit and scholarship of civic engagement (Boyer, 1987). It should be noted that service-learning partnerships characterized by all, or even a majority of, the collaborative dimensions highlighted in the questions I have posed are limited, considering that many of these partnership dimensions are just beginning to evolve (Engstrom and Tinto, 2000). In proposing the following models, I have briefly described the first two, using only generic examples. In the hope of encouraging us to move toward the collaborative model, I have provided more detail and specific institutional examples.

The Clearinghouse Model

A majority of service-learning or community service offices based in student affairs provide important clearinghouse functions and resources to faculty and community agencies. Such offices offer faculty and students an array of possible service sites and other information to consider in designing service-learning activities. For example, the clearinghouse might offer guides for students that outline the steps involved in securing a volunteer position, hints for having a successful experience, databases and materials about community sites, strategies for identifying community placements compatible with service-learning course objectives, and transportation options. The staff might also present workshops or class sessions on many of the above topics and host community service fairs that enable volunteer coordinators to meet students and faculty.

Many community service or service-learning offices offer additional resources to faculty, including sample service-learning course syllabi, reflection exercises, course evaluations, information about grant or professional development opportunities, and assistance with administrative issues such as learning contracts and liability.

Although all these resource functions are essential to faculty, the clearinghouse model does not require much in the way of relationships between faculty and student affairs. In cases where there is little meaningful communication about service-learning, it is possible that the information and services offered do not fully meet faculty needs. Certainly, faculty and student affairs professionals would not challenge each other to consider doing their work in different ways.

The Cooperative Model

Many cooperative ventures between faculty and student affairs professionals engaged in service-learning work have emerged, resulting in significantly enhanced learning experiences for students. In fact, it is probable that a majority of service-learning partnerships between student affairs and academic affairs today fit within the cooperative model.

One typical example of the cooperative model is the service-learning credit, or fourth-credit, option that is offered at numerous colleges and universities. The following description of the service-learning credit option is a composite of several actual programs. Often the service-learning credit option is administered by a service-learning center housed in student affairs. One great advantage of this type of program is that it enables students to add an additional credit to a regular three-credit course by contracting to do a significant number of hours of community service (usually forty to fifty-five hours per semester) and relating the service to course content (Enos and Troppe, 1996). Although students generally may add a service-learning credit to courses in any discipline, as long as the faculty member agrees, in practice the option is exercised primarily in the social sciences, English, and theology (Engstrom and Tinto, 1997).

The student is generally responsible for identifying and securing the service site, completing a learning contract, attending a mid-semester seminar with other service-learning credit students, and writing a series of reflective essays designed to encourage students to consider the connections between their service experiences and course material. The professor is responsible for reading and evaluating the student essays, determining how unsatisfactory performance in the site will impact the student's grade, and assigning the course grade.

The service-learning center takes on several key responsibilities in this type of partnership. The center promotes the program to faculty and students and assists students in finding potential service sites. Center staff members develop the basic learning contract and sign the contracts, along with the professor, the student's home college dean's office, and the student. Staff also facilitate the required reflection sessions that are designed to challenge students to consider the pedagogical dimensions of service and learning from interdisciplinary perspectives (Engstrom and Tinto, 1997). Both the essays and the reflection sessions push students to relate their learning experiences to social problems, policy questions, and ethical dilemmas.

Center staff usually contact the community site supervisor at least twice during the semester to gather feedback about student performance. They inform students who are in jeopardy of failing to meet the responsibilities outlined in the learning contract and alert the faculty member.

It is important to note that this faculty–student affairs partnership is a two-way relationship. The service-learning credit option could not happen without the service-learning center staff and faculty each taking on essential roles and responsibilities. The functions assumed by each partner are well defined and tend to tap what is typically and traditionally considered to be each partner's strengths and expertise. Student affairs professionals exercise their skills in project administration, risk management, group facilitation, and relationship building with community agencies. Faculty members evaluate the quality of the students' academic work. Both faculty and student affairs staff have enormous opportunities to learn more about local communities and the problems they face, challenges involved in promoting critical thinking and citizenship among students, and how concrete experience can enrich student learning.

However, what else can be observed about this type of student affairs–academic affairs partnership? Relationships are often limited to one course or one semester, with individual faculty members entering and leaving the system with little impact on the overall program. It is not critical that faculty and student affairs staff develop shared goals for the students' service-learning experience or work together to develop activities that support an integrated notion of learning. For example, the student affairs staff member who facilitates the reflection sessions may take a social justice or multicultural education approach. This focus may or may not be shared by the faculty member who analyzes and grades student essays. Shared assumptions about teaching and learning are not required, and, as a result, opportunities for student affairs staff and faculty to learn from each other are rather limited. The traditional notions of the roles assumed by faculty and student affairs staff remain more or less intact and unchallenged.

The Collaborative Model

Developing relationships through cooperative and even clearinghouse models often sows the seeds necessary to develop more collaborative endeavors. The examples of collaboration between student affairs and academic affairs that follow will provide insight into strategies useful in moving institutions of higher education to systematically and intentionally create holistic learning experiences for students and a means to institutionalize civic engagement. I contend that individuals involved in collaborative relationships are dedicated to promoting and working in "learning organizations"

(Senge, 1990) in which students, faculty, student affairs, and community partners come together as co-learners and co-teachers.

University of Utah

Clearly, the relationships between faculty and staff of the Lowell Bennion Center for Community Service at the University of Utah are exemplary in exhibiting a majority of dimensions of the collaborative model. For more than ten years, the efforts of faculty and student affairs staff have been intimately intertwined as they have developed a comprehensive service-learning program that has become increasingly institutionalized across departmental structures (Engstrom and Tinto, 1997). Housed in the division of student affairs, with reporting lines to both academic affairs and student affairs, the center is highly respected across the institution.

Student affairs staff attribute their success to the strong faculty relationships and leadership that were nurtured since the inception of the center (American Association for Higher Education, 2001). Early in its development, the director of the Bennion Center created, and granted critical responsibilities to, a Faculty Advisory Committee. Consisting of representatives from each college and school, this group worked closely with center staff to develop a shared purpose for, and commitment to, service-learning that emphasizes service-learning's role in developing "socially responsive knowledge" that would contribute directly to society (American Association for Higher Education, 2001).

The group advocates for service-learning at all levels of the university. Other important roles that this group has assumed include developing criteria for designating a course as a service-learning course; approving courses for service-learning designation; developing a statement and rationale for the value of integrating service-learning within departmental, college, and administrative structures; coordinating the faculty awards program; and lobbying for the development of criteria for use across schools and colleges in evaluating service-learning efforts in the tenure and promotion process. The group also was successful in soliciting funding from the president, the vice president for student affairs, and the vice president for academic affairs to develop initiatives to encourage academic departments to build service-learning into their courses so that the courses are designated as service-learning courses, irrespective of who teaches them (Engstrom and Tinto, 1997). More than forty departments offer service-learning courses involving more than eighty faculty and two thousand students. The director of the Bennion Center stated that the "Faculty Advisory Committee has helped us select our strategies and approaches wisely" (American Association for Higher Education, 2001). High levels of trust have evolved over the years. In addition, the Bennion Center has been willing to relinquish some degree of control of its domain as it has allowed the Faculty Advisory Committee to help shape the center's priorities and actions.

The infrastructure, particularly as it relates to staffing and resource allocation, has promoted faculty and student affairs staff working side by side on the daily activities involved in developing, implementing, and assessing service-learning initiatives. For example, faculty who are teaching service-learning classes for the first time are assigned one of twenty teaching assistants funded, trained, and supervised by the Bennion Center. The teaching assistant typically takes responsibility for arranging the site placements and facilitating the reflection components of the courses.

Through the awards program developed by the Faculty Advisory Committee and the Bennion Center, faculty and staff come together to recognize faculty accomplishments in service-learning and to promote future innovative work. One award grants faculty members release time to develop service-learning courses; another provides faculty with financial support to design and implement projects that have significant potential to contribute to the community. The Faculty Mentor Award program selects seasoned service-learning faculty to mentor faculty new to service-learning pedagogy.

Bennion staff and faculty also work together to design and implement faculty development programs. Student affairs professionals regularly attend new faculty orientations to introduce service-learning and offer individual consultations. The center often hosts roundtable discussions by experienced service-learning faculty. Finally, assessment is a joint endeavor of faculty and Bennion staff. The center conducts ongoing evaluations of service-learning courses and provides specific course information to instructors. Aggregate data are used to recognize effective practices and to identify recommendations for change.

The Bennion Center's partnerships with academic affairs avoids slotting faculty and student affairs professionals into traditional roles. Although all partners make contributions from their particular areas of expertise and influence, faculty and student affairs staff share responsibilities for teaching, learning, administration, and assessment (American Association for Higher Education, 2001).

Chandler-Gilbert Community College

A Maricopa Community College located in Chandler, Arizona, Chandler-Gilbert Community College (CGCC) also works intentionally to foster long-term, collaborative partnerships among faculty and student life staff. The college integrates service-learning into its required general education courses and a variety of other courses in English, biology, math, psychology, and music. Similar to the University of Utah, CGCC pulled together key faculty, student affairs staff, and senior administration from the beginning into a working group to provide leadership and institutional advocacy for service-learning. The director of the service-learning program states that its success is a result of "the enthusiastic and collaborative nature of how our program was established. Both sides of the house (student services and instruction) came together to support and build service-learning opportunities" (American Association for Higher Education, 2001).

The service-learning program is organizationally located in the Office of Student Life but coordinated by a twelve-member Leadership Team comprising the dean of students, the dean of instruction, faculty, and service-learning center staff. The work of the team, which meets weekly, includes designing and leading workshops about service-learning pedagogy for new faculty and providing concrete ideas for course implementation.

Student life staff meet regularly with faculty new to service-learning and have created detailed instructions and criteria for faculty use in evaluating service-learning essays. Faculty assist in the selection of undergraduate service-learning assistants who are supervised directly by the Office of Student Life (Jacoby, 1999).

This example highlights several dimensions that are critical to establishing and sustaining collaborative relationships. CGCC has developed structures for faculty and student affairs to work on multiple aspects of service-learning, including a joint mission and assessment of the program's success in meeting shared student-learning goals. As is the case with the University of Utah, these practices recognize that student affairs staff are invaluable sources of knowledge not only in traditionally recognized domains but also in areas such as pedagogy, curriculum development, and evaluation of learning.

University of Michigan

Two noteworthy examples at the University of Michigan in Ann Arbor highlight additional ways in which academic affairs and student affairs work together in a truly collaborative partnership. For more than twenty-five years, the University of Michigan's Edward Ginsburg Center for Community Service and Learning (CSL) and faculty in the sociology department have collaborated on Project Community (also known as Sociology 389: Practicum in Sociology), a group of academically accredited service-learning courses that enroll more than seven hundred students annually. In these courses, students spend time each week serving in a community agency, participate in a weekly reflection seminar with a student facilitator, read assigned articles on sociology, keep a log of their observations and reactions, and write analytical papers that draw connections between their field experiences and the sociology literature (Edward Ginsburg Center for Community Service and Learning, 2002).

The mission, goals, pedagogical model, and course requirements were initially, and continue to be, jointly developed by sociology faculty and student affairs staff. The program is run by three CSL staff, a one-quarter-time sociology faculty member, four or five sociology teaching assistants, and more than forty students who facilitate peer-led weekly seminars. These graduate and undergraduate seminar facilitators are the key players in guiding the student learning process in Project Community. They are trained by the CSL staff and sociology faculty about how to promote students' reflections on their field experiences and how to link these experiences with the literature. The sociology teaching assistants provide facilitators with reading lists that address sociological issues relevant to the students' service sites (Edward Ginsburg Center for Community Service and Learning, 2002).

Chesler contends that this program requires ongoing creativity, flexibility, and risk taking by all partners in that they are required "to think of themselves as change-agents and as instruments of innovation and reform in the University" as they promote a pedagogy that is quite different from traditional pedagogies found in premier research institutions (Edward Ginsburg Center for Community Service and Learning, 2002).

A more recent initiative at the University of Michigan, the Michigan Community Scholars Program (MCSP), is a residentially based program open to two hundred first- and second-year students from all schools and colleges. In this program, spearheaded by the College of Literature, Sciences, and the Arts (LSA) and the Housing Office, faculty and student affairs staff provide rich opportunities for students to make connections between their coursework, living environment, and the broader community in ways that recognize that the academic and social domains of learning are intertwined (D. Schoem, personal communication, May 2001). The program structure and activities clearly reinforce the seamless nature of learning. Through courses, social activities, study groups, peer assistants' tutoring of new students, and service projects, "students strive to model an ideal community in terms of friendship, values, responsibilities, diversity, social justice, celebration, collaboration, and caring" (Michigan Community Scholars Program, 2002). In the fall semester, new students take the one-credit transition-to-college seminar with the program director and one of the fifteen three-credit first-year seminars that involve long-term service-learning projects and are taught by faculty from various colleges and schools (D. Schoem, personal communication, May 2001). A variety of service-learning courses is offered in the winter, many of which count toward distribution requirements.

Schoem attributes the success of the MCSP student affairs–faculty partnership in part to the long-standing history of deep and respectful relationships across campus on behalf of service-learning (personal communication, May 2001). In addition, the staffing pattern intentionally promotes intensive, integrated learning experiences for students. Specifically, the faculty director and the program director (a student affairs professional) share the leadership for program development, implementation, and evaluation. The faculty director works 50 percent of his or her time on this project and is funded by LSA. Funds for the full-time program director position come from both LSA and the Housing Office.

The faculty director recruits faculty colleagues to teach the interdisciplinary service-learning seminars, teaches one of the seminars, works collaboratively with the program director on advising and programming initiatives, and regularly attends Housing Office staff meetings. The program director teaches the one-credit transition-to-college seminar each fall and supervises the graduate assistants, resident advisers, peer advisers for community service, and programming board. Peer advisers in community service and resident advisers work together to sponsor programs for residents and work with faculty teaching freshman seminars to develop educational programs related to the course material (W. Zeller, personal communication, June 2001). This innovative sharing of responsibilities leads to occasional ambiguity, but the creativity that results overshadows any momentary frustration (D. Schoem, personal communication, May 2001).

The above examples of collaborative partnerships reinforce the importance of developing a mutual understanding of the purpose and values of service-learning. Faculty and student affairs staff can work quite interdependently, rather than autonomously, to promote student learning and development. These partnerships cross organizational boundaries that generally tend to hinder the development of integrated learning experiences. All parties benefit when faculty and student affairs professionals critically examine and creatively share roles and responsibilities in the student learning process.

Conclusion

What can be learned from institutions that promote and sustain collaborative partnerships in which faculty and student affairs professionals work together across cultural differences and forces of specialization and fragmentation? What recommendations can be shared to promote learning-centered and civic-minded engaged campuses that recognize the interrelatedness of in- and out-of-class educational experiences?

A consistent theme across the collaborative partnerships described in this chapter is the presence of strong, active leadership or advisory teams comprised of both faculty and student affairs professionals. In successful collaborations, these teams develop a shared vision and purpose for their service-learning initiatives and work side by side to develop and implement processes critical to the quality and sustainability of their programs. Such teams provide opportunities for members to demonstrate courage, flexibility, and risk taking as they challenge and begin to unravel traditional disciplinary and functional area boundaries. Members learn from one another and value the knowledge and experiences that each brings (Engstrom and Tinto, 2000). They also become a major stimulus for identifying and promoting other collaborative relationships.

Collaborative, interdisciplinary partnerships for service-learning blossom in an environment in which the vision of senior administrators includes a focus on student learning, community engagement, and the development of student citizenship. Institutional support is also reflected in administrative and faculty reward systems. Senior-level administrators should support collaborative initiatives by celebrating those relationships that require the most time, risk, and innovation because of the cross-disciplinary, coherent nature of their activities. The recognition of service-learning as a factor in promotion and tenure decisions is also critical to allow the participation of junior faculty. This requires institutional leaders to adopt a more inclusive view of faculty work that values interdisciplinary, integrated approaches to teaching and broadens the definition of research to include the development of knowledge that addresses local community issues. As Engstrom and Tinto argue, "Without these paradigm shifts in how scholarship is viewed, it is not hopeful that partnerships between student affairs and faculty will reflect anything more than fragmented efforts at the periphery of campus life" (2000, p. 446). Finally, it cannot be forgotten that innovations in teaching and learning do not come cheap (Barr, 1998). Administrators must provide adequate resources in the areas of staffing, facilities, program development, and assessment in order for service-learning initiatives to be created and sustained.

This chapter offers opportunities and models for establishing collaborative partnerships between faculty and student affairs. It critically analyzes how student affairs and faculty can conduct their work as fully collaborative partners. Clearly, such partnerships are powerful vehicles for transforming our institutions into learning-centered organizations that promote individual and institutional civic responsibility and enrich our students, our institutions, and our society.

References

American Association for Higher Education. [http://www.aahe.org/service/models.html]. 2001.

American Association for Higher Education, American College Personnel Association, and National Association of Student Personnel Administrators. *Powerful Partnerships: A Shared Responsibility for Learning.* Washington, D.C.: American Association for Higher Education, American College Personnel Association, National Association of Student Personnel Administrators, 1998.

American College Personnel Association. *The Student Learning Imperative: Implications for Student Affairs.* Washington, D.C.: American College Personnel Association, 1994.

Barr, R. "Obstacles to Implementing the Learning Paradigm: What It Takes to Overcome Them." *About Campus,* 1998, 2(3), 18–25.

Blake, E. S. "Classroom and Context: An Educational Dialectic." *Academe,* Summer 1979, 65, 280–292.

Boyer, E. L. *College: The Undergraduate Experience in America.* New York: HarperCollins, 1987.

Boyer Commission on Educating Undergraduates in the Research University. *Reinventing Undergraduate Education: A Blueprint for America's Research Universities.* Stony Brook, N.Y.: State University of New York, 1998.

Bringle, R. G., and Hatcher, J. A. "Institutionalization of Service Learning in Higher Education." *Journal of Higher Education,* 2000, 71, 273–290.

Edward Ginsburg Center for Community Service and Learning, University of Michigan. [http://www.umich.edu/~mserve]. Jan. 2002.

Engstrom, C. M., and Tinto, V. "Working Together for Service Learning." *About Campus,* 1997, 2(3), 101–105.

Engstrom, C. M., and Tinto, V. "Developing Partnerships with Academic Affairs to Enhance Student Learning." In M. J. Barr and M. K. Desler (eds.), *The Handbook of Student Affairs Administration.* San Francisco: Jossey-Bass, 2000.

Enos, S. L., and Troppe, M. L. "Service-Learning in the Curriculum." In B. Jacoby (ed.), *Service-Learning in Higher Education: Concepts and Practices.* San Francisco: Jossey-Bass, 1996.

Jacoby, B. "Partnerships for Service-Learning." In J. Schuh and E. Whitt (eds.), *Creating Successful Partnerships Between Academic and Student Affairs.* New Directions for Student Services, no. 87. San Francisco: Jossey-Bass, 1999.

Kezar, A., and Rhoads, R. "The Dynamic Tensions of Service Learning in Higher Education: A Philosophical Perspective." *Journal of Higher Education,* 2001, *72*(1), 148–171.

Kuh, G. D. "Guiding Principles for Creating Seamless Learning Environments for Undergraduates." *Journal of College Student Development,* 1996, *37*(2), 135–148.

Love, P. G., and Goodsell Love, A. *Enhancing Student Learning: Intellectual, Social, and Emotional Integration.* ASHE-ERIC Higher Education Report, no. 4. Washington, D.C.: George Washington University, 1995.

Michigan Community Scholars Program. [http://www.lsa.umich.edu/MCS/mainRight.html]. Jan. 2002.

National Association of State Universities and Land-Grant Colleges. *Returning to Our Roots: The Student Experience.* Washington, D.C.: National Association of State Universities and Land Grant Colleges, 1997.

Robinson, G., and Barnett, L. *Best Practices in Service Learning: Building a National Community College Network, 1994–1997.* Washington, D.C.: American Association of Community Colleges, 1997.

Schroeder, C. C. "Developing Collaborative Partnerships That Enhance Student Learning and Educational Attainment." ACPA Senior Scholars Trend Analysis Draft Essays. [http://www.acpa.nche.edu/srsch/charles_schroeder.html]. 1998.

Schroeder, C. C. "Forging Educational Partnerships That Advance Student Learning." In G. Blimling and E. Whitt (eds.), *Good Practice in Student Affairs: Principles to Foster Student Learning.* San Francisco: Jossey-Bass, 2000.

Senge, P. M. *The Fifth Discipline: The Art and Practice of the Learning Organization.* New York: Doubleday, 1990.

Terenzini, P. T., and Pascarella, E. T. "Living with Myths." *Change,* 1994, *26*(6), 28–32.

Wingspread Group on Higher Education. *An American Imperative: Higher Expectations for Higher Education.* Racine, Wis.: Johnson Foundation, 1993.

Chapter Five

Partnerships with Students

Irene Fisher and Shannon Huff Wilson

In this chapter we proceed from a philosophical perspective that students can best develop as active citizens on campuses that model democratic practices internally and also reach out to create authentic partnerships with their communities. We believe that students are essential partners in service-learning, and we suggest that partnerships with students be evaluated by the same benchmarks that are applied to relationships between campuses and external partners. We present examples of how these benchmarks can be adapted to partnerships between students and institutional leaders, service-learning program administrators, faculty, and alumni. We also describe partnerships between students and the community, as well as with state and national organizations. Finally, we explore possibilities for extending the reach of democratic policies and practices beyond student service-learning partnerships to encompass all aspects of campus life. Deeper partnerships indeed become possible as fully engaged faculty and students move beyond the campus arena into co-created, community-based scholarship and community work.

Benchmarks for Partnerships with Students

The *Benchmarks for Campus/Community Partnerships* (Torres, 2000), cited in Chapter One, provide a useful starting point for developing democratic, reciprocal relationships between campuses and communities. Using the benchmarks as a lens for viewing partnerships with students can serve as a tool to strengthen those relationships. Just as service-learning practitioners have recognized the propensity of campuses to "do unto" community partners through relationships built on unhealthy power imbalances, practitioners are too often prone to "act upon" students and regard them as less knowledgeable, less able, less worthy of trust in the context of service-learning partnerships. The Campus Compact benchmarks are loosely grouped into three stages (Torres, 2000). Below we briefly review these stages, adapt the eight benchmarks to focus on partnerships with students, and provide examples of how the benchmarks might play out in practice.

Stage I: Designing the Partnerships

The first benchmark for campus-community partnerships states that genuine democratic partnerships are founded on a shared vision and that "in collaborative conversation, partners develop a vision of how their immediate environment—the community in which they live and work—can be strengthened" (Torres, 2000, p. 5). *Community,* in the context of partnerships with students, becomes both the campus itself and the broader community. Adapting this concept to student partnerships, there are numerous ways in which students can and should be involved in all aspects of developing the vision, mission, and goals of service-learning centers or programs. In the curricular arena, students can be equal partners with others on committees that set criteria for service-learning course designation and determine which courses should be so designated.

The second benchmark in Stage I relates to tangible benefits for partners that satisfy some of the unique self-interests of each in addition to shared interests. In a faculty-student partnership in which both share an interest in providing service-learning opportunities to other students, the faculty member might acknowledge a personal self-interest in strengthening her student course evaluations for her tenure portfolio, while the student acknowledges the desire for personal growth and the need to build a résumé for postgraduate employment. A program administrator and student leaders in a service-learning center might share broad program goals: the administrator holds a personal interest in ethical development and the student leaders want to hone their leadership skills.

Stage II: Building Collaborative Relationships

As with campus-community partnerships, relationships with students must be characterized by "trust and mutual respect; equal voice; shared responsibilities; risks and rewards; forums to support frequent and open communication; clear lines of accountability; shared vision; and mutual interest" (Torres, 2000, p. 6). Administrators and faculty should view students as vital and essential partners, not token representatives, in visioning, planning, managing, and evaluating service-learning programs and courses. In the ideal scenario, students would be seen in leadership roles as frequently as others.

The fourth benchmark posits that strong collaborative relationships are multidimensional in order to best address complex problems (Torres, 2000). Numerous multifaceted problems arise in the course of campus-community partnerships, service-learning reflection, and various aspects of institutional governance. Involving a diverse range of students in problem solving enables them to make unique contributions as well as to learn important lessons they can apply in other situations. This benchmark cautions us to be prepared for the culture clashes that may occur when individuals with different perspectives are invited to the table (Torres, 2000). While students may challenge ideas and values in unexpected ways, conflict with civility should be welcomed as a powerful learning experience.

Readily adaptable to partnerships with students, the final benchmark in Stage II emphasizes the importance of clear organization and dynamic leadership (Torres, 2000). Both faculty and student affairs professionals know that with an appropriate degree of structure, guidance, and clarity of purpose, students can make powerful contributions and be strong leaders. For example, students should be included on committees that evaluate service-learning courses, review faculty proposals for service-learning course development grants, and select faculty for awards as outstanding service-learning educators. Similarly, within individual courses, students can work with faculty to determine the number of service hours required, consider options for service sites, and design reflection activities.

Stage III: Sustaining Partnerships over Time

The sixth benchmark elucidates that sustaining partnerships over time requires that they be integrated into the institutional mission and that the work of the partnership be spread throughout the institution (Torres, 2000). To adapt this benchmark to partnerships with students, the institutional mission statement could call for students to be involved in campus governance, and supporting documents could define how this will occur at various levels and in various aspects of the governance structure. To support service-learning, students must be involved in bodies that make decisions related to the curriculum. Students can be tremendously effective partners in fund-raising efforts for service-learning because they can tell potential donors firsthand about the benefits that both students and communities derive.

Similarly, partnerships that are sustained over time are grounded in opportunities for consistent communication and the initiation of positive change. Adapting the seventh benchmark to student partnerships could involve the creation of regular forums for open communication between administrators and students. A service-learning advisory board that includes several student members is one way to institutionalize the partnership. In addition, campus spaces can be established to encourage genuine, inclusive dialogue.

The emphasis of the final benchmark is on evaluation. In a genuine democratic partnership, students would fully participate in defining the desired outcomes of service-learning experiences for all parties and then in designing measures to assess the degree to which they are achieved.

Profiles of Successful Partnerships

This section offers specific examples of reciprocal, democratic service-learning partnerships with students. These examples represent a wide range of higher education institutions and organizations and are readily adaptable for replication.

Student Partnerships with Institutional Leaders

"Being involved with service-learning has helped me gain leadership skills and develop my values," says Jason Johnson, a student at Ferris State University in Grand Rapids, Michigan (personal communication, March 2001). Administrators at Ferris State believe that open dialogue about service-learning practices helps maintain the validity and value of the program. Student leaders from the Student Volunteer Center engage in regular conversations regarding service-learning issues with university president William Sederburg. Recent topics of discussion have included minimizing liability for students in the community, the types of service that should be offered, and including Campus Compact membership dues in the institutional budget (J. Johnson, personal communication, March 2001).

"It's been two and a half years now since I graduated, and I don't know if President Stone has any idea how much of an impact he had on my life and future," says Amanda Schafer, an alumna of Michigan's Alma College who became community director at George Washington University's Community Living and Learning Center (personal communication, October 2001). Anne Ritz, service-learning coordinator at Alma College, says that the work President Alan Stone and Schafer accomplished was an example of a strong president, a strong student, and a "natural fit" (personal communication, October 2001). Schafer had access to President Stone through regular meetings he routinely schedules with the student body president and the editor of the school newspaper. Schafer, as both student body president and external coordinator for Students Offering Service (SOS), consulted with Dr. Stone about her concern with the deterioration of that service organization. President Stone's counsel, encouragement, and letters of support enabled Schafer to successfully compete for a Michigan Campus Compact grant to restructure the SOS program into what has become a more vital and effective entity. Says Schafer, "President Stone pushed me to organize bigger things" (personal communication, October 2001).

"What students remember of their college experience is being taken as a colleague," says Jeremy Cohen, associate vice provost for undergraduate education at Pennsylvania State University (personal communication, October 2001). Cohen's belief in students led him to seek committed students to work with him to initiate what has become the Mt. Union Nutrition Project, a partnership between the institution and a small, rural farming community about an hour from the campus. Three communication students, and later several nutrition students, responded to Cohen's invitation to present workshops to middle and senior high school students in Mt. Union over spring break in 1997. The program became a "wild success" and has achieved permanency within the College of Health and Human Development. Cohen gives credit for success of the program to his student partners and says his roles were to be an advocate on campus, to help "lower walls and fences," to provide mentoring, to be sure reflection was a strong part of the program from the beginning, and "to be there symbolically for the students and the institution—to say this is important" (personal communication, October 2001).

Open communication allows presidents and top administrators to understand the benefits and challenges of service-learning and encourages them to support it. Partnerships with presidents and other administrators offer students the empowering experience of acceptance as colleagues in the educational enterprise.

Student Partnerships with Service-Learning Program Administrators

Successful centers for service-learning incorporate student talents in multiple ways. Some provide students with democratic decision-making experiences within the center itself. Students who serve in such positions as program directors, community liaisons, office staff, or members of the center's advisory board have the opportunity to hold the power and responsibility of true leaders. Students at the Center for Service-Learning at Brevard Community College in Cocoa, Florida, are called just that: service-learning leaders. Selected through a rigorous application process, these students have five main responsibilities: to recruit student volunteers; to schedule, orient, and train volunteers; to develop and maintain strong community partnerships; to study the process of service-learning; and to solve problems as they arise. Terri Bridson, who now coordinates the America Reads program at Brevard, became engaged in service as a student in an education course and is now a service-learning leader. Her increased role has helped her maintain her excitement about service-learning and learn more about the challenges she may face in her future teaching career. While her professors provide the necessary theoretical frameworks and technical skills in curriculum development and classroom management and the service director provides support, Bridson is responsible for the overall direction of the America Reads program and the students who are involved in it (R. Henry, personal communication, February 2001).

"Partnering with students is my greatest challenge and my greatest joy," says Judy Rauner, director of the Office for Community Service-Learning at the University of San Diego (USD). "The challenge involves collaboratively increasing the quality of their leadership development. They bring such creativity to the process. Students run our programs" (personal communication, October 2001). USD's Office for Community Service-Learning utilizes faculty-student leader teams to facilitate service-learning logistics and reflections for the thirty to thirty-five service-learning courses offered each semester in an array of disciplines. In advertising community service leader positions to students, the first benefit mentioned is the opportunity to collaborate with a professor to empower fellow students. Students who have worked as community service leaders with a faculty member can continue as associates and design their own leadership roles through the Office of Community Service-Learning. In addition, students have equal representation, with faculty and community partners, on the office's advisory committee (J. Rauner, personal communication, October 2001).

Without official designation as leaders, a group of visionary students led by Dan Gregory created the Center for Service-Learning at Pima Community College in Pima, Arizona. Because these students felt their peers in all disciplines could benefit from serving the community while acquiring academic knowledge, they approached Pima students, faculty members, and administrators, as well as community agencies, to enlist their support in developing a service-learning program. Realizing that both faculty and agencies control student access to service-learning opportunities, the students began recruiting faculty members to join an organization called Service-Learning in College (SLIC). The students and faculty approached community agencies together to garner support. More than fifty agencies wrote letters, which were included in "The Book," a compilation of materials supporting the project. Using the common goals of strengthening their understanding of service-learning and providing students with creative projects, faculty and agencies then met at workshops in which they created partnerships with a strong academic focus. These partnerships and "The Book" were the catalysts the administration needed to create a formal center for service-learning, including an advisory committee, that has become a strong institution on the campus (Homan, 1996).

Students at the University of Utah engaged in a similar process as they sought to design a Service-Learning Scholars Program. Andy Cooley, newly elected student body president, commissioned three students to approach faculty members and administrators with the idea of creating the program. Within one year, these students received approval from the University's academic senate and board of trustees to institute a program, administered through the Lowell Bennion Community Service Center, in which students who completed ten semester hours of service-learning course work, four hundred hours of documented service, and a service-learning capstone project receive a service-learning designation on their diploma and special recognition at commencement (I. Fisher, personal communication, January 2001).

Student Partnerships with Service-Learning Faculty

As service-learning class members or as teaching assistants, students can be invaluable partners for service-learning faculty. They bring incredible energy and insight to both the service and the learning. At Fresno State University in Fresno, California, Chris Fiorentino is a faculty member who teaches two courses, service-learning 1 and service-learning 101. He is continually impressed with the outstanding student learning and involvement that occur in these classes. Freshman Amanda Whitten took service-learning 1 to fulfill a requirement for her honors program. After learning about the methodology of service-learning and its value as a classroom teaching technique, Amanda began advocating for more service-learning courses at Fresno State. At Fiorentino's invitation, Amanda represented students among many faculty members at a service-learning task force retreat. Amanda insisted that the students' perspective drive the twenty-three goals that the task force declared important for the furthering of service-learning at Fresno State. She is pleased with the outcomes and recommendations of the task force because she feels that the goals reflect real possibilities for faculty who are just becoming aware of the power of service-learning (C. Fiorentino and A. Whitten, personal communication, March 2001).

Gary Daynes, professor of history at Brigham Young University in Provo, Utah, reflects on his experience with one of the many teaching assistants he works with to teach American Heritage, a general education course, which has enrolled more than 2,200 students last semester: "There was some point where the faculty-student thing disappeared. We became colleagues, friends, co-authors" (personal communication, October 2001). Ellen Rife, one of Daynes' thirty teaching assistants who began teaching with Daynes as a junior and is now a second-year graduate student, says, "Having Gary's respect (and it was hard to call him Gary for a long time) is just a gift. He's amazing with teaching assistants. We meet weekly to design the class, to evaluate and make changes, to write exams" (personal communication, October 2001). Each teaching assistant, or "co-teacher" in Daynes' words, leads a weekly reflection section for students engaged in one of four modes of civic engagement, including service-learning. Honesty and openness characterize Daynes' relationship with his teaching assistants. He describes a session in which his teaching assistants told him that he had not been clear in his previous lecture section. Rife voices the amazement she and the other teaching assistants felt when Daynes went into the class the next week, told the class he knew he had not been clear the previous week, and covered the material again. Daynes explains the mutual dependence that has evolved between him and his teaching assistants: "I can't possibly teach 2,268 students, and many of my TAs feel like they can't possibly handle four discussion sections of thirty students. But I can make a better attempt at it together with them" (personal communication, October 2001).

Chris West, a senior majoring in biology, and Stephanie English, a senior majoring in English and minoring in values, ethics, and social action, together coordinate the student-initiated Service-Learning Challenge at Allegheny College in Meadville, Pennsylvania. As director of community service within the Allegheny Center for Experiential Learning, David Roncolato is the students' link to the institution, but "leaves the ball in our court," says English (personal communication, October 2001). Originally conceptualized by two students as a challenge that all students engage in a service experience, Service-Learning Challenge has become a program in which teams of two students work with a faculty member to teach a course with a service component. During the fall semester, West and English select students who introduce service-learning into the course, prepare and monitor a service project related to course material, lead reflection sessions, and evaluate the course. Asked why he has taken on this work, West says that it is because he really believes in service-learning and thinks it's an "awesome" learning tool. He likes getting other students involved and views it as very empowering for him and for other students (C. West, personal communication, October 2001).

Involving students as teachers requires faculty to modify or even abandon traditional teaching methods. The benefits of teaching partnerships with students, including more engaging class discussions, more meaningful and relevant reflection, and closer contact with community partners, to say nothing of shared workload, are likely to far outweigh the loss of control that may accompany less reliance on traditional pedagogy.

Student Partnerships with Communities

At several universities, students who have taken service-learning classes or participated in staff-led service have gone on to enter into direct community partnerships. In most cases, the students' involvement in projects in a particular community led them to identify an unfilled need and to work with community agency and/or neighborhood representatives to design a program to address it. As Veronica Francis, a student at Springfield College's School of Human Services, in St. Johnsbury, Vermont, explains: "I now see community as a group of connectedness. We must listen to our communities to solve problems" (personal communication, March 2001).

Springfield College's School of Human Services requires students to conduct a twelve- to sixteen-month service-learning project after taking a course on community issues and research. They then divide into groups, and each group is assigned an adviser. The adviser is a "sounding board" only and has no control over the direction the students take. In 1994, Francis and two women classmates became interested in women's issues. They began by spending several months listening to diverse women, including housewives, factory workers, single mothers, landowners, and professionals. As a result of their research, the students determined that in their rural location, the greatest problems faced by women were economic insecurity and feelings of isolation. In response, these three students received an $80,000 grant to create the Women's Rural Entrepreneurial Network (WREN). In its first year, WREN assisted ten women through skill-building classes, discussion forums, and subgrants to create their own businesses. Since then, WREN's membership has increased to five hundred, two hundred of whom own and run their own businesses. Francis admits that the idea for this type of organization had been in her mind for some time, but without the framework and course content provided by the college, it never would have gotten off the ground. Service-learning is a powerful vehicle for social change and community building when students have the tools they need to become real partners (personal communication, March 2001).

In the fall of 1998, two students at the University of Maryland in College Park, Ken Liffiton, a government and politics major, and Sheila Somashekhar, a biology and art major, took an introductory urban studies course that involved service-learning. Dr. Bill Hanna, the faculty member teaching the course, had developed an ongoing partnership with residents of Langley Park, a community with a large percentage of recent immigrants with high unemployment and low family incomes that is located within a stone's throw from the campus. To fulfill their service requirement, the students in the course taught English to Langley Park adults who had not yet acquired English language skills. The students were shocked at how little the community members knew about the university and at how little they knew about Langley Park. The following year, they formed Beyond These Walls, a student organization with the mission of bridging the gap between the campus and the Langley Park community. Among other programs, Beyond These Walls volunteers operate an after-school art and reading program at the local elementary school and evening adult literacy classes. Members of Beyond These Walls also regularly attend meetings of Action Langley Park, a community group supported by Hanna, to forge additional linkages between the university and the community (B. Jacoby, personal communication, July 2001).

Learning for Life (L4L), another example of students partnering with a community, has a unique twist: the "community partner" exists right on the campus. L4L began as an idea to conduct an adult literacy program for employees with limited literacy skills at Swarthmore College in Swarthmore, Pennsylvania. Early in the program's development, its student leaders realized that by calling it a literacy program, they would force participants to reveal themselves as illiterate. Professor Diane Anderson, in Swarthmore's education program, helped the students realize that there are many kinds of literacy and that we conceptualize literacy too narrowly if we focus only on reading and writing. L4L has helped the entire campus learn that almost anything can be a literacy activity. In its current form, still directed by a student, the program matches individuals who want to learn a new skill or concept with a learning partner with similar interests. Learning partnerships are between Swarthmore students and employees who work maintaining facilities, in dining services, and as environmental service technicians. The program started in 2001 with fifty matched learning partners and hopes to quickly double this number. Partner teams have learned to knit, swim, prepare for the GED, develop driving or athletic skills, expand computer knowledge, and much more. One staff member from Vietnam was a newspaper reporter in her own country but knew no English and was earning minimum wage at Swarthmore. She worked with a Vietnamese student who had never known her native language and expanded her own grasp of English.

Susie Ansell, currently a senior, has directed the program since she was a freshman. Ansell guided the program through an initial problem phase when supervisors thought employees would be taking off time irresponsibly in order to participate. The real experience was that the employees worked faster and better. The institution has been supportive from the beginning and funds one to three hours of paid time for each employee who participates. Recently, Ansell instituted a coordinating committee of students, employees, and faculty. Pat James, director of community service learning programs at Swarthmore, who says she "mostly watches in amazement," concludes that "Swarthmore College is a better place because we are a better community" (S. Ansell and P. James, personal communication, October 2001).

Student Partnerships with Alumni

According to Scott Warnick, University of Utah Bennion Center alumni president, the purpose of the alumni organization is "to support students in their current service work and demonstrate a lifelong ethic of service" (personal communication, March 2001). In 1999, former Bennion Center student leaders spent six months developing an alumni organizational structure to engage alumni and support current students in a variety of roles. After creating a written charter, alumni leaders invited other Bennion Center alumni to volunteer for alumni leadership roles. They began sponsoring regular one-time service projects, offering assistance to current student leaders, and participating in Bennion Center fundraising. The Alumni Cabinet, the leadership team for the group, meets regularly to explore additional ideas that can reengage alumni in meaningful community work (S. Warnick, personal communication, March 2001).

In 1988, as the celebration of the twentieth anniversary of the Youth Educational Services (Y.E.S.) Program at Humboldt State University in Arcata, California, approached, a student suggested that former students who had shaped this successful program should be included in the celebration. Y.E.S. is an energetic service-learning program that each year sponsors twelve to fifteen student-run programs that are based on community needs. Current students involved in Y.E.S. launched an alumni campaign and succeeded in identifying nearly two hundred alumni of the program, most of whom still lived in the area. Y.E.S. alumni now serve on steering committees, advise current programs, contribute resources, participate in service activities, and receive annual newsletters. Those alumni who work as staff at local community agencies also create new service-learning partnerships with students (C. Douglas, personal communication, February 2001). As these two examples illustrate, active service-learning alumni can offer lifelong opportunities for service to fellow alumni, support the institution and service-learning programs through contributions of their own skills and resources, and serve as role models for current students.

Student Partnerships with State and National Organizations

Student partnerships with state and national service-learning organizations enrich the organizations, campus-community partnerships, and the experience of the students involved. In some cases, the organizations have initiated opportunities to partner with students; in others, students have themselves created the organizations.

Student Partnerships with State Campus Compacts

Several state Campus Compacts have partnered with students in different ways. For example, Michigan Campus Compact has created a formal network of students from all thirty-five member institutions. Two students from each serve as Student Community Action Network (SCAN) representatives, who meet one Friday each month to network, problem solve, and discuss issues pertaining to community service. "It is critical to establish networks and work in collaboration with others to improve programs," says Katie Koski, a student at Central Michigan University (personal communication, March 2001). Kimberly Lane, SCAN adviser, is continually impressed by the in-depth discussions at these student-led meetings and the complexity of the issues the students bring to them. Often information from SCAN meetings influences the decisions of faculty and administrators of Michigan Campus Compact regarding community issues and program development. For Koski, a three-year SCAN representative, the opportunity to learn from her peers improves her university's service-learning programs and enhances the development of her own sense of values. Learning from others gives her a broader perspective on her role in the community (K. Koski and K. Lane, personal communication, February and March 2001).

In the spring of 1998, students from fifteen Minnesota campuses met to create a statewide student network, Students Together for Action, Networking, and Development (STAND), to operate within the Minnesota Campus Compact and to support the efforts of student leaders across the state. More recently, the state Compact has initiated the STAND Leaders Program, as part of the AmeriCorps education award program. A corps of fifty student leaders serves as coordinators and leaders of service-learning projects (J. Myhre, personal communication, March 2001).

Student Partnerships with National Campus Compact

Campus Compact, whose members are college and university presidents, recognizes the importance of partnerships with students. In 1998, Campus Compact received funds from the Templeton Foundation for a project that initiated conversations between student leaders and presidents at 122 campuses across the country. The conversations enabled the students to learn about the presidents' commitment to civic and character education and how they regard service-learning as a vehicle for that education (Campus Compact, 1999). Through these dialogues, students also told their presidents about the benefits they derived from involvement in service-learning and how the presidents could take an active role in providing additional opportunities and support for service-learning. A number of the students published articles based on their conversations in campus or local media. As a result, broader conversations have occurred, and support for service learning has increased at many participating institutions (P. Boylan, personal communication, February 2001).

In March 2001, Campus Compact convened a student summit at the Johnson Foundation's Wingspread Conference Center in Racine, Wisconsin. It assembled thirty-five juniors and seniors from across the country who were heavily engaged in service. Campus Compact staff deemed the event very successful because the students brought important new perspectives to the organization. The summit explored, among other topics, how students view the connections between service-learning and civic education and whether involvement in service leads students to deeper civic engagement. Plans are under way for a second summit to convene earlier in their college careers students with less service-learning experience (K. Heffernan, personal communication, April 2001).

National Organizations Created by Students

In 1985, a group of recent college graduates formed the Campus Outreach Opportunity League (COOL) to encourage students to serve their communities. Since then, COOL has supported thousands of student-initiated service projects, and more than two thousand students attend COOL's annual conferences (Jacoby, 1996). Each year COOL hosts its national conference on a different campus. Supported by national COOL staff who spend time at the host institution, students work closely with the staff and serve as conference planners. All decisions are made by consensus. Prior to the 1999 COOL conference held at the University of Utah, two national staff members from COOL moved to Salt Lake City for the academic year prior to the conference, worked out of the Bennion Center, and developed a strong partnership with a working group of students who provided the leadership for the conference planning and implementation (I. Fisher, personal communication, March 2001). Justin Olsen, a student conference committee member, recalls his experience as a powerful combination of learning about group process and making individual contributions: "Realize your role, but stand up for your beliefs" (personal communication, March 2001).

In 1989, Lisa Madry and Clay Thorpe, two students at the University of North Carolina–Chapel Hill who were deeply interested in literacy education, came to the realization that many campus literacy programs lacked the support they needed to fully serve their clients. Believing that young people can make a tremendous contribution to literacy education, Madry and Thorpe began the process of creating a nonprofit organization to connect campus literacy programs that sought help with those that could provide it. Today, the Student Coalition for Action in Literacy Education (SCALE) is a comprehensive network of students, adult learners, administrators, literacy educators, and community partners that is part of the School of Education at the University of North Carolina. SCALE provides a full range of technical assistance to students and member institutions, including on-site training, consultation via telephone and e-mail, regional and national conferences, grants, publications, and network referrals. All the services and resources SCALE provides "reflect SCALE's commitment to participatory literacy and college student leadership" [www.unc. edu/depts/scale, 2001].

Started ten years ago by campus-based Public Interest Research Groups (PIRGs) and USA for Africa, the National Student Campaign Against Hunger and Homelessness (NSCAHH) is the largest student network in the country working directly on these issues. More than six hundred institutions in forty-five states are members of the coalition. NSCAHH helps students organize Hunger and Homelessness Awareness weeks on their campuses and has involved 110,000 volunteers in service projects to raise more than $1 million for domestic and international relief through the Annual Hunger Cleanup. The organization offers publications and training to students and community members regarding strategies for creating or enhancing service programs. It also organizes antipoverty political efforts and establishes food salvage programs to channel surpluses from restaurants to food banks and shelters. Like COOL, NSCAHH holds its annual conference at a different campus each year and involves students at the host institutions in all aspects of conference planning and implementation [www.pirg. org/nscahh, 2001].

Making Student Partnerships Work: Lessons Learned

From conversations with service-learning practitioners and our own experiences, we offer five "lessons learned" as potential guideposts for educators seeking to create or strengthen partnerships with students. As is true regarding the other kinds of partnerships described in this book, and human relationships in general, high-quality, lasting partnerships with students require considerable time and energy.

The students, faculty, and service-learning administrators we interviewed consistently stated that respect for students and a belief in their power to achieve important outcomes are the core values essential to successful partnerships. When students truly share power with other service-learning practitioners, when they understand that others believe that they can achieve, and when appropriate supports are in place, desired learning and service outcomes can be achieved. Faculty and staff who find it challenging to believe in the capacity of students to be full partners often need only to confer with colleagues and students to find concrete examples of students who have succeeded in making a positive difference as partners in service-learning. This chapter contains several such examples. Needless to say, when a community service director says to a student, "You are in charge of this program," the partnership can only succeed if subsequent actions truly reinforce that leadership charge.

Our own experiences, reinforced by comments of others, lead us to the second lesson: building partnerships with students requires an ability to live with ambiguity. The balance between student development and accountability is continually challenged. Campus leaders must keep one eye on commitments to concrete outcomes for community partners, while maximizing learning and leadership opportunities for students. Successful partnerships with students must hold all participants accountable, but within a power-sharing, supportive environment that avoids reasserting "power over" students when a fear or actuality of failure looms. Allowing for the varying motivations and interests of students and their partners to guide their joint efforts is essential for successful partnerships.

Conversations with successful campus partners suggest that colleges and universities should offer a wide range of service-learning experiences intentionally designed for students at different points in their education and at various stages of development (Jacoby, 1996). A key to attracting student partners is providing them with choices that appeal to them. These should be selected in partnership with students and could include curricular opportunities, such as working with faculty in research and serving as teaching assistants; cocurricular opportunities for both individual and group service; and paid positions through Federal-Work Study or AmeriCorps/VISTA. When students are encouraged to choose opportunities that fit their own interests, values, and needs, they are more likely to be dedicated to the causes for which they work. Likewise, when students are satisfied with their roles, they are more likely to be successful and continue with their service involvement.

As service-learning educators seek to create partnerships with students, they could use as models other kinds of partnerships in which student affairs professionals have traditionally engaged students. For example, students routinely serve in such paraprofessional positions as resident assistants and orientation advisers. There is much to be learned from residence hall and orientation program staff about how they select, train, supervise, and support their student partners. A national model of student leadership that has great potential for adaptation to the campus level is the National Association for College and University Residence Halls (NACURH). This nonprofit organization is completely student-run. Students fill the three national administrative positions and the three administrative positions for each of the eight regions, as well as serving as chapter presidents on their home campuses. The unique structure of this organization allows students to determine the direction of residence hall involvement, create programming to meet identified student needs, control resources for implementation, and hold annual regional and national conferences (E. Lofgren, personal communication, February 2001).

We have found that successful service-learning partnerships with students reflect the culture and the needs of the students of the specific campuses on which they are created. As faculty, staff, and students attempt to design new programs or revitalize existing ones, it is useful to study models that work at other institutions. However, models that work at urban institutions may not readily adapt to rural environments, programs at residential campuses may not work at commuter institutions or community colleges, and successful efforts at large research universities are often difficult to translate to small college settings.

Conclusion

If, as we and an increasing number of service-learning educators believe, the purpose of service-learning relates strongly to the development of the values and skills of active citizenship, authentic partnerships with students require that institutions of higher education themselves serve as models of democratic practice. Astin states that "campuses are modeling certain values in the way they conduct themselves professionally: how students are treated in and out of class, how professional colleagues deal with one another, and how institutions are run. If those in higher education want students to acquire the democratic virtues of honesty, tolerance, empathy, generosity, teamwork, cooperation, service, and social responsibility, then they must model these same qualities not only in individual professional conduct but also in their curriculum, teaching techniques, and institutional policies" (1999, p. 37).

In the specific instance of service-learning, democratic practice would entail involving students in the development of service-learning policies and practices. Democratic practice in the classroom, as described by Reeher and Cammarano (1997), would become more commonplace. The shared learning associated with service-learning pedagogy would, in some cases, replace the traditional classroom model in which faculty are the expert disseminators of knowledge while students are the recipients (D. Lisman, personal communication, February 2001).

As described in Chapters Ten and Eleven, student-faculty partnerships for community-based research can and should be expanded. Such partnerships would be particularly well suited to research institutions that seek to involve undergraduates in research and could enable faculty to involve larger numbers of students than more traditional research models.

Further, faculty-student partnerships could encourage service-learning faculty to accompany rather than send their students into the community. Active partnership within the classroom is important, but a deeper type of partnership can evolve as students and faculty work side by side to address community needs and issues. Opportunities for true mentorship become more frequent as the artificial barriers that often separate students and faculty crumble in the urgency of shared work of real significance.

Finally, in this chapter we suggest that authentic partnerships with students can serve as a catalytic force for the development of democratic processes across entire campuses over time. Institutions grounded in democratic practice, in turn, are more able to develop democratic partnerships with their communities.

References

Astin, A. W. "Promoting Leadership, Scholarship, and Democracy: What Higher Education Can Do." In R. G. Bringle, R. Games, and E. A. Malloy (eds.), *Colleges and Universities as Citizens*. Needham Heights, Mass.: Allyn & Bacon, 1999.

Campus Compact. *Progress Report, College Students Interview Presidents About Civic Responsibility*. Providence, R.I.: Campus Compact, 1999.

Homan, M. "A Little Something for Dessert." [http://www.mc.maricopa.edu/academic/compact/ccc/dessert.html]. Sept. 1996.

Jacoby, B. (ed.). *Service-Learning in Higher Education: Concepts and Practices.* San Francisco: Jossey-Bass, 1996.

Reeher, G., and Cammarano, J. (eds.). *Education for Citizenship: Ideas and Innovations in Political Learning.* Lanham, Md.: Rowman & Littlefield, 1997.

Torres, J. (ed.). *Benchmarks for Campus/Community Partnerships.* Providence, R.I.: Campus Compact, 2000.

Chapter Six

Developing an Infrastructure for Service-Learning and Community Engagement

Jennifer M. Pigza and Marie L. Troppe

In this chapter we propose three models of campuswide infrastructure that supports service-learning and community engagement. The more broadly and deeply the infrastructure is constructed, the more effective service-learning initiatives will be and the more likely they will lead to a campus culture of community engagement. The literature that informs this discussion is based on research on institutionalizing service-learning and cultivating a campus community that supports civic engagement.

Three assumptions provide the foundation for this exploration. First, no one method or structural framework can work for all colleges and universities. Aspects of the three models presented here can be adapted to meet the character, needs, and mission of particular campuses and communities. Second, developing a campuswide infrastructure for service-learning involves the entire institution as well as community partners. Service-learning, by definition, requires numerous connections and partnerships—among faculty, students, and staff; between the university and the community; and between those being served and those doing service. Lastly, a campus committed to institutionalizing service-learning does not promote service-learning solely for its own benefit or for its students' educational opportunities. Service-learning must be grounded in reciprocal, authentic partnerships with the community. It is most likely to thrive in an institution that pursues an engaged campus identity. Institutionalizing service-learning entails not only a shift in policies and practices that support service-learning as a valid form of teaching, research, and service but also a commitment to civic engagement by the institution as a whole.

This chapter begins with an overview of relevant theoretical frameworks. With these concepts in mind, we present three models of infrastructures that in varying degrees support service-learning and community engagement. Nine benchmarks accompany the models and serve as an institutional self-assessment tool. Just as no one model provides a blueprint for institutional infrastructure, no one institution serves as a perfect example for others. Thus this chapter utilizes examples from several colleges and universities to illustrate effective practice. Finally, we offer suggestions for action and present an agenda for future directions and research.

Theoretical Frameworks

The theoretical foundation for our work begins with Boyer's (1990) four dimensions of scholarship: discovery, integration, application, and teaching. He expands the traditional view of scholarship and paves the way for the concept of the scholarship of engagement. In 1994, Boyer envisioned a "New American College" that would "connect thought to action" and "organize cross-disciplinary institutes around pressing social issues" (p. A48). Bringle, Games, and Malloy (1999) build on Boyer's work by examining the institutional landscape and promoting the concept of colleges and universities as citizens. Like Boyer, Checkoway (1997) calls on educators to think deeply about the purposes of higher education and to create a new vision of scholarship. Checkoway considers campus and community as co-learners, examines access to knowledge, and expresses concern about knowledge utilization.

Saltmarsh (1998) and Bringle (2001) provide new insights into the nature of relationships between campuses and communities. Saltmarsh discusses definitions of community, the relative weight of sets of relationships over the impact of geography, and issues of coexistence and common interest. Drawing on his background in psychology, Bringle compares tasks in the development of personal relationships to the tasks in campus-community partnership development. He notes components of closeness that can characterize both personal relationships and campus-community partnerships.

In addition to the above perspectives, several practical assessment tools enable institutions to determine their degrees of service-learning institutionalization and civic engagement. Holland (1997) proposes a matrix that relates levels of commitment to service from low relevance to full integration, with characteristics of key organizational factors at each level, including mission, faculty involvement, and campus publications. The *Presidents' Declaration on the Civic Responsibility of Higher Education* (Campus Compact, 1999) ends with a series of questions for use in assessing campus commitment to civic engagement. The Comprehensive Action Plan for Service-Learning (CAPSL) model (Bringle and Hatcher, 1996) identifies ten principal activities that support the success of service-learning to be pursued by faculty, students, the institution, and the community. A three-year study of forty-three colleges and universities outlines the defining characteristics of how campuses move along the continuum of service-learning institutionalization and differences in that movement between types of institutions (Furco, 2001). The conceptual work of rethinking the purposes of higher education, creating new visions of scholarship, and adjusting the lens through which we view community, plus the practical application of assessment tools, led to the development of the three models that follow.

Three Models of Infrastructure for Service-Learning and Community Engagement

The models in this chapter were adapted from models developed during a 1999 project, "Establishing Benchmarks for the Engaged Campus," funded by Campus Compact. The University of Maryland, one of ten institutional grantees, created a team of twenty-one university and community representatives (students, faculty, academic and student affairs staff, city employees, and professionals from local nonprofit agencies and public schools), which was chaired by the authors of this chapter, to discuss the concept of the engaged campus. By design, the team was broad in scope and represented both the institution's current, positive community partnerships and its aspirations for engagement. After several intensive meetings, the group produced a report intended to provide a snapshot in time of the nature and scope of the university's role as an "engaged campus" (Pigza and Troppe, 2000). Although the models were developed to address the concept of the "engaged campus," they are expanded here to address issues of building a campuswide infrastructure for service-learning and community engagement.

We present three models for infrastructure development: concentrated, fragmented, and integrated (see Figure 6.1). While the third model is the most desired, the first two provide valued benefits to the community and university. A university should maximize the positive features of these three models as they fit its context and community. As Checkoway (1997) reminds us, "No single structure fits all universities; the key is to fit structure to situation" (p. 312). The three models are based on an institutional perspective rather than a programmatic one. In other words, each model demonstrates how a whole institution as opposed to a single program or entity such as a centralized service-learning center expresses its community engagement. The same principles apply to building campuswide infrastructure for service-learning. A network of committed units enables wider and deeper service-learning infrastructure than individual units acting in isolation.

The diagram for each model includes a university and its internal components, indicated by a large circle with smaller enclosed circles, and community partners, indicated by squares. The degree of the commitment, knowledge, and resources of any component is represented by the shading of the circle or square: the darker the shading, the greater the degree of commitment, knowledge, and resources to the partnership. Arrows represent a relationship between two entities and the prevailing direction of communication. Finally, each model is described in terms of five factors: communication, access, resources, engagement, and responsibility.

Concentrated Model

In the concentrated model of engagement, the arrows in the diagram represent closed circuits; activities are highly structured but limited to discrete areas of the institution. These specific units

Figure 6.1. Models of Infrastructure for Service-Learning and Engagement

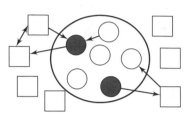 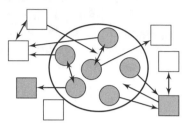

Concentrated

Communication
Communication with the community is largely one-directional and controlled by the university. Very little communication within the institution.

Access
Significant barriers to access for the community with the university. Few, if any, partnerships.

Resources
Community is not recognized for strength, knowledge, and resources.

Engagements
Engagement occurs in specific ways with specific entities.

Responsibility
Responsibility for engagement is concentrated in and limited to designated units within the university.

Fragmented

Communication
Limited communication within the institution. Increasing communication between community partners.

Access
More partnerships and easier access.

Resources
Units of the university begin to recognize the strength, knowledge, and resources of community partners.

Engagements
Broad and varied engagement, but little or no coordination of expertise or information.

Responsibility
Many university units contribute a little, but there is no centralized strength or coordination of efforts.

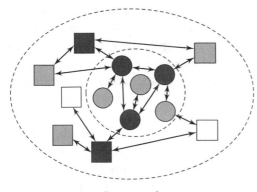

Squares = Community
Partners

Circles = University Units

Darker Shading = Increasing
Engagement

Arrows = Relationship and
Communication

Integrated

Communication
Communication inside and outside the university
is facilitated by established connections. Mutual
ongoing evaluation and assessment of the
partnerships are part of communication.

Access
University boundaries are permeable, and the
university is viewed as part of the community.

Resources
Expertise both in the community and the
university is recogized. Resources are shared
willingly when possible.

Engagements
Grow and adapt through time and build social
capital for future success. Relationships are built
on mutually defined goals and objectives.

Responsibility
Expertise and resources are centered in specific
units of the university and community. These
coordinate and promote engagement throughout
the entire system.

within the university are charged with the responsibility of campus-community partnerships. Personnel, knowledge, and resources are concentrated in these units; little or no responsibility for engagement, or knowledge of the activities and ethos of engagement, is evidenced in other areas of the institution. Additionally, in the concentrated model of engagement, the context and content of the relationships with community entities are largely determined by the university and its needs and desires. The relationship is rather one-directional, and community access to university resources is often minimal.

Holland's (1997) research reveals that the concentrated centers of expertise and resources "were often seen as fully responsible for sustaining institutional service efforts and, in some cases, were judged to inhibit the interest of others on campus ('they do service in that center, so I don't have to think about service in my work')" (p. 36). The benefits of amassing expertise and resources in concentrated locations include easy identification and inventory of efforts, less chance of duplication, and clear access points for community partners. The drawbacks, however, such as lack of integration of community engagement throughout the campus culture, prevent the university and community partners from realizing many potential benefits.

Fragmented Model

The second model of engagement is characterized by fragmentation. Communication, access, and resources are much more fluid than in the concentrated model, but because of the distributed nature of the efforts, the university is often accurately described as disorganized and unaware of the efforts and relationships happening on its own campus. As a result, community partners are often "tapped" by multiple units of the university, community members' requests and questions may be lost or not directed to the most appropriate university resource, and there is frequent duplication of efforts within the university. The arrows in the diagram here represent open circuits; activities are prevalent across the institution and less rigid than in the concentrated model, but they often lack the organization needed to provide lasting impact.

The benefits of this model include the growing recognition of the resources of community partners and their ability to be in more equal relationships with university entities. There is also increased communication among community partners and within the university. The lack of centralized coordination and responsibility, however, prevents maximum successful engagement.

Integrated Model

Finally, the integrated model reflects what Checkoway (1997) describes as "a commitment to collaboration among co-learners on campus and in the community" (p. 312). The walls between the university and potential community partners become more permeable, and a greater understanding of the university as a *part of* the community rather than *apart from* the community is strong. This model incorporates the best aspects of the first two models, expands the capacity of all parties to engage in mutually beneficial relationships, and attempts to answer the question, "How well does our campus create structures that generate a more porous and interactive flow of knowledge between campus and communities?" (Campus Compact, 1999, p. 7).

The arrows in the integrated model diagram represent coordination and communication of service-learning efforts. Dark circles represent centers of expertise and facilitation; gray circles represent gateways to service-learning and engagement. Activities can be readily adapted to fit the needs of campus-community partnerships; more or less structure can be negotiated to keep advancing the effort. If momentum for a particular initiative gets roadblocked in one area, it can be rerouted elsewhere to accomplish its purpose. Not only do campus units link community partners together, but community partners also link campus units together.

Within the university, overall responsibilities are coordinated in specified units, but a culture of engagement permeates the institution throughout multiple academic and nonacademic departments. A critical mass of individuals and units in the university engages with the community, creating synergy that enhances the capacity of both the community and the university to meet their shared and individual goals. In the integrated model, the campus builds sustainability rather than simply focusing on meeting immediate needs.

While the integrated model is ideal, its manifestation is unique to each campus. By its very nature, there is no one simple "integrated model." The model suggests characteristics of effective infrastructure, and these features must be adapted to a particular institution rather than overlaid onto a campus wholesale.

Indicators of a Campus Infrastructure That Supports Service-Learning and Community Engagement

Several indicators to guide institutions in a self-assessment of their progress toward developing a campus infrastructure that supports service-learning and community engagement flow from the three models. Three concepts are key to using the benchmarks as an assessment tool: impact, intentionality, and visibility.

A college or university must be prepared to specify the *impact* that service-learning and engagement create in relation to each benchmark. Impact may be measured in concrete terms, such as the number of children tutored, housing units refurbished, or service-learning courses offered. It is equally important, however, to note the intangible benefits that strengthen a community's social capital and capacity. One such intangible benefit might be the extent to which new leadership continually emerges and develops within the community.

Evaluating the benchmarks from the perspective of intentionality and visibility is also important. The lens of *intentionality* challenges the university to determine the extent to which programs and policies result from a specific desire to connect the university with the community and from the recognition of interdependency between university and community partners. Intentionality involves coherent, deliberate action rather than simply capturing the unintentional byproducts of actions. It is about directing action toward certain outcomes. *Visibility* implies the extent to which those inside and outside the institution are aware of the university's engaged activities and can understand and access information and resources. The lens of visibility is not a campaign to promote good deeds but comes from a standpoint of building collaborative relationships and sustaining ongoing development within the community.

The following nine benchmarks are stated in their ideal form. While each has a specific focus, the benchmarks operate interdependently. In concert they ask these fundamental questions: What are we doing? How are we doing it? How well are we doing it? To what end are we doing it?

1. *Institutional mission.* The *Wingspread Declaration on Renewing the Civic Mission of the American Research University* (Boyte and Hollander, 1999) encourages presidents of colleges and universities to actualize the promise of civic responsibility that is often included in mission statements. Holland (1997) highlights institutional mission as one of the seven factors used to evaluate an institution's commitment to service-learning. The campus is cognizant of the extent to which its mission supports service-learning and community partnerships. Students, faculty, and staff as well as community members understand the university's mission, recognize that service-learning actualizes the mission, and participate in the mission's fulfillment.

2. *Internal and external points of access.* This benchmark "requires recognition that both the individual and the institution have responsibility for knowledge utilization and that formal structures are necessary for the process" (Checkoway, 1997, p. 311). This accessibility occurs through personal interactions as well as print resources such as "catalogs, strategic plans, recruitment materials, annual reports, alumni publications, newsletters, and even budgets" (Holland, 1997, p. 38). Potential community partners in service-learning can easily find the institutional resources they seek and receive quick and accurate referrals to them. The institution assesses constituents' satisfaction with its responsiveness to their requests and concerns. The campus also evaluates its capacity to initiate activities and provide information about resources, facilities, and opportunities.

3. *Cocurricular opportunities.* Because service-learning occurs in both curricular and cocurricular venues, the campus encourages student involvement in activities and organizations that promote university-community partnerships and foster a culture of civic engagement. Examples of this involvement include community service organizations, fraternities and sororities, residence halls, faith communities, and other student groups. Cocurricular service-learning enables students to practice leadership skills, develop meaningful relationships with peers and staff, reflect on values and

purpose, deepen their understanding of human difference and commonality, and apply knowledge acquired in classes. A discussion of service-learning becomes part of academic advising, and cocurricular transcripts record service-learning experiences.

4. *Curriculum infusion.* The campus provides opportunities within the curriculum for students to make connections between their academic pursuits and real-world issues. Service-learning, "a pedagogy in which students serve the community and learn from the experience, is one way to reintegrate social values into the curriculum" (Checkoway, 1997, p. 314). Through service-learning courses, action research, internships, and other forms of experiential learning, faculty encourage students to think of themselves as responsible in some way for the advancement of society. The local community is viewed as a rich partner in providing active learning opportunities for students that also benefit the community.

5. *Authentic community partnerships.* Authentic community partnerships are characterized by an acknowledgment of the assets of community partners as well as those of the college or university. "Partnership in this sense would mean more than providing willing volunteers to local service agencies" (Saltmarsh, 1998, p. 7). The university and community value reciprocity. They recognize the realistic parameters of the relationship, accept respectful disagreement, and honestly communicate their limitations and needs. In an institution committed to service-learning and community engagement, there is a mutually understood process by which all parties interact, set priorities, and take action. The overall goal is to increase the capacity of all involved. Faculty development for service-learning occurs with community partners who are seen as co-teachers in the field. Communities are encouraged to name their own issues, goals, assets, and problems; universities are part of this process but not the driving force. Institutions involve community partners in decisions that affect both the service-learning program and the community.

6. *Faculty: teaching, research, and service in the balance.* Various types of research (including action research), curricular infusion of service-learning, and collaborative efforts across academic departments are encouraged and validated through the promotion and tenure process. Reaching this benchmark implies a major cultural shift in academe. Specifically related to service-learning, insti-

tutions can institute faculty development grants for course enhancements, support interdisciplinary efforts, and provide discipline-specific resources such as the American Association for Higher Education's *Series on Service-Learning in the Disciplines* (for example, Battistoni and Hudson, 1997). Faculty are encouraged to strengthen the service-learning currently under way, initiate new projects, and develop the skills to enhance and evaluate student outcomes of service-learning.

7. *Identifying, collaborating, capitalizing on engagement.* Institutionalized, regular information sharing about campus-community partnerships leads to a discussion of shared goals, the recognition of connected agendas, and the development of a common language germane to service-learning and community engagement. These internal relationships extend the university's capacity to respond to the community more effectively and promote collaboration across the campus for similar projects. Institutionalized communication also encourages campus units to recognize their cross-campus support and to develop a critical mass for espousing continual campus culture change. In the integrated model, hubs for service-learning information and collaboration ease faculty access and connection to resources and like-minded colleagues, provide multiple opportunities for students to reflect on service and engagement, and organize a campuswide dialogue about the role of the institution and the individual in social change.

8. *Assessment and generation of knowledge related to service-learning and engagement.* The campus assesses and generates knowledge locally and contributes to the general scholarship of service-learning, engagement, and civic responsibility. The university and community have specific methods for evaluating and assessing their activities, recognizing that university and community partners might define success differently. Research and assessment in areas of student skills and competencies, changes in the local community, and efforts to connect discipline-specific information to service-learning are viewed as important and regularly occur on the campus. In the broader scope, campuses participate in a national dialogue about service-learning and issues of engagement through refereed journals, research centers, and professional organizations.

9. *Administration and resource allocation.* The campus states its commitment to service-learning and community partnerships at

the presidential level and acts upon that commitment throughout the institution. The service-learning program has a secure funding base in the institutional budget; it is not forced to exist from grant to grant. The administrative leadership of the university supports and promotes service-learning, community engagement, and community access to institutional resources. This includes appropriate resources for training, development, implementation, and assessment. Systems for accountability also permeate the institution and indicate the campuswide commitment to service-learning and engagement activities.

The Integrated Model in Practice

Thus far, we have discussed the theoretical foundation for this work, proposed three models for developing an infrastructure that supports service-learning and community engagement, and offered nine benchmarks to serve as self-assessment tools. While no institution is likely to meet each benchmark completely, we contend that striving toward them is critical. This section creates a vision of an integrated campus by drawing examples from multiple institutions. It discusses centers of expertise and facilitation as well as evidence of gateways to universitywide commitment to service-learning.

Centers of Expertise and Facilitation

One of the central features of the integrated model is the balance between centers of service-learning expertise and facilitation and shared responsibility for institutionalizing service-learning in gateways throughout the entire campus and community. Responsibility for engagement is shared throughout the institution, but coordination and communication are facilitated by concentrations of key players. These centers might also be construed as networks of promoters of service-learning or incubators for new projects. They recognize the strength of community partners and involve them heavily in planning and partnerships. On the integrated model diagram, they are indicated by black circles and black squares. In practice, these centers of expertise and facilitation are involved in three major efforts: supporting service-learning initiatives across the institution, developing long-range vision and research agendas, and building relationships between faculty and community partners.

Facilitating Service-Learning Initiatives

In 2000, Tufts University created the University College of Citizenship and Public Service (UCCPS). As a center of expertise and facilitation, it supports and reinforces the efforts of all Tufts schools and departments to foster active citizenship throughout the curriculum. From the beginning of this endeavor, the institution decided that as a guiding principle, UCCPS would coordinate but not centralize efforts to promote active citizenship across the curriculum. It exemplifies the benchmark of identifying, collaborating, and capitalizing on engagement because it supports efforts in departments across the campus rather than locating projects within its own center. UCCPS helps advertise various initiatives, attracts students to participate in them, and otherwise serves as the infrastructure behind the projects. UCCPS addresses another benchmark, authentic community partnerships, by locating access points within three key community partnerships: one with local public schools, a second with the Chinatown neighborhood, and a third with the Mystic Watershed Collaborative. In the latter example, half the collaborative's members are community partners and the other half are directly affiliated with Tufts. The group meets monthly to work on improving the Mystic River watershed.

Spelman College in Atlanta is in the process of initiating its own center of expertise and facilitation of service-learning. To honor past president Johnetta B. Cole, the board of trustees created an endowment to support service-learning. The Johnetta B. Cole Institute for Community Building and Community Service will serve as a think tank with the express purpose of institutionalizing service-learning and servant leadership.

Developing Vision and Research Agendas

Another critical function of centers of expertise and facilitation is to involve the institution and the community in developing a vision and strategy for institutionalizing service-learning and community engagement. They build sustaining resources, follow the progress of changing campus attitudes and culture, conduct research about

salient issues, and promote service-learning externally to local officials, alumni, community associations, and others. Georgetown
University and the University of Minnesota represent these kinds
of centers.

Building on a long tradition of service and social justice,
Georgetown University in Washington, D.C., created in 2001 a new
entity, the Center for Social Justice Research, Teaching and Service. Following a strategic planning process based on listening sessions with faculty, students, staff, and community representatives,
the Center fashioned its mission statement: "In order to advance
justice and the common good, the Center integrates and promotes
community-based research, teaching and service by collaborating
with diverse partners and communities" (Center for Social Justice
Research, Teaching and Service Mission Statement, October 2001).
That mission will guide this center of expertise and facilitation as
it strives to consolidate and develop work in its three key areas: service, curriculum, and research. The Center's mission reflects the
larger mission of the university and thus exemplifies the institutional mission benchmark.

First, under the leadership of the director of volunteer and
public service, the Center will incorporate and build on the vibrant
student work of direct service and the learning it fosters in areas
ranging from tutoring and mentoring to arts education to job
training. Second, under the leadership of the director of curriculum and pedagogy, the Center will promote and help develop curricular offerings that incorporate community-based work and
service directed toward social justice. Third, in the newest arena,
under the leadership of the director of research, the Center will
consolidate and advance the exciting collaborative, community-
based research projects already under way in several of the under-
resourced neighborhoods of Washington, D.C. These projects
address the reduction of violence and crime among adolescents, the
enhancement of planning and community organization, and
the development of new neighborhood-based economic opportunities. Finally, it is expected that the synergy of the collaboration
of the three branches of the Center will lead to service deepened
by analysis, teaching grounded in experience, and research stimulated by creative service and dynamic pedagogy. While many cam-

puses focus on student participation in direct service and faculty development for service-learning, Georgetown goes a step further by incorporating research as one of three functions in its Center. It thereby embodies the benchmark on assessment and generation of knowledge related to engagement.

The University of Minnesota in Minneapolis formed a universitywide Task Force on Civic Engagement to clarify the meaning of civic engagement and strengthen the institution's civic mission across the full range of university activities. The Task Force defined civic engagement as an institutional commitment to public purposes and responsibilities intended to strengthen a democratic way of life in the twenty-first century. In keeping with its comprehensive charge, the Task Force was organized around six major topics: civic mission, public scholarship, civic learning, community partnership, institutional priorities, and institutional connections. Its final report contains practical proposals for incorporating civic engagement as an ongoing dimension of core university activities, including research, teaching, and outreach. By developing a comprehensive vision and change agenda, this example encompasses all benchmarks of an infrastructure that supports service-learning and community engagement. Of particular interest are the benchmarks concerning points of access and the assessment and generation of knowledge related to engagement. The Task Force website makes information about engagement accessible to the general public. During the coming years the Task Force will continue to assess the impact of their initiatives within the university and in the larger community (S. M. Engelmann, personal communication, May 2001).

Fostering Faculty and Community Relationships

Finally, a campus concerned with institutionalizing service-learning and community engagement must have a deep commitment to fostering relationships between faculty and community partners. The success of service-learning depends on faculty willingness to expand the ways in which they view scholarship, teaching, and service. They must be responsible and responsive change agents on their campuses and in their communities. Building connections between faculty and community partners results in success when the academic pursuits of disciplines are matched well with community assets and needs in a reciprocal relationship. Unity College and Lehigh University are meeting with success in these endeavors.

Unity College in Unity, Maine, prepares students for careers in environmental sciences, natural resource management, wilderness-based outdoor recreation leadership, and related fields. This environmentally centered college holds community engagement as a priority and combines academic rigor with equally demanding field experience. Service-learning has been integrated across the five core courses in the environmental stewardship curriculum. In 1997, a group of faculty created a structure to support multidisciplinary community-based projects. They sought to develop partnerships with organizations that ideally were within walking distance of the campus, address an issue that would involve a wide range of classes and large numbers of students, last for several years, and involve multiple partners. With those criteria as a guide, the process resulted in the highly successful Lake Winnecook Water Quality Project. The following six goals describe the project and the products it generated: to monitor the water quality of the lake and feeder streams; to develop outreach materials to educate and mobilize the public; to identify the social issues that affect the water quality of the lake; to establish a protocol for coliform bacteria testing and conduct ongoing tests; to compile a "rule book" of municipal, state, and federal rules and regulations concerning the lake and its shorelands for lay readers; and to conduct a natural resource inventory of the lake. For example, in a course called Great Issues in World Civilization, students investigated public priorities and social issues affecting water quality and made recommendations to the Lake Association. Mammology students reported results of their wildlife tick study to the Maine Lyme Disease Project. The project goals are evidence of the benchmark of authentic community partnerships. The criteria for strategically choosing partnerships assist in coordination of service efforts achieving depth, continuity, and impact.

At Lehigh University in Bethlehem, Pennsylvania, the partnership between students, faculty, and community organizations is centered on student-facilitated research. In 1997, Lehigh's College of Business and Economics began developing a multidisciplinary, experiential, team-based program in regional and urban economic development. Although the curriculum is hosted in one college, teams of students from all three undergraduate colleges run Lehigh Community Research and Policy Service (Lehigh CORPS). Lehigh CORPS teams work on three different types of projects: quantitative analysis of public data sources, original survey research, and qualitative urban policy analysis and planning. Student teams have analyzed transportation barriers to successful welfare-to-work transitions, surveyed businesses to assess the importance of broadband access in their selection of location, and developed a geographic information systems database to track quality of life and health indicators for children living in high-poverty neighborhoods. Lehigh's CORPS program exhibits the benchmarks related to curricular infusion and the faculty's great effort to balance the demands of teaching, research, and service. Faculty involved in the CORPS program benefit from the ability to combine quality teaching, original research, and service within one activity. Thus, through CORPS, faculty build their tenure and promotion portfolio while engaging in service-learning.

Gateways to Service-Learning and Community Engagement

In addition to the centers of expertise and facilitation, the integrated campus also includes gateways that serve as the front door of service-learning and are evidence of a campuswide commitment to service-learning. These gateways (smaller units indicated by gray circles and squares in Figure 6.1) manage discrete projects while remaining connected to one another and to the centers of expertise and facilitation. Because they are connected to the campuswide infrastructure for service-learning, they provide appropriate referrals to students, faculty, staff and community partners seeking additional service-learning resources, information, and opportunities. Gateways offer initial access to the activities and concepts of service-learning through cocurricular, curricular, and information-exchange programs.

Cocurricular Service-Learning
Johnson County Community College in Overland, Kansas (JCCC), offers an excellent gateway to service-learning specifically designed for its student body. JCCC sends teams of faculty and students for

intensive short-term service projects to Las Pintas, Mexico. As a cocurricular activity, the Las Pintas program does not offer academic credit, but it does challenge students to utilize professional and personal skills in areas such as nursing, dental hygiene, and construction. This exemplifies the cocurricular-opportunity benchmark because it offers a cross-cultural experience, draws connection between professional skill and human need, and fosters nonpositional leadership. To support this program, the college assumes the majority of the expenses for the trips with supplemental fund-raising done by students and faculty. JCCC demonstrates commitment to the benchmark related to administration and resource allocation by dedicating faculty time to the project and enabling students with financial constraints to participate. These trips have greatly increased visibility and support for the college's overall service-learning program.

Curricular Service-Learning

Bryn Mawr College in Pennsylvania successfully integrates practice and theory through "Praxis: A Community-Based Learning Program" that combines intensive academic study with rigorous fieldwork. The Praxis program uses the term *fieldwork* or *community-based learning* to represent what we would call service-learning. Students work with organizations that serve the community in some way, but not all the organizations are nonprofits or community service agencies. In Praxis I departmental courses, fieldwork constitutes 25 percent of the total coursework; the student makes one field visit per week and spends three to four hours in the field each visit. In Praxis II interdepartmental seminars, the percentage of fieldwork increases to 50 percent, with field visits numbering two per week for a weekly total of six to eight hours of fieldwork. In Praxis III independent studies, 75 percent of the course consists of fieldwork: three field visits for a total of nine to twelve hours of fieldwork weekly. Praxis I and III courses can be offered in every department depending on faculty and student interest. Praxis II courses involve several departments, as in the course on "Innovative Teaching Methods in Math and Science" that involves the math, chemistry, education, and physics departments. Praxis field placement coordinators support Praxis faculty and develop, coordinate, and evaluate placements. Faculty retain control over course readings and discussion, rigorous reflection, and student evaluation.

In relation to the curriculum infusion benchmark, Praxis provides a clear structure to address the question of academic rigor, makes service-learning widely available across the curriculum, and enables students to follow a developmental path in their acquisition of knowledge and experience. The Praxis program acts as a gateway because all students have the opportunity to take Praxis courses; it therefore reaches students who might not choose other types of service-learning. In addition, it introduces a broad cross-section of faculty to service-learning pedagogy.

Information-Exchange Programs

While the Las Pintas and Praxis programs provide curricular and cocurricular points of access to service-learning, Portland State University's Center for Academic Excellence has designed a database that provides faculty, staff, community partners, and students with descriptive information about the more than two hundred service-learning courses offered yearly. The database documents the following: course description, faculty name and contact information, the community organizations that work with the students in the course, and a description of the projects the students in the course have completed. The database currently profiles more than 400 total courses. The Center for Academic Excellence collects information for the database from individual faculty and from the coordinator of the Capstone Program, which accounts for 140 service-learning courses a year.

Portland State University's database is useful in a number of ways. Faculty who are interested in pursuing community-based learning may use it to generate ideas for their courses and to identify community partners. Students use the information in the database to locate courses, faculty, and community partners. Community partners access the database for similar purposes. Finally, administrators find that the database informs program assessment, grant writing, and further partnership development. Thus the database greatly facilitates internal and external access to information related to service-learning initiatives. Meeting this benchmark helps avoid some of the lack of coordination often found in large institutions and the confusion that results. Associated with providing points of access, this database also excels in another benchmark of an infrastructure that supports service-learning: identifying, collaborating, and capitalizing on engagement by offering information that encourages the expansion of service-learning across the campus and community.

A campus committed to an integrated model of service-learning and community engagement requires centers of expertise and facilitation that provide coordination, vision, research, and partnership development opportunities, as well as multiple gateways to service-learning through cocurricular, curricular, and information-exchange programs. Although the integrated model suggests characteristics of effective engagement, contextual factors, including each university's historical relationship with the community, size, geography, the strengths and limitations of its faculty expertise, and its financial health, influence the degree of institutionalization of service-learning and community engagement. A diagram representing the university's move toward institutionalization would reveal additional lines of communication and increased evidence of service-learning and engagement activities.

Next Steps for Taking Action

Developing a campus infrastructure that supports service-learning and community engagement involves understanding and working within the contexts of how institutional mission affects policy and actions, how campus constituents respond to change, and how management decisions are made and communicated. It requires institutional change that must engage all stakeholders and be based on shared goals and vision, as reflected in the models of engagement and nine benchmarks that involve both grassroots and top-level administrative commitments.

One of the first steps in developing a campus infrastructure that supports service-learning and community engagement is for faculty and administrators to learn about the strength of the current campus infrastructure and community resources. There are many assessment tools for use by campus and community partners for understanding and evaluating their commitments to service-learning and the pieces of infrastructure that are in place. Using the questions from the *Presidents' Declaration* (Campus Compact, 1999), the Holland (1997) matrix, or the CAPSL model (Bringle and Hatcher, 1996) mentioned earlier in this chapter can stimulate dialogue as a key step toward advancing the service-learning infrastructure. While these tools specifically address change related to service-learning, others address general change processes in higher education institutions. For example, publications of the American Council on Education provide resources and reflection questions to help guide institutions through change. The first in their series is *On Change I: En Route to Transformation* (Eckel, Hill, and Green, 1998).

There are many actions that service-learning practitioners and advocates should regularly engage in to assist the development of infrastructure that supports service-learning and engagement. First, be an entrepreneur on your own campus and seize opportunities to link service-learning with other campus priorities such as retention and diversity. Identify allies and related activities that might support service-learning by scanning campus publications for relevant people, research, and programs and sharing information with appropriate faculty and administrators. Second, pay attention to official documents like mission statements and strategic plans, refer to them when appropriate, and participate in processes to develop or modify them to ensure the inclusion of service-learning and engagement. Third, cultivate relationships with both positional and informal leaders and create a network of sympathetic faculty, administrators, students, and community partners. Fourth, document faculty members' research interests, disciplinary association memberships, and community involvement activities. Use this information to engage faculty effectively as resources, direct appropriate resources to them, and reward service-learning and engagement activities. Finally, use local media to showcase service-learning and community engagement efforts that portray campus involvement with the local community. Seek ways to describe more accurately and deeply the interdependency of campus and community partners, so that partnership activities become more than photo opportunities.

In addition to your campus-based work, join the many service-learning professionals who are involved in service-learning research as well as practice. The models and benchmarks presented here provide a rich framework for research. As a beginning point, an investigation of their application to different institutional types will reveal much about how these theoretical frameworks are actualized. The field will also benefit from a comparative analysis of institutions that do and do not have extensive campus infrastructures to support service-learning and the potentially differing outcomes for student learning and community development.

Also consider studying the qualities of campus-community partnerships in various stages of development to learn more about what makes them work for both the campus and the local community. Investigation of the long-term effects of campus engagement with communities in terms of community growth and development is also needed. Faculty members should be encouraged to explore how teaching and learning are affected by service-learning and how students integrate course knowledge with community experiences. In addition, integrate questions about civic engagement and service-learning into general student experience surveys in order to follow changes in student learning and experience over time.

Conclusion

The three models and nine benchmarks presented in this chapter provide a framework for establishing and evaluating a campus infrastructure that supports service-learning and community engagement. The vision of the integrated model and institutional examples illustrates how these benchmarks can be actualized and how the integrated model can work.

While service-learning can occur without the institutional support of an engaged campus, the development of a campuswide infrastructure that supports service-learning necessitates an expanded conversation focused on creating a campus culture of community engagement. The integrated model of engagement is a clarion call for reinvestment in the social and civic responsibilities of higher education. We must dream big about the possibility of a campus fully engaged with its local community, where service-learning is de rigueur and reciprocity and learning flourish at the core of campus-community partnerships. Students, faculty, staff, and community partners must embark upon institutional change—

not only to institutionalize service-learning but to institutionalize a new way of thinking about higher education and its relationship to society.

References

Battistoni, R. M., and Hudson, W. E. *Experiencing Citizenship: Concepts and Models for Service-Learning in Political Science.* Washington, D.C.: American Association for Higher Education, 1997.

Boyer, E. L. *Scholarship Reconsidered: Priorities of the Professoriate.* Princeton, N.J.: Carnegie Foundation for the Advancement of Teaching, 1990.

Boyer, E. L. "Creating the New American College." *Chronicle of Higher Education,* Mar. 9, 1994, p. A48.

Boyte, H., and Hollander, E. *Wingspread Declaration on Renewing the Civic Mission of the American Research University.* Providence, R. I.: Campus Compact, 1999.

Bringle, R. G. "Civic Engagement: Relationships and Service Learning." Paper presented at the American Association for Higher Education Conference, Washington, D.C., Mar. 2001.

Bringle, R. G., Games, R., and Malloy, E.A. *Colleges and Universities as Citizens.* Boston: Allyn & Bacon, 1999.

Bringle, R., and Hatcher, J. "Implementing Service Learning in Higher Education." *Journal of Higher Education,* 1996, *67*(2), 221–239.

Campus Compact. *Presidents' Declaration on the Civic Responsibility of Higher Education.* Providence, R.I.: Campus Compact, 1999.

Center for Social Justice Research, Teaching and Service Mission Statement. Washington, D.C.: Georgetown University, Oct. 2001.

Checkoway, B. "Reinventing the Research University for Public Service." *Journal of Planning Literature,* 1997, *11*(3), 307–319.

Eckel, P., Hill, B., and Green, M. *On Change I: En Route to Transformation.* Washington, D.C.: American Council on Education, 1998.

Furco, A. "Institutionalizing Service-Learning in Higher Education: Findings from a Three-Year Study (1997–2000)." Paper presented at The Forum on Volunteerism, Service, and Learning in Higher Education, College Park, Md., June 2001.

Holland, B. "Analyzing Institutional Commitment to Service: A Model of Key Organizational Factors." *Michigan Journal of Community Service Learning,* 1997, *4,* 30–41.

Pigza, J. M., and Troppe, M. L. "Establishing Benchmarks for the Engaged Campus: The University of Maryland Report." [http://www.inform.umd.edu/CampusInfo/Departments/commute/CSP/ServiceLearning/engaged.html]. 2000.

Saltmarsh, J. "Exploring the Meanings of Community/University Partnerships." *National Society for Experiential Education Quarterly,* Summer 1998, 6–22.

Chapter Seven

Partnerships Among Colleges and Universities for Service-Learning

James Birge, Brooke Beaird, and Jan Torres

Since its founding in 1636, American higher education has clearly articulated and demonstrated its public purposes. Parks Daloz, Keen, Keen, and Daloz Parks (1996) state, "[Colleges and universities] steward intellectual and material resources vital to the life of the commons" (p. 223). Despite what has appeared to some as a departure from their explicit public purpose, American colleges and universities are, in fact, exercising civic leadership by addressing our nation's critical issues, including education, health, housing, the environment, and public safety. In addition, higher education in its civic role is addressing crumbling urban infrastructures, increasing incivility in our communities, growing social and cultural enclaves that challenge our collective sense of community, and declining participation in the democratic process by young adults (Ehrlich, 2000).

Higher education leaders recognize the strong potential of institutional collaborations to make a difference in society. Indeed, it was four college presidents who gathered in 1985 to form Campus Compact, a coalition of presidents committed to the public purposes of higher education, which now includes more than 850 members. This compact among presidents was an agreement to work together toward a common set of goals in a nationwide collaboration with a state-based infrastructure. At this writing, twenty-seven states have formed Campus Compacts, with six others in the development process. This type of broad partnership facilitates a unique opportunity, often noted by its member presidents, for public and private colleges to work together, and lays the foundation for additional partnerships at the local level.

The blossoming practice of service-learning on campuses leads to partnerships among higher education institutions, as well as with communities. Increasingly, colleges are recognizing that partnerships for a common purpose or project offer opportunities to maximize impact, increase resources, provide more links to community-based organizations, and leverage the support of local corporate, government, or foundation interests. Chitgopekar and Swaba (1999) demonstrate service-learning's utility as a mechanism for institutions to address community issues, as well as to break down institutional barriers that separate two- and four-year colleges, weaving together a fabric of diverse educational institutions and communities into one cloth. In this chapter we address the principles and practices of building service-learning partnerships between and among institutions.

Benchmarks for Partnerships Among Institutions

Although the partnership frameworks offered in Chapter One focus on partnerships between institutions and communities, they are easily applicable to partnerships among institutions. *The Benchmarks for Campus/Community Partnerships* (Torres, 2000) identify three stages that build from the relationship up, shaping the partnership from a base of shared vision, values, and trust to mutually beneficial outcomes to long-term collaborations dictated by critical and tangible outcomes (Torres, 2000). They also represent the three distinct stages that define the evolution of successful partnerships among institutions of higher education.

A few examples illustrate how the Campus Compact benchmarks serve partnerships among colleges and universities. In the initial design phase, it is critical that each partner be able to identify clear benefits that serve its particular self-interest. The work of the partnership may support the teaching agenda of one institution, the research agenda of another, and the public service agenda of yet another. As they grow, strong partnerships are built upon a diversity of voices, skills, and resources. Partnerships must reflect a collaboration of multiple dimensions in order to develop comprehensive responses to complex problems. The "value added" of partnership among different types of institutions is the different strengths and perspectives that each brings. Sustainability and success of partnerships over time require that the work of the partnership be tied to each institution's mission and purpose. Although the key players in a partnership may represent different sectors of their institution's organizational structure, it is important that the president demonstrate support for the partnership in whatever manner is most appropriate for each institutional partner.

Ramaley's (2000) lessons, while drawn from examples of university-community partnerships, also apply equally well to partnerships among institutions for service-learning and community engagement. Her admonition that any partnership must be grounded in the academic strengths and philosophy of an institution amplifies the Campus Compact *Benchmarks* emphasis on integration with institutional mission. Ramaley describes an ideal partnership as one that matches the academic strengths and goals of the university with the assets and interests of the community. Thus, an ideal partnership among several institutions synchronizes the partners' multiple academic strengths and goals with multiple facets of community interests. Conversely, Ramaley points out that each institution must carefully weigh what it actually can bring to a partnership. As resources become more limited, institutional leaders will be forced to scrutinize more closely what they can offer without causing adverse effects on core functions. Thus, partnerships among institutions with varying assets become essential in addressing issues shared with the community. She also highlights the mutual learning that evolves from and, in turn, nurtures university-community partnerships. Likewise, faculty, staff, and students from partnering institutions stand to learn a great deal from one another and to gain fresh perspectives on their work. It should not be overlooked that institutions working together to address community issues have the opportunity to create a "culture of evidence," in Ramaley's terms (2000, p. 242), that can enhance their image and esteem in the eyes of the public, governing bodies, and funders.

Challenges to Creating Strong Partnerships Among Higher Education Institutions

Forging strong, sustainable partnerships between and among colleges and universities has never been easy. Studies of higher education collaborations highlight the difficulties inherent in establishing such partnerships (Thomas, 1999; Chitgopekar and Swaba, 1999). As a result, there are relatively few examples of good practice to serve as models. However, Thomas and Chitgopekar and Swaba have documented existing partnerships that reveal both obstacles and strategies for addressing them. These obstacles, or challenges, fall into seven categories: the complexity of higher education; the autonomous nature of colleges and universities; poor planning and design; failure to maintain communication and relationships; weak, divided, or inconsistent program leadership; clash of different cultures; and lack of clarity about goals.

The Complexity of Higher Education

Broadly speaking, higher education as a social institution is diverse and complicated. The *2001 Higher Education Directory* (Rodenhouse and Torregrosa, 2001) describes the ten Carnegie classifications of institutions. Multiple distinctions among the types of higher education institutions reflect vast differences in size, scope, mission, students, and programs. To exemplify the complexity of this classification system, one of the categories, "specialized institutions," comprises nine subcategories, including theological seminaries, medical schools, and schools of engineering and technology.

Individual higher education institutions are complex organizationally as well. Each has a variety of distinct governance structures, such as one or more external governing boards, different forms of student government, faculty senates, and various institutional administrative councils. Separate and autonomous departments and numerous funding sources, including government appropriations, tuition, fees, sales, grants, private gifts, and endowment interest, add to the complexity. In addition, a wide range of distinct constituencies make up the modern American college or university—students, faculty, administrators, staff, alumni, donors, and trustees. Subgroups, stratifications, and hierarchies are embedded in each of these groups. Each group has distinct roles and responsibilities and, in many cases, conflicting interests with other groups of institutional constituents. This intricate web of relationships is often the root cause of the glacial pace of change in higher education and can also discourage and slow the formation of sustainable partnerships among institutions.

The Autonomous Nature of Colleges and Universities

It is well known that competition for students, funding, and prestige exists between institutions, even between institutions in the same system. Further, competition for departmental funding, recognition, and, increasingly, technology resources *within* institutions also exists. As Thomas (1999) notes, the most successful partnerships among institutions involve those that have "demonstrate[d] a history of collaboration both *internally and externally*" (p. 13). As a result, in order for institutions to work together on service-learning initiatives, they must transcend their autonomous natures on two levels. Chapter Six addresses how colleges can establish an internal infrastructure that supports service-learning partnerships.

Poor Planning and Design

In the eagerness to get started, programs that require solid interpersonal relationships often do not take the time to form those relationships before beginning the programmatic work. The only way that partnership work can be accomplished is in the context of interpersonal relationships based on trust and mutual respect. Indeed, partnerships may be viewed as a series of interpersonal relationships built one on top of the other to create a bond between institutions. In addition, successful service-learning partnerships need a clear vision and action plan from the very beginning to ensure that goals are met and the program achieves an appropriate level of sustainability. Poor design of the partnership process hinders the work to be accomplished. Institutions inexperienced with partnerships often fail to develop a project team and empower it to define the partnership, initiate the work, provide resources for the partnership, and assess the accomplishments and challenges.

Failure to Maintain Communication and Relationships

Maintaining communication in an atmosphere of equal voice and shared responsibilities is essential. For many individuals in higher education, working collaboratively feels unnatural and awkward and is contrary to their leadership style. For those who are accustomed to functioning alone and making independent decisions, it may be difficult to adjust to working with multiple others as equals in decision making. The problem most frequently identified by campus partnerships is a breakdown in communication challenged by personal style, geography, scheduling and conducting meetings, and friction caused by one person moving ahead without consulting all the partners.

Weak, Divided, or Inconsistent Program Leadership

Strong leaders are needed to organize the resources necessary for establishing an infrastructure for developing, implementing, and sustaining service-learning partnerships. However, when leaders focus on their own institutions rather than the partnership, the risk of leadership conflict escalates. Turf issues may impede cooperation as partners vie for control, resources, and publicity. In the absence of leaders committed to the partnership, communication can break down and partners may begin to take sides. Leaders who are skilled at negotiating conflicts can assist in resolving these challenges. Another obstacle is the turnover of key leaders, causing a gap in program continuity and often the collapse of projects. By designing a partnership with more than one leader, this challenge can often be avoided or at least diminished.

Clash of Different Cultures

Partnerships that include multiple partners across sectors, both within and outside of higher education, are more likely to face challenges. For example, large research universities, community colleges, and private religiously affiliated institutions may have more differences than similarities. In addition, as described in Chapter Twelve, higher education, nonprofit community organizations, and corporations likewise have vastly differing cultures, missions, and practices. Sometimes the difficulties may be as simple as campuses operating on different academic schedules. In other cases, the demographics and learning goals of the students may be quite different. In yet other situations, the higher education partners, no matter from which sector, have different motivations and goals for working with the community. The complexity increases as corporate and community partners enter the scene. In the early developmental stages of cross-sector partnerships, it is important that time be allotted for the key players to learn about one another's cultures.

Lack of Clarity About Goals

Finally, prolonged ambiguity about purpose causes partnerships to dwindle and leads to their early dissolution. Although uncertainty and lack of clarity early in the partnership can provide an opportunity for the parties to work together to develop purpose, the partnership will likely dissolve quickly if the direction remains undefined. Although all partnerships require an ability to withstand a healthy degree of ambiguity so that they can respond to the changing forces that shape their work, lack of focus on mutually determined outcomes threatens sustainability.

Characteristics of Strong Partnerships

Campus Compact has both convened experts and studied, through a number of pilot programs, the anatomy of campus-community partnerships. The Campus Compact National Center for Community Colleges has also evaluated partnerships between two- and four-year colleges. Documentation from these and other partnerships among colleges and universities indicates several characteristics of effective collaborations that have emerged out of good planning, intentional efforts, and trial and error. This information reveals that, although forming partnerships between and among higher education institutions is not easy, the field has much to learn from the few that have negotiated these mostly uncharted waters.

The existing documentation we reviewed shows that there are key characteristics of partnerships that are effectively working to address the challenges and obstacles that surface when two or more institutions of higher learning consider establishing partnerships. In conjunction with the benchmarks described earlier that define the stages in partnership development, these characteristics can be used to guide our work.

Involving All Stakeholders in Defining the Issues and Mutual Benefits

The partnerships that we reviewed for this chapter placed a high value on involving all stakeholders in the definition of the issues to be addressed. People and institutions are motivated to join a partnership to satisfy a need or to gain benefits. If, for example, the work of the partnership focuses on an environmental issue in the community, it would likely pique the interest of natural sciences faculty and students from the partnering institutions, no matter to which sector of higher education they belong. Individuals are also drawn to partnerships that allow them to attract others to issues or practices that are important to them. For example, a community college faculty member involved in action research may join a partnership to mentor university faculty members who express interest in a community-based research project. Stakeholders may also come to partnerships out of a desire to belong to a community of people committed to working for positive change. This kind of commitment is qualitatively distinct from the commitment that is based on interest in the topic and reflects a focus on the concept of participation in community life as a fundamental role of a citizen.

Institutions have ample opportunities to realize benefits from defining issues collaboratively. Each partner may contribute a unique element or enriched perspective to the partnership that is actualized when the problem or issue is defined jointly. Motivated by a need to increase expertise in a particular area, cultural diversity, prestige, or access to other organizations or opportunities, each partner will slowly realize that collaboration can yield much more than working alone. For example, an institution wishing to begin a project in a Hispanic neighborhood on the opposite side of the city would benefit from partnering with an institution that has deep roots in that area. Similarly, a suburban university that requires access to the city government to retrieve municipal records would benefit from working with an urban institution that can provide that access. In a variety of situations, one partner might be able to facilitate financial resources in exchange for access or information.

Complementing the Strengths of Each Partner

The distinct academic cultures of colleges and universities determine everything about the institution, including values, mission, policy, instruction, research, and student profile. Although it can be challenging to find common ground among institutional cultures, it is possible when institutions openly recognize their distinctions and creatively bring them to bear on partnerships. An inventory of each institution's assets is helpful in defining strengths.

Chitgopekar and Swaba (1999) document the benefits of combining assets in their study of the partnership between Mesa Community College (MCC) and Arizona State University (ASU): "From an institutional perspective, the value of MCC and ASU's collaboration to benefit poverty-experienced women through mentorship and action research lies in the fact that neither institution would be fully capable of such successful mentoring and research without the other" (p. 11).

The partnership between MCC and ASU integrated distinct campus dynamics that grounded the partnership's efforts to create access to higher education for women whose lives were in transition. While a group of MCC students and faculty associated with the Center for Public Policy and Service created a mentoring and support program for women on welfare or who were escaping abusive environments, students and faculty associated with ASU's Center on Urban Inquiry had an interest in conducting an action research study of the experience of such women. This partnership represents an outstanding example of the integration of public problem solving, academic coursework, and community outreach made possible by a collaboration between two very different institutions.

Using Service-Learning at Individual Institutions to Stimulate Partnerships

Strong partnerships among institutions frequently evolve out of preexisting, campus-based service-learning initiatives. In several examples we reviewed, core stakeholder populations of experienced participants created the foundation of the partnership that attracted new stakeholders. It is also important to note that rarely did the emerging partnership supplant the existing service-learning initiative. In many cases, participants in the activities of the partnership were meeting preexisting curriculum protocols or course objectives through their contributions to the partnership. Such a program development dynamic appears to lead institutions toward deepening and broadening their commitments to civic engagement.

In each instance of interinstitutional partnerships we reviewed, service-learning opportunities were expanded at all partnering institutions. Institutions with strong service-learning programs can stimulate service-learning activities at partner institutions with less developed programs. At the same time, partnerships among institutions also generate new campus-based initiatives. For example, a partnership between Hocking College and Ohio University focused upon environmental issues associated with the local Monday Creek watershed. Although both institutions had promoted service-learning on their campuses, they had not worked collaboratively on any projects despite common interest in the watershed and their close proximity to it. Elaine Dabelko from Hocking College and Scott Miller from Ohio University worked together to identify two community agencies that were actively involved in environmental issues related to the watershed. The representatives of the four partnering organizations then established a set of goals and developed service-learning projects that would contribute to enhancing the quality of life for local communities.

Environmental studies students from both institutions worked on monitoring, researching, and engineering methods for improving the health of the watershed. Students and faculty integrated water sampling and analysis techniques into environmental studies courses at both. They conducted a detailed analysis of the water quality, categorized orders and classes of insects in and around the watershed, and created a biological sampling system for the Monday Creek Restoration Project, the partnership-based organization that emerged from the collaboration between the institutions and the community organizations.

As a result of the Monday Creek project, more faculty at both institutions have become interested in the practice of service-learning. At Hocking College, a faculty member in the recreation and wildlife technology department engaged his students in service-learning activities that exposed them to local history and culture issues. Another Hocking faculty member from the same program and a biology professor at Ohio University involved their students in macro invertebrate sampling within the polluted streams of the watershed. A faculty member at Ohio who teaches a first-year orientation course integrated watershed projects into his syllabus. Thus, whereas this partnership has brought the resources of higher education institutions to bear on the persistent community problem of water quality, it has also led to the development of additional service-learning pedagogy on both campuses.

Breaking Down Barriers Between Institutions

Successful partnerships require the eradication of long-held stereotypes about individual institutions or types of institutions. In defining the benefits both individuals and institutions seek from the partnership, similar, even common, motivations may result. When this is not the case, frank sharing of motivations among the partners often leads to deeper understanding and appreciation of the differences among institutions. Finding opportunities for shared reflection, teaching, and learning helps to reduce the barriers among institutions. This point is clearly articulated by a participant in a partnership between Middlesex Community College and Bentley College, both in Massachusetts:

> The Middlesex and Bentley collaboration has served to break through institutional barriers that previously have separated two-year and four-year institutions, as it has also broken barriers between ethnically diverse segments of the community. It is responsible for a shift in attitudes among participating faculty about the depth and breadth of the institutional divide separating community colleges and four-year institutions. We have learned

that this gulf may be bridged through hard work, patience, commitment, and perseverance. The partnership has opened new
vistas for community college students to see that the practical
realities of higher education need not end with an Associate
Degree [Chitgopekar and Swaba, 1999, p. 54].

The partnership helped to reduce barriers in a variety of ways.
First, as a result of the shared service-learning experiences between
Middlesex and Bentley students, the two-year students were more
likely to consider continuing their education at a four-year institution. Moreover, four-year students realized that as a result of the
common learning experiences, academic study in two-year and
four-year institutions can involve similar pedagogy—in this case,
service-learning. Finally, as a result of this formal institutional partnership, both colleges established a model for developing future
institutional partnerships.

Valuing Patience, Persistence, and Reflection

Because of the competitive and autonomous nature of institutions,
partnerships require significant amounts of time to become established. It is not unreasonable to expect to take a year to identify
leaders, define the issues to be addressed, and develop relationships among partners. Thomas' (1999) study suggests that partnerships that realize change must last at least seven to ten years.
This length of time allows the partners to build a broader base of
campus support for the partnership, to examine the recurring
themes of success of the partnership, and to demonstrate partners'
commitment to the work over the long haul. Thomas' study suggests that partnerships lasting fewer than seven years are less likely
to create meaningful transformation. See Chapter Two for further
discussion of transformational partnerships.

As a result, long-term commitments from institutional and
other stakeholders to a partnership are necessary. The partnerships
we reviewed demonstrated such commitments from all partners.
In addition, successful partnerships intentionally create opportunities for participants to share their thoughts about their work.
Although this element of reflection was consistent among most of

the partnerships we reviewed, it was also noted to be one of the most challenging elements to initiate and sustain. The constraints of time and geography test the resolve of individuals and the organization of the partnerships. Nonetheless, opportunities for all participants to reflect on their work was deemed a critical factor for success.

Strategically Seeking Funding

It goes almost without saying that funding of partnerships is fundamental to sustain them. Minigrants and short-term funding can provide an initial catalyst to mobilize partnership stakeholders. In many cases, these types of funds help to attract partners, establish the focus of the partnership, frame the work to be done, and help to bring the community issue to the attention of the institutions. However, small grants do not contribute to the sustainability of partnerships. Short-term funding should be used to get the program started and for documenting and sharing results as preparation to leverage additional funds. An example is the Indiana Campus Compact, which is a coalition of higher education institutions to promote service-learning and the civic development of college students throughout the state. Indiana obtained a $5,000 seed grant from the national office of Campus Compact to establish its organization. An administrative coordinator organized meetings among service-learning practitioners to exchange information about their programs and to explore methods for building on effective practices. Although the meetings helped practitioners strengthen their work on their campuses, they also developed shared service-learning initiatives among Indiana institutions. Within several years, the Indiana Campus Compact was well enough organized to receive funding from the Corporation for National and Community Service in order to establish a statewide Faculty Fellows program and to expand their work in other ways. The initial seed grant also allowed the coordinator to arrange meetings among Indiana college and university presidents, enabling them to leverage additional funding from the Lilly Foundation. Indiana Campus Compact now has a budget in excess of $2 million.

Developing Strong Leadership

Strong leaders are able to mobilize resources, inspire others, and influence the levels of involvement of the partnering institutions. Leaders of partnerships among institutions should be able to work well with a variety of individuals and to recognize this skill in others. They also must be able to coordinate multiple projects simultaneously, think in terms of systems, and possess a deep commitment to the principles and potential benefits of service-learning.

Because true partnerships are collaborative relationships founded on equality, the challenge of the partnership leaders is to spread resources, responsibilities, and rewards as evenly as possible among the stakeholders. The strongest partnerships delegate important responsibilities to each partner and clarify lines of accountability. New leaders must be continually identified and trained so that the partnership can survive despite changes in personnel. Partnerships require individuals to serve in a variety of leadership roles, using their unique skills and experiences. For example, some partners may act as project managers, using their organizational or financial management skills. Others may serve as advocates to sell the mission of the partnership and recruit financial or political support. Some may be skilled facilitators to translate ideas, values, or needs among the stakeholders.

In this vein, the leadership of the Philadelphia Higher Education Network for Neighborhood Development (PHENND) lies in two places. Its co-chairs are academic leaders from four local universities (David Bartelt, professor of geography and urban studies at Temple University; Maurice Eldridge, executive assistant to the president at Swarthmore College; Ira Harkavy, associate vice president and director of the Center for Community Partnerships at the University of Pennsylvania; and Robert Palestini, dean of graduate and continuing education studies at St. Joseph's University) who serve as its advisory group. In addition, it has developed a group of key contacts at institutions, community service and service-learning directors who feel strong ownership for PHENND (H. Aisenstein, personal communication, 2001).

The co-chairs frame the focus of PHENND's work to engage higher education institutions in the lives of their communities.

Representing institutions with different missions, the co-chairs demonstrate to other institutions that PHENND is an association that all institutions can join and that engages all institutions in the work of revitalizing communities. The co-chairs also help to leverage institutional as well as federal funds to support PHENND's organizational infrastructure and projects.

An effective partnership will build in a system to obtain feedback on its leadership, in the same way it would assess the effectiveness of its programs. Assessment of partnerships is the subject of Chapter Three.

Empowering Student Leadership

The partnerships we reviewed provide opportunities for students to assume roles in which they can develop their leadership skills and contribute to the work. These include planning and directing projects of the partnership, leading discussions among partners, and representing the partnerships in public meetings. The partnership between Gannon University and Mercyhurst College, both in Pennsylvania, to provide academically at-risk college youth with corporate mentors and, in turn, to empower the college students as mentors of at-risk elementary students reported to Campus Compact that the college students improved in the areas of team building, leadership, communication, organization skills, flexibility, tolerance, and creativity. College students worked with myriad community agencies as mentors for at-risk youth. Activities varied greatly. Some students organized social events for a center for emotionally disturbed children and a homeless shelter. Others hosted field trips, a college night, skating parties, or building projects to assist community agencies. These activities, in turn, enhanced the college students' skills and self-esteem as they mentored the children. Involving college students in significant leadership roles justifies the value of the partnership in the eyes of institutional leaders, faculty, and funders. The partnership's advocates are careful to demonstrate how student participation and leadership in its activities prepare future leaders to understand complex social issues, enhance critical thinking, and develop the skills necessary to sustain our democracy.

These examples illustrate how a variety of service-learning partnerships among institutions embody the characteristics of strong partnerships that we have identified. The following case study describes how these characteristics combine to create a strong, sustainable partnership.

A Snapshot of a Partnership in Action: The Philadelphia Higher Education Network for Neighborhood Development

Ira Harkavy and his colleagues formed the Philadelphia Higher Education Network for Neighborhood Development (PHENND) in the early 1990s as a consortium of colleges and universities in the Philadelphia area. PHENND works to create a collective vision among higher education institutions to bring their resources to bear on the problems of urban poverty such as K–12 education reform, homelessness and hunger, and "digital divide" barriers (H. Aisenstein, personal communication, 2001). In 1992 PHENND institutions participated in the Philadelphia Summer of Service project, which was the precursor to AmeriCorps, by helping to immunize children in the city. This initial concrete outcome of the group's meetings enabled the partners to test the waters of collaborative action while gaining visibility for their network. By 1993, with funds from the University of Pennsylvania, PHENND was able to hire a graduate student to help organize regular meetings as well as an annual workshop for higher education institutions and community-based organizations in the region to examine and expand the role of higher education institutions in their communities. The Corporation for National and Community Service provided funding in 1997 to formalize the PHENND partnership, allowing it to hire full-time professional staff, offer subgrants to campus and community partners, and provide training and technical assistance.

PHENND continues to build the capacity of its member institutions to develop mutually beneficial, sustained, and democratic community-based service-learning partnerships. The consortium actively seeks to revitalize local communities and schools and to foster civic responsibility among forty-four of the region's seventy colleges and universities. As an association of institutions in a focused geographic area, PHENND can determine the gaps and overlaps of service delivery in the greater Philadelphia area and then work with institutions to engage more efficiently and effectively in their communities. For example, Hillary Aisenstein, executive director of PHENND, recently discovered that two Philadelphia institutions each had a tutoring program at the same elementary school, yet they did not coordinate any of their work. With PHENND's assistance, the institutions have now revised their programs to include common training programs for their students and to coordinate their efforts at the school.

Another strategic benefit of the PHENND multi-institutional partnership is the promotion of partnerships between single institutions and community agencies or schools. For example, through its newsletter, PHENND connected a Turner Middle School teacher with a LaSalle University communications professor to work on a census project. The professor read about the teacher's efforts to involve her class in collecting census data in West Philadelphia, a minority neighborhood that underreported census data. The professor offered to have his communication class students help design a marketing strategy for the students to promote the census in the community. The result was that West Philadelphia had the highest census return rate of any community in the city.

This partnership also leverages resources to mobilize the assets of the institutions and the communities and to build their capacity to address problems of urban poverty. This work includes helping to identify public space on campuses for community organizations to meet and connecting institutions and community agencies with local foundations. For example, in the summer of 2001, PHENND organized a series of meetings with foundation executives who addressed topics such as board and program management and corporate relationship development. In addition, a cadre of higher education faculty and staff and community members provide training and technical assistance around literacy, student leadership, after-school programs, and school-university partnerships. Members of the partnerships have also initiated efforts to improve health care service delivery, advance community-based research, and reduce poverty in local communities.

As a result of their meeting at the PHENND-sponsored Poverty Action Seminar in February 2000, Professors Jon Van Til of Rutgers University–Camden and Timothy Peterson of Messiah College–Philadelphia have begun to link their research, teaching, and service with examining the quality of life in urban America. Both Van Til and Peterson teach introductory courses on urban poverty and are interested in the issues around formulating and utilizing neighborhood indicators of urban livability and poverty. They are now working together to create opportunities for comparative research and collaborative teaching. Peterson and his students, who work and study in North Philadelphia, are using the same neighborhood indicators model that Van Til uses. Van Til's students, who work and study in Camden, New Jersey, are using Peterson's model. The two classes have had joint discussions and are sharing their research with one another. As a result of the work performed by the students, a photographic database of abandoned and vacant properties in North Philadelphia has been submitted to the city's Office of Housing and Community Development in order to demonstrate the need to place a high priority on the city's urban renewal of the North Philadelphia neighborhoods. Ultimately, Van Til and Peterson hope to expand this collaboration to other universities in the region (H. Aisenstein, personal communication, 2001).

PHENND's growth in the immediate future will be to focus on other major social issues in the area. The institutions in the network have asked PHENND to take a more active role to help them identify and address key issues. This expansion might create a network of institutions and communities to focus on health. For example, PHENND is beginning to create a strategy for bringing health and medical faculty from several local institutions to meet with community health activists in order to define urgent community health needs that institutions can address, particularly through service-learning practice. Through their efforts to participate in a network of social institutions that deal with acute and chronic health issues, the partners hope to make a substantial impact on health issues at the neighborhood and city levels.

Conclusion

Institutional partnerships for service-learning extend and deepen the public purposes of higher education by addressing pressing social needs. Service-learning is one of the most purposeful ways in which colleges and universities embrace their role as responsible citizens of their communities, the nation, and the world. Institutions seeking to work on public issues through service-learning can substantially increase their capacity by partnering with other institutions both similar to and different from themselves. The weight of institutional resources that can be assembled through partnerships among institutions and brought to bear upon positive social change is compelling and fundamental to higher education's civic role. Although American colleges and universities compete with one another for student enrollment, funding, recognition, and faculty, they share a common tradition of responding to the needs of society. In this chapter we provide rationale, incentives, and models to encourage institutions to move beyond competition to collaboration in addressing the local, national, and global issues that move us toward a brighter future and, in turn, demonstrate for our students the value of mutually beneficial partnerships.

References

Chitgopekar, A. S., and Swaba, J. (eds.). *Where Is the Common Ground?: Insights into Service Learning Collaborations Between Community Colleges and Universities.* Mesa, Ariz.: Campus Compact National Center for Community Colleges, 1999.

Ehrlich, T. *Civic Responsibility and Higher Education.* Phoenix: Oryx, 2000.

Parks Daloz, L. A., Keen, C. H., Keen, J. P., and Daloz Parks, S. *Common Fire: Leading Lives of Commitment in a Complex World.* Boston: Beacon Press, 1996.

Ramaley, J. A. "The Perspective of a Comprehensive University." In T. Ehrlich (ed.), *Civic Responsibility and Higher Education.* Phoenix, Ariz.: Oryx, 2000.

Rodenhouse, M. P., and Torregrosa, C. H. (eds.). *2001 Higher Education Directory.* Falls Church, Va.: Higher Education Publications, 2001.

Thomas, N. "An Examination of Multi-Institutional Networks." New England Resource Center for Higher Education Working Paper #23. Boston: New England Resource Center for Higher Education, 1999.

Torres, J. (ed.). *Benchmarks for Campus/Community Partnerships.* Providence, R.I.: Campus Compact, 2000.

Chapter Eight

Principles and Profiles of Exemplary Partnerships with Community Agencies

Susan R. Jones

"We love the youthful enthusiasm that students bring to our organization."

"These students don't have a clue about life 'on the other side.'"

"The assessment project conducted by these students enabled us to collect important data we need but didn't have time to gather ourselves."

"It's hard sometimes to find enough work to be done when we have to accommodate students' requests on their timelines."

"I wish all college students had the opportunity to witness, first-hand, complex social issues and then to develop the skills and the commitment to do something about what they see."

These illustrative quotations from research and assessment projects conducted by this author with community service agency staff represent the potential benefits and challenges inherent in partnerships developed in the context of service-learning. At the heart of service-learning is a commitment to community, defined by Saltmarsh (1998) as both a place and a set of relationships. Few would argue about the integral role that community agencies play in service-learning as students' community service work frequently takes place in these organizations. However, great care must be taken to design and sustain partnerships with community agencies that enable student-learning objectives to be realized while advancing community agency goals and activities. This requires a reconceptualization of the more typical ways in which universities understand and interact with the communities in which they reside such that "the valid self-interests of the university are indistinguishable from the interests of a community" (Saltmarsh, 1998, p. 7).

Heightened interest in, and attention to, the creation of partnerships with community agencies is occurring within the larger context of the call for university-community partnerships. In part a direct response to demands both external and internal to the academy for attention to broad social issues and local problems, the mandate for higher education includes increased involvement and engagement with the community. This imperative is framed in terms including *Universities as Citizens* (Bringle, Games, and Malloy, 1999), the "Engaged Institution" (Kellogg Commission on the Future of State and Land-Grant Universities, 1999), and *Presidents' Declaration on the Civic Responsibility of Higher Education* (Campus Compact, 1999). Integral to the realization of this vision for higher education is the creation of reciprocal partnerships with the community. As the Kellogg Commission suggests, "Such partnerships are likely to be characterized by problems defined together, goals and agendas that are shared in common, definitions for success that are meaningful to both university and community" (1999, p. 27). This vision stands in contrast to the prevailing patterns evident in the relationships between higher education and their communities. For meaningful and effective reciprocal partnerships to be developed, "Communities cannot be viewed as pockets of needs, laboratories for experimentation, or passive recipients of expertise" (Bringle, Games, and Malloy, 1999, p. 9).

The literature on service-learning is replete with references to the reciprocal nature of relationships with community agencies. In fact, reciprocity is frequently described as the most fundamental ingredient for high-quality service-learning programs (Mintz and Hesser, 1996). Reciprocity exists when all involved in the service-learning partnership are teaching and learning, giving and receiving (Kendall, 1990; Porter Honnet and Poulsen, 1989; Radest,

1993; Rhoads, 1997; Sigmon, 1979). Implicit in these conceptions of reciprocity is the idea that such equality in relationships is both possible and desirable. As Kendall (1990) articulated, "In service-learning, those being served control the service provided; the needs of the community determine what the service tasks will be. It is this sense of reciprocity that creates a sense of mutual responsibility and respect between individuals in the service-learning exchange" (p. 22). However, the achievement of this frequently purported essential criterion for service-learning requires attention to complex issues: "To learn what it means to be part of a community is to participate in the life of the community in such a way that power and its relations are analyzed and critiqued in the context of a reciprocal relationship—what affects me affects the wider community, and what affects the wider community affects me. The consequences are indistinguishable. This is true reciprocity" (Saltmarsh, 1998, pp. 7, 21).

Little in the research and literature on service-learning provides evidence that the accomplishment of indistinguishable consequences, or true reciprocity, is actually achieved. And the literature that does exist is almost exclusively written from the university point of view. How different might the stories of partnerships be if told from the community agency perspective? The goal of creating authentic reciprocal partnerships between universities and community service agencies is one to which all aspire when designing partnerships for service-learning. How then are authentic reciprocal partnerships with community service agencies created and sustained?

Principles for University–Community Agency Partnerships

Advocates for reciprocity in service-learning have advanced principles of good practice to undergird the design and implementation of effective and responsible service-learning, including the Campus Outreach Opportunity League's "Critical Elements of Thoughtful Community Service" (1993), Rhoads's "Critical Community Service" (1997), Sigmon's "Three Principles" (1979), and *Principles of Good Practice in Combining Service and Learning* (Porter Honnet and Poulsen, 1989). Mintz and Hesser (1996) suggest that existing principles of good practice are understood and practiced differently by the primary partners in service-learning—college and university faculty and staff, students, and community. As a result, they propose the idea of examining these principles through the intersecting lenses of collaboration, reciprocity, and diversity (Mintz and Hesser, 1996). Still other literature takes a more logistical and procedural approach to describing campus-community partnerships (Cotton and Stanton, 1990; Gugerty and Swezey, 1996; Vernon and Ward, 1999). Without exception, these principles and approaches emphasize the integral role that community organizations play in the design and implementation of service-learning. However, less clear is the prevalence of community voices and involvement in the creation of such principles, as well as the translation of these principles into effective design of actual partnerships with community agencies.

More recently, principles for campus-community partnerships have emerged to address the need for a more explicit framework for the relationships that anchor service-learning activities. In the exhibits in Chapter One, three sets of such principles are reproduced in their entirety. These principles speak to the design of effective partnerships and to the values that serve as the foundation of such relationships. The *Benchmarks for Campus/Community Partnerships* (Torres, 2000) clearly reflect values integral to the partnership relationship and offer criteria upon which to base the design and implementation of partnerships with community agencies. They are useful in providing a framework for thinking about important factors contributing to authentic partnerships. Particularly helpful is the idea of the "partnership process," as this suggests the more dynamic, nonlinear, and fluid aspects of partnering with community service agencies. A strong partnership process is characterized by frequent communication among all involved in the partnership, a method for revisiting the essential goals and fundamentals of the partnership, and a structure that is flexible and resilient enough to allow for growth and change (Torres, 2000).

The Campus Compact document is also valuable because it includes some reference to the complexities of the process with descriptions of barriers to the design of reciprocal partnerships, including the development of trusting relationships and the sometimes enormous cultural differences between universities and community agencies. It is not uncommon for university faculty and staff who are developing partnerships for service-learning to invest time in working to overcome years of skepticism and cynicism about the university's interests in and commitment to the community.

Community-Campus Partnerships for Health (CCPH) is commonly identified as one of the most effective models of partnership because of the organization's longstanding commitment to engaging campuses and community agencies in the common work of improving health education and health in local communities. The nine principles of partnership developed by CCPH are transferable to settings outside the arena of health education. They also emphasize the importance of such qualities as trust, respect, and shared decision making (Seifer and Maurana, 2000). Further, they are written in such a way as to suggest that the locus of control in the partnership is the partners themselves. Other statements leave the actors involved in the partnership process more vague. While it is presumed that partnerships are collaborative, it is less clear who creates the conditions needed for collaboration and reciprocity to occur. In the absence of specificity in this area, the presumption is that the partnership relationship is primarily initiated and created by university actors who then approach community agency staff about their interest in participation. While unintended, this reifies the partnership relationship as essentially university-driven.

Despite the existence of principles of good practice, creating and sustaining truly reciprocal partnerships with community agencies is rarely as neat and tidy a process as the principles may suggest. While these principles provide frameworks and consequently greater direction in forming and sustaining partnerships with community agencies, they fail to capture the significant contextual and cultural influences on partnership development, which makes the process all the more complex and idiosyncratic. Thus, the principles identified above are important in thinking through the design of effective partnerships and in clarifying roles, responsibilities, and resources in a partnership, but the implementation of partnerships based upon these principles rarely reflects all the aspirations, values, and goals implicit in such principles. Peter Hocking (2000) of the Swearer Center for Public Service at Brown University in Providence, Rhode Island, hints at this reality: "Among our strategies is to see individual programs [supported by the Center] . . . as discrete centers of innovation and practice. Because each program works with different community partners and within distinct cultural contexts, program leaders begin planning with those differences and particularities in mind, collaboratively crafting methods and goals that are shared and tailored to specific needs, beliefs, and contexts" (p. 2).

Moving from Rhetoric to Reality: Putting Principles to Work

When thinking about partnerships with community service agencies, it is important to recognize that not only is there great diversity *among* these organizations with respect to mission, staffing, and resources but also *within* the organizations themselves. For example, service-learning partnerships may be created with a staff member at a particular organization, such as an executive director or volunteer coordinator, but the nature of the partnership is significantly affected by other staff, members of the board of directors, volunteers, and recipients of the services provided by the agency. Further, the research on service-learning has largely focused on student-learning outcomes and university benefits, with much less attention to the nature and outcomes of partnerships from the community agency perspective. Those studies that have focused on community involvement in service-learning illuminate some of the more logistical aspects of partnerships and satisfaction with student volunteers (Bringle and Hatcher, 1996; Ferrari and Worrall, 2000; Gray, Ondaatje, Fricker, and Geschwind, 2000). For example, Vernon and Ward (1999) surveyed directors of community service agencies and found that community members generally have positive perceptions of partnering campuses and working with students in the context of service-learning. They concluded that partnerships between campuses and community service agencies could be strengthened through increased communication among all partners about purposes and expectations, coordination of projects and activities, and collaboration in recruiting and training students. In addition, Bringle and Hatcher's (1996) Comprehensive

Action Plan for Service Learning (CAPSL) provides a useful model for identifying the activities, tasks, and outcomes associated with working with community representatives in service-learning.

After reviewing the service-learning literature, Ward and Wolf-Wendel (2000) advocated a community-centered approach to service-learning that represents a departure from the more typical strategy of universities *doing for* community service organizations. To move toward an approach of *doing with* community service agencies, Ward and Wolf-Wendel (2000) offer five recommendations for developing campus partnerships with community organizations: connect through commonalities; blur boundaries between campus and community; consider the position, history, and power (or powerlessness) of all involved in service relationships; encourage reciprocal assessment; and rethink service missions to include and reward public service and genuine community partnerships (pp. 774–776). Underlying each of these is a focus on empathy and empowerment.

Cruz and Giles (2000) summarize common claims about the community dimensions of service-learning: service-learning contributes to community development, bridges town-gown gaps, and offers benefits to community partners. To deepen understanding of community in the service-learning paradigm, Cruz and Giles suggest that "the strategic direction for research on the value of service-learning communities should focus less on evaluating 'community outcomes' and more on developing greater skills in using research as a process for sustained collaboration between universities and communities" (p. 29). In particular, they recommended research that focuses on the partnership as the unit of analysis, models principles of good practice in service-learning, uses action research, and highlights community assets (Cruz and Giles, 2000).

How then might we translate the theoretical frameworks of the partnership principles and the research and literature on community perspectives on service-learning partnerships to the actual design and implementation of partnerships with community service organizations? In other words, how can we put the principles to work in the service of creating and sustaining authentic partnerships with community agencies in the context of service-learning? The characteristics that follow represent a synthesis of those factors that appear to be most effective.

Time

Effective partnerships with community agencies are developed over time and take time to cultivate and nourish. When conceptualized as relationships (Bringle and Hatcher, forthcoming), campus and community agency partnerships can develop the kind of trust and respect that does not occur with one phone call, one class, or one project. If partnerships are truly based upon real community interests, then in most cases, the commitment extends well beyond an initial contact and develops into full immersion into many aspects of the life of the community agency. Responsible and responsive partnerships with community service agencies take time, intentional effort, and consistent attention.

In order to sustain partnerships with community agencies, service-learning programs and activities should emerge from a developing partnership. This is in contrast to the more typical (and more expedient) pattern in which the service-learning activity is the impetus for interest in a partnership. This pattern may enable the service-learning to occur, but it does not necessarily contribute to building an ongoing relationship. Further, faculty and staff seeking to initiate partnerships must take the time to truly get to know the organizations with which they would like to partner. This includes developing a working knowledge of mission, services, programs, staffing, and clientele, and is best accomplished by spending time on site at the community agency.

Fit

For partnerships with community service agencies to be most effective, there must exist a close match between the university's objectives and intended student-learning outcomes and the community organization's mission, activities, and timelines. Without such a match, partnerships will always serve university and student interests first. Fit includes both the nature of the work to be accomplished and the time needed to complete it. Do service-learning partnerships fit with the natural flow of work in the agency, or do they disrupt it? Community service agencies rarely function on the semester or quarter cycle of most universities. Rather, they constantly balance the urgent needs of day-to-day existence and the longer-term battles with complex social problems such as homelessness, illiteracy, hunger, and AIDS. Responsible and responsive partnerships, then, must be cultivated and sustained based upon the individual and collective interests and needs of all those involved and sensitive to the rhythms and routines of community organizations.

Attention to Power Dynamics

In most cases, service-learning relationships begin with a real or perceived power differential between universities and the community service agencies with which they seek to partner. Unless this power dynamic is acknowledged, the partnership will replicate the very inequalities that service-learning is intended to help eradicate. Once acknowledged, the potential partners must address this issue through an equitable distribution of tasks and resources such as staff and funding. All too often, universities initiate the partnerships and then turn over to the community agencies the management of the logistics of student training and supervision. Instead, the university should make efforts to relieve the burden of training and supervising students at the community site. In addition, the university should recognize and reward community service agency staff who function as teachers, trainers, and on-site supervisors for their contributions to the service-learning experience.

Effective partnerships require that both community service agencies and universities have the infrastructure and the organizational capacity to support such partnerships if they are to be successful over time. This may require shifts in resource allocation so that community agencies have the staffing, supplies, and financial resources needed to support service-learning activities. Equitable distribution of resources increases the likelihood of a more reciprocal relationship between campuses and community service agencies.

Communication

Often, communication between university and community agency personnel focuses on "setting up" the service-learning site placements. After an initial investment of time, university faculty and staff tend to back away from the day-to-day facilitation of the partnership.

As a result, community partners become frustrated by the lack of attention, involvement, and communication from their would-be university partners. It is critical that faculty and university staff who design service-learning programs remain active participants.

Effective partnerships with community agencies are characterized by consistent communication and dialogue throughout all aspects of the partnership process. For example, both agencies and students participating in service-learning need orientation to their work together with identification of clear expectations and guidelines. Initial conversation to ensure clarity of goals must be supplemented by ongoing communication about the extent to which expectations are being met. Regular dialogue, as well as flexibility, is essential as conditions, issues, and student inclinations and motivations change. In addition, community agency priorities and staffing often change quickly. Consistent communication permits renegotiation of partnership expectations as necessary.

Acknowledging Expertise

For partnerships with community service agencies to be effective, university faculty and staff must recognize that expertise exists in many forms and resides in multiple places. Recognizing and cultivating the expression of expertise of community partners requires a shift in thinking. Campus leaders often simply do not consider community agency staff in the teaching of courses or agency staff and clients in the facilitation of on-site reflection. In addition, navigating the terrain of learning in the context of partnerships takes students, university faculty and staff, and community service agency representatives into uncharted territory.

For faculty, in particular, the integration of community service into courses and working collaboratively with community agencies present challenges. These include a departure from traditional teaching methods, relinquishing control of what and where learning takes place, and making sense, together with students, of what happens in the community and its relationship to course content. For these reasons, Howard (1998) refers to service-learning as a counternormative pedagogy that requires a reconceptualization of the teaching and learning process. Anticipating the issues that may emerge from truly reciprocal teaching and learning has tremendous potential to enhance learning.

Evaluation and Assessment

Successful and effective partnerships with community service agencies must be continually assessed and evaluated, with all participating in the process. Often, this dimension of the partnership is minimized or neglected, particularly from the community partner's perspective. The terms *research, assessment,* and *evaluation* are frequently used interchangeably, yet important distinctions exist (Waterman, 1997). Research emphasizes the development of theory and the advance of knowledge in a particular field, while evaluation focuses on decision making regarding program quality, including planning, implementation, and outcomes. Assessment is a form of evaluation and focuses on "defining, measuring, collecting, analyzing, and using information" to guide good practice (Erwin, 1996). Often, assessment serves as the initial stage for evaluation as the results of data collection, analysis, and interpretation inform the design of a program evaluation. Assessment and evaluation rely on both quantitative methodologies, such as surveys, and qualitative methodologies, including focus groups, interviews, and participant observation.

Most common forms of assessment and evaluation include assessing student learning outcomes and evaluating service-learning programs. Less frequent are assessment and evaluations of outcomes for community participants. For partnerships to be strengthened and sustained, mutually agreed upon strategies for assessment and evaluation that include all partners must be developed. This begins with the identification of measurable outcomes for the community agency as well as for the partnership. As noted in Campus Compact's *Benchmarks for Campus/Community Partnerships,* "Assessment, like every other facet of a partnership, needs to be tailored to the specific values and goals of your work. Thus, in order to achieve useful results, you will need to have clearly articulated what those goals are. What constitutes success?" (Torres, 2000, p. 34). Criteria for success should consider not only student performance and completion of tasks but also community benefits from student participation onsite, specific outcomes for the community agency and its clients, and the nature of the partnership itself. Community involvement in assessment might include not only volunteer staff but also those with whom students come into contact through their community service work. Further, assessment should occur in all phases of the partnership so that it informs not only a final analysis of the service-learning partnership but also the day-to-day functioning of the partnership relationship (Torres, 2000). What constitutes success? Bringle and Hatcher (1996) offer this perspective on evaluating the success of university and community organization partnerships: "Evidence that a stable, meaningful, mature relationship is evolving would include continuity in the relationships across time, consensus that mutual needs are being met, collaboration in advocacy and grant proposals, formal and informal participation by the agency staff in the university context (for example, team teaching), and formal and informal participation by the faculty, alumni, and students in the agency (for example, advocacy, board of directors, consultants)" (p. 236).

Profiles of Successful Partnerships

A message posted to the service-learning listserv (sl@csf.colorado. edu) in the preparation of this chapter requesting examples of successful partnerships with community service agencies produced more than one hundred responses. This author found it heartening that some of the responses described partnerships that had been sustained over time, reflected a close match between desired student learning outcomes and community agency mission, and demonstrated reciprocity in planning and implementation. Other responses, however, exhibited a lack of clarity about the relationship to service-learning or a vague sense of purpose of the partnership they represented. The following partnership profiles were chosen for diversity of institutional and partnership type, evidence of strength of the partnership, and explicit connection to service-learning.

The Homelessness Prevention Network Project and Purdue University

The partnership between the Homelessness Prevention Network and Purdue University in Lafayette, Indiana, is part of the Engineering Projects in Community Service (EPICS) program. Now a national service-learning program, EPICS was initiated at Purdue in 1995. Through the EPICS program, undergraduate students in engineering enroll in courses that require participation in long-term projects working with community organizations. Students receive academic credit over the several semesters during which they are involved. This enables them to make a commitment to see the project through from initial design to completion. The projects are defined, designed, built, and implemented through a collaborative process involving partnerships between community service organizations, engineering faculty, and industry advisers (Oakes and others, 2001).

The integration of service-learning into the engineering curriculum enables students and faculty to work closely with community agencies. While working on real community problems that require their technical expertise, the students also develop an enhanced understanding of engineering, including "the role of the partner, or 'customer,' in defining an engineering project; the necessity of teamwork; the difficulty of managing and leading large projects; the need for skills and knowledge from many different disciplines; and the art of solving technical problems. They also learn many valuable lessons in citizenship, including the role of community service in our society; the significant impact that their engineering skills can have on their community; and that assisting others leads to their own substantial growth as individuals, engineers, and citizens" (Oakes and others, 2001, p. 1).

The purpose of the Homelessness Prevention Network (HPN) is to maintain an accurate count of homeless individuals in the Greater Lafayette area and then to coordinate services provided by agencies serving those who are homeless. The agencies associated with the HPN requested the formation of an HPN EPICS team to design, develop, deploy, and support a database system that would enable the agencies to count and describe their clients, track services provided to each client, enable case management that spanned all agencies and services, and create accurate reports without violating clients' confidentiality. The HPN EPICS team has been working together for more than five years.

The success of the partnerships created through the EPICS program is evident in this comment from Joyce Field, former director of HPN: "The HPN project team has had a significant impact on the accomplishment of the mission of the agencies in the network by providing a necessary client management system that will help each agency assess the quality of services provided by each agency and the network as a whole. . . . I am a tremendous supporter of the EPICS program and the way the program allows students to work in real life settings on real life problems that affect the community" (personal communication, March 2001).

The HPN EPICS team is a model of true partnering with community agencies. The ideas for technical assistance come from the community; designs and planning are constructed by teams that include all involved; and student-learning objectives are clear, explicit, and connected both to the development of expertise in engineering and to citizenship skills (F. R. DeRego Jr., personal communication, March 2001).

Hispanic-Latino Service-Learning Partnership and Colorado State University

The Service Integration Project (SIP) was initiated in 1992 to expand faculty interest in and use of service-learning as a teaching strategy (Mintz and Hesser, 1996). As the project grew, a necessary emphasis on the partnerships needed to support and sustain service-learning developed. Ongoing working relationships with a number of community service agencies drew attention to issues and concerns that all partners shared. One such compelling focus was on the success of Hispanic-Latino youth. This common concern resulted in the development of service-learning courses and programs to address youth development and leadership in the Hispanic-Latino communities in close proximity to the Fort Collins campus. The SIP approach to working with community agencies by focusing on an issue of common concern leads to partnerships of greater depth and increased possibilities for addressing community needs in a more sustained and systemic manner.

In order to arrive at a deeper and common understanding of the needs in the community, SIP sponsored a "learning circle" including Colorado State faculty, community partners, and students. The opportunity for discussion and dialogue among these groups resulted in a number of ideas for programs and projects. One such initiative was the Hispanic-Latino Service-Learning Partnership. This partnership is anchored in existing relationships with a number of community agencies and schools, each with an interest in the success of Hispanic-Latino youth. For example, a foreign language professor partnered with community members to integrate service-learning into a national training model, the Hispanic-Latino Leadership Institute. The three-day institute then produced additional opportunities for collaboration, including a Hispanic community newsletter, a health services coalition for Hispanic families, and a volunteer group working to provide tutoring and mentoring services for Hispanic-Latino youth.

With a strong foundation in place, SIP is now working to deepen the partnerships in the context of service-learning. This spring, SIP is facilitating a six-week Service-Learning Scholars institute on the issue of Hispanic-Latino retention. Participants in the institute include six faculty and six community partner representatives who will engage in a planning process to deepen their service-learning partnerships. Intended outcomes include an increase in the number of service-learning courses from a broad range of academic disciplines that will focus on Hispanic-Latino youth in the community.

Community agency staff clearly perceive the partnerships with Colorado State as mutually beneficial. As Amy Maheras-Lopez, volunteer coordinator for the Family Center/La Familia, one of the partnering community service agencies, wrote: "Service-learning is a vital part of the Family Center's programming. . . . Service learners have contributed a great deal to the success of Family Center programs as well as to university students by promoting greater awareness of social and cultural issues within the community. The rewards on both sides outweigh any of the negative" (personal communication, April 2001). Partnerships in this model focus on a common issue of concern to many in the Fort Collins community. This approach provides the opportunity for depth in the partnerships with community agencies as well as for a diversity of strategies to address the multiple issues involved in the success of Hispanic-Latino youth (C. Cleary, personal communication, March 2001).

Project Open Hand-Columbus and The Ohio State University

The very small office of the executive director of Project Open Hand (POHC) was nestled in the basement of an urban church and was filled with books, educational pamphlets about AIDS, and food packaging materials. It was a hot summer day, and the temperature in the office mirrored the heat and humidity outside the doors of the church. As a faculty member interested in service-learning and familiar with the volunteer needs of this organization whose mission focuses on preparing and delivering nutritious meals to people living with AIDS, I approached the executive director about how Ohio State students might help them accomplish their goals. At first blush, she was incredulous that a faculty member was interested in engaging students in the community as part of an academic course. In fact, her first response was, "You want to do what?"

I explained that my commitment to this community agency was to provide trained student volunteers every quarter and that graduate students interested in service-learning would facilitate training, ongoing supervision, and evaluation of students on site to relieve the potential burden that the student volunteers might unintentionally present. She expected that this idea would turn into yet another "hit-and-run" approach by the university to share its expertise with those in need, only to disappear when the quarter ended, the grant funding ran out, or the research was completed. However, the somewhat skeptical executive director decided to give this "partnership idea" a try.

Now, eleven quarters later, nearly one hundred undergraduate students enrolled in a leadership in community service course and thirty graduate students in the higher education and student affairs program who have completed coursework in service-learning in higher education have spent a minimum of three hours a week working at Project Open Hand. The partnership is "owned" by both Ohio State faculty and Project Open Hand staff and clients. In addition, because of the visibility of so many students affiliated with Project Open Hand, involvement from other university faculty and students has grown. Likewise, Project Open Hand was added to the list of community agencies to which Ohio State faculty and staff may direct their charitable giving through the

Greater Community Shares program. Undergraduate students have played a major role in the Columbus AIDSWALK, a major fund-raising event upon which Project Open Hand depends for a substantial portion of its income.

The partnership between Project Open Hand and Ohio State is successful because of the in-depth involvement of faculty and staff in the agency, frequent communication between agency staff and university faculty, and the ongoing commitment to the organization from students who first became aware of Project Open Hand through their service-learning classes. The executive director, herself a product of service-learning classes at Ohio State, which introduced her to Project Open Hand, commented, "The benefits of having OSU student volunteers at POHC are unmatched. Not only do students provide a vital source of volunteer support, such as cooking and delivering meals, which our agency depends on; but they also bring an enthusiasm that reenergizes staff, current volunteers, and clients. In addition to our agency benefiting from this partnership, students also learn valuable lessons from their experience. . . . They definitely come away from their community service experience wiser and in many cases committed to staying involved with our agency" (T. Fortkamp, personal communication, March 2001).

Stone Soup and California State University–Fresno

The partnership between a local nonprofit organization, Stone Soup of Fresno, and California State University–Fresno was created to address community needs, educate students, and involve faculty in tackling problems facing a neighborhood adjacent to the university. The partnership began in 1992 when a group of concerned community members and organizations began exploring strategies for addressing problems in a neighborhood known as El Dorado Park, which is just west of the campus. The neighborhood had many children living in poverty and was identified as a high-crime area, with gang violence, illiteracy, and a number of other issues prevalent. Ongoing meetings of concerned citizens resulted in the creation of Stone Soup of Fresno to serve the needs of this disadvantaged community. California State University–Fresno was an initial partner in the development of Stone Soup. The intent of the partnership was to combine the resources of the university with the resources and assets of the community to focus on a particular neighborhood's needs.

The university's role in the partnership with Stone Soup includes raising grant funds to support Stone Soup programs and dedicating human resources of more than seventy faculty and staff members and three hundred students each year who provide direct services to the El Dorado Park community through Stone Soup. Faculty have developed service-learning courses that address areas of interest and need in the community. For example, theatre arts–drama faculty and students develop and sponsor puppetry shows and workshops for the children served by Stone Soup. The shows focus on issues such as violence prevention, cultural sensitivity, and substance abuse. Students in health science and nursing classes share information on nutrition, dental health, hygiene, and childhood immunizations with neighborhood residents. Additional service-learning courses with site placements in the El Dorado Park community are offered in sociology, counseling, consumer sciences, education, industrial technology, and gerontology. This partnership is exemplary because of the integration of university faculty, staff, and students into the work of Stone Soup. Likewise, Stone Soup staff and volunteers function as co-teachers working directly with faculty and students, modeling the principles of mutuality and reciprocity that anchor effective service-learning and partnership development (C. Fiorentino, personal communication, March 2001).

House of Peace and Education and Mount Wachusett Community College

While connecting to their communities has long been considered a hallmark of community colleges, many presume that students attending community colleges do not have the time or inclination to participate in community service. The unique partnership between the House of Peace and Education (H.O.P.E.) and Mount Wachusett Community College in Gardner, Massachusetts contradicts this presumption. The President of Mount Wachusett Community College (MWCC) was interested in a curriculum that integrated the development of academic skills with community service. His goal was to establish service-learning as a collegewide pedagogy to offer all students the opportunity to bridge theory with real-life experience, to acquire skills in their fields of study, and to develop strong connections in their community.

Around the same time, the H.O.P.E. program began as a mentoring and educational program for women and children in the area who had experienced violence in their lives and the resulting loss of self-esteem. Students enrolled in service-learning courses at MWCC started to work with the children and women served by H.O.P.E. Often, MWCC students found themselves tutoring the children of other MWCC students, which provided unique lessons in the reciprocity and mutuality of service-learning. The faculty and H.O.P.E. staff work so closely together that they often refer students to one another. For example, MWCC faculty refer students in need of additional academic assistance to H.O.P.E., and H.O.P.E. encourages women who have gained skills and self-confidence to enroll in courses at the college. In fact, through the service-learning partnership between MWCC and H.O.P.E., the missions of the two institutions have become intertwined, each based upon respect for all individuals and a commitment to student success (S. McAlpine, personal communication, February 2001).

Conclusion

Partnerships with community agencies are essential for service-learning. Principles of good practice provide a framework for thinking about the nature of partnerships as well as an articulation of the values that serve as the foundation for relationships with community agencies. They encourage reciprocal partnerships between campus and community, with all involved sharing in the design, working together on implementation, addressing the challenges, and reaping the benefits of such relationships. However, the translation of principle to practice is often a messier process than the principles might suggest. Without careful attention to the complex dynamics of partnership relations, "the best of community service learning will not be about community, the service provided will be directed toward the students, and the learning fostered will ultimately tend to perpetuate the social system that produces the inequality, impoverishment, and injustice students witness" (Saltmarsh, 1998, p. 22).

Given national trends in higher education, interest in the "engaged campus" and in developing citizenship skills and practices among students will continue. If colleges and universities are serious about promoting engagement as both a process and an outcome, then higher education institutions themselves must be transformed. This does not suggest only the presence of institutional commitment and the support of the leadership, but also a rethinking of who can teach (and learn) and where teaching and learning can occur. As colleges and universities link economic development with campus-community partnerships, the nature of these relationships becomes more complex. For example, campus "revitalization" efforts are perceived and experienced very differently by those at the university driving these initiatives and those in the community who feel disenfranchised by such efforts. The engaged campus cannot be one that merely reaches out into the community; instead, the boundaries that separate campus from community should disappear and become impossible to differentiate. This suggests the need for increased involvement of community members in the life of the university. Further, if partnerships between campuses and community agencies are to be effective means of engagement, the university has a role in helping agencies create and sustain an infrastructure to support service-learning initiatives. It is under the conditions of shared resources and reciprocity that campuses and community agencies can develop the mutual capacity to support service-learning partnerships that enrich both.

While engagement implies partnerships on the institutional level, it is important to remember that partnerships with community agencies are, in fact, often based in partnerships among individuals. Service-learning partnerships bring people together from very different life circumstances and experiences. This dynamic introduces the central factor of caring that is fundamental to the partnership relationship. Noddings (1984) captures this important connection: "When we see the other's reality as a possibility for us, we must act to eliminate the intolerable, to reduce the pain, to fill the need, to actualize the dream. When I am in this sort of relationship with another, when the other's reality becomes a real possibility for me, I care" (p. 14).

Partnerships between campuses and community agencies, mutually constructed and collaboratively implemented, hold the potential for cultivating relationships anchored in caring and respect. Conversely, caring and respectful relationships between individuals can lead to broader and deeper partnerships between campus and community. As Lawrence-Lightfoot discovered in her recent research, "Respectful relationships also have a way of sustaining and replicating themselves" (1999, p. 10). This is the hope for the creation of partnerships between campuses and community agencies in the context of service-learning.

References

Bringle, R. G., Games, R., and Malloy, E. A. *Colleges and Universities as Citizens.* Needham Heights, Mass.: Allyn & Bacon, 1999.

Bringle, R. G., and Hatcher, J. A. "Implementing Service Learning in Higher Education." *Journal of Higher Education,* 1996, *67*(2), 221–239.

Bringle, R. G., and Hatcher, J. A. "Campus-Community Relationships: The Terms of Engagement." *Journal of Social Issues,* forthcoming.

Campus Compact. *Presidents' Declaration on the Civic Responsibility of Higher Education.* Providence, R.I.: Campus Compact, 1999.

Campus Outreach Opportunity League. *Into the Streets: Organizing Manual, 1994–95 Edition.* St. Paul, Minn.: COOL Press, 1993.

Cotton, D., and Stanton, T. K. "Joining Campus and Community Through Service Learning." In C. Delve, S. D. Mintz, and C. M. Stewart (eds.), *Community Service as Values Education.* New Directions for Student Services, no. 50. San Francisco: Jossey Bass, 1990.

Cruz, N. I., and Giles, D. E., Jr. "Where's the Community in Service-Learning Research?" *Michigan Journal of Community Service Learning,* Special Issue, 2000, 28–34.

Erwin, T. D. "Assessing Student Learning and Development." In S. Komives and D. Woodard (eds.), *Student Services: A Handbook for the Profession* (3rd ed.) San Francisco: Jossey-Bass, 1996.

Ferrari, J. R., and Worrall, L. "Assessments by Community Agencies: How 'the Other Side' Sees Service-Learning." *Michigan Journal of Community Service Learning,* 2000, *7*, 35–40.

Gray, M. J., Ondaatje, E. H., Fricker, R. D., Jr., and Geschwind, S. A. "Assessing Service-Learning: Results from a Survey of 'Learn and Serve America, Higher Education'" *Change,* Mar.–Apr. 2000, 30–39.

Gugerty, C. R., and Swezey, E. D. "Developing Campus-Community Rela-
    tionships." In B. Jacoby (ed.), *Service-Learning in Higher Education:
    Concepts and Practices.* San Francisco: Jossey-Bass, 1996.
Hocking, P. "Introduction." In *Push.* Providence, R.I.: Swearer Center for
    Public Service, Brown University, 2000.
Howard, J.P.F. "Academic Service Learning: A Counternormative Peda-
    gogy." In R. A. Rhoads and J.P.F. Howard, *Academic Service Learning:
    A Pedagogy of Action and Reflection.* San Francisco: Jossey-Bass, 1998.
Kellogg Commission on the Future of State and Land-Grant Universities.
    Returning to Our Roots: The Engaged Institution. Washington, D.C.:
    National Association of State Universities and Land Grant Colleges,
    1999.
Kendall, J. C. *Combining Service and Learning: A Resource Book for Commu-
    nity and Public Service.* Raleigh, N.C.: National Society for Internships
    and Experiential Education, 1990.
Lawrence-Lightfoot, S. *Respect: An Exploration.* Reading, Mass.: Perseus, 1999.
Mintz, S. D., and Hesser, G. W. "Principles of Good Practice in Service-
    Learning." In B. Jacoby (ed.), *Service-Learning in Higher Education:
    Concepts and Practices.* San Francisco: Jossey-Bass, 1996.
Noddings, N. *Caring: A Feminine Approach to Ethics and Moral Education.*
    Berkeley: University of California Press, 1984.
Oakes, W. C., and others. "EPICS: A Student Perspective of Service-Learn-
    ing in Engineering. " Paper presented at the American Society for
    Engineering Education, West Lafayette, Ind., Mar. 2001.
Porter Honnet, E., and Poulsen, S. *Principles of Good Practice in Combining
    Service and Learning.* Racine, Wis.: Johnson Foundation, 1989.
Radest, H. *Community Service: Encounter with Strangers.* New York: Praeger,
    1993.
Rhoads, R. A. *Community Service and Higher Learning: Explorations of the Car-
    ing Self.* Albany: SUNY Press, 1997.
Saltmarsh, J. "Exploring the Meanings of Community/University Part-
    nerships." *National Society for Experiential Education Quarterly,* Sum-
    mer 1998, 6–22.
Seifer, S. D., and Maurana, C. A. "Developing and Sustaining Community-
    Campus Partnerships: Putting Principles into Action." *Partnership
    Perspectives,* 2000, 7–11.
Sigmon, R. "Service-Learning: Three Principles." *Synergist,* 1979, *8*(1).
Torres, J. *Benchmarks for Campus/Community Partnerships.* Providence, R.I.:
    Campus Compact, 2000.
Vernon, A., and Ward, K. "Campus and Community Partnerships: Assess-
    ing Impacts and Strengthening Connections." *Michigan Journal of
    Community Service,* 1999, *6,* 30–37.

Ward, K., and Wolf-Wendel, L. "Community-Centered Service Learning: Moving from *Doing for* to *Doing with.*" *American Behavioral Scientist,* 2000, *43*(5), 769–780.

Waterman, A. S. *Service-Learning: Applications from the Research.* Hillsdale, N.J.: Erlbaum, 1997.

Chapter Nine

Partnerships with Elementary and Secondary Education

Terry Pickeral

Partnerships between higher education and K–12 schools are part of the heritage of American education. From laboratory schools to student teacher placements, higher education has traditionally worked with K–12 schools as settings where college students learn academic content, acquire skills, and prepare for their careers. There are many reasons that K–12 schools and higher education have created partnerships, including improving student achievement by identifying what students are expected to know and be able to do in preparation for college, easing the transition from high school to college by aligning curricula and admissions standards, increasing access to higher education by creating pathways to college that are clearly marked and easily navigated by students, enhancing teacher preparation by developing a shared understanding of student learning goals, and accessing grant opportunities from funding organizations requiring or giving priority to existing partnerships.

As more and more elementary and secondary schools incorporate service-learning into the curriculum, colleges and universities have found another avenue for collaboration. In fact, partnerships between institutions of higher education and K–12 schools are the most popular form of service-learning partnership. Campus Compact indicates that students at 61 percent of their member institutions tutor children in math and that at 77 percent, students tutor in reading and writing. Further, 65 percent of Campus Compact institutions work with preschools, 89 percent with elementary schools, 77 percent with junior high and middle schools, and 65 percent with high schools in campus-based service-learning projects (Campus Compact, 2001).

Moreover, many service-learning advocates have come to realize that the future of service-learning in higher education is closely tied to K–12 education. As service-learning pedagogy and practice increase in elementary and secondary schools, it has become clear that students' precollege experiences will, for better or worse, shape their attitudes toward collegiate service-learning. In 1999, the U.S. Department of Education reported that students participate in community service activities arranged or recognized by their school in 64 percent of all public K–12 schools and 83 percent of all public high schools (Office of Educational Research and Improvement, 1999). Every year more individual schools and school systems are integrating service-learning into the formal curriculum and requiring it for high school graduation. As a result, students are coming to college with preformed opinions of service-learning that may be positive or negative: "To the extent that they perceive their service and reflection activities attractive and valuable, students will seek opportunities to continue service when they enter higher education. Hence, students may 'vote with their feet' in favor of institutions with well-developed service-learning programs. . . . To the extent that service-learning becomes institutionalized in K–12 education, then, colleges and universities will encounter a steady stream of students seeking service-learning as part of their postsecondary educational experience" (Droge, 1995, cited in Jacoby, 1996, pp. 327–328). Similarly, if colleges and universities are to be successful in developing active and socially responsible democratic participants, it is important that K–12 civic education programs be of high quality.

This chapter posits that higher education institutions must extend and enhance their partnerships with elementary and secondary schools to advance service-learning on both levels. It examines higher education/K–12 partnerships, with an emphasis on how service-learning enhances partnerships. It also offers policy implications, examples, challenges, strategies, and recommendations for moving partnerships to greater depth, scope, quality, and reciprocity. Finally, it concludes with a view of the future based on the concept of partnerships beginning at the preschool level and extending beyond the baccalaureate.

A Historical Perspective on Education Partnerships

Despite all the eminently logical reasons for K–12 systems and higher education to work closely together, this has not always been the case and is not always true even today. Haycock (1994) maintains that the two systems, K–12 and higher education, grew apart as each evolved during the course of the twentieth century. For example, when college faculty believe that entering students lack adequate preparation, they often lobby for the addition of new admission requirements without consulting the K–12 system to understand the implications of their action.

As Haycock states, "The movement toward separation—indeed toward virtual neglect—began to reverse" during the late 1960s and early 1970s (1994, p. 17). However, while the first wave of school-college partnerships enabled a college education to become a reality for many young people who never would have even considered going to college, the programs were "collaborative in name only" (Haycock, 1994, p. 18). Unfortunately, "neither college- nor school-level administrators seemed to want to explore deeper roots to the problems of underrepresented minority students, especially those embedded in the educational systems" (Haycock, 1994, p. 18).

By the late 1970s, declining scores on college entry tests and rapid increases of first-year students requiring remedial coursework led to a second wave of higher education focus on the schools. A number of reports accused K–12 schools of "grade inflation" and declining standards. Haycock indicates that the eventual response by higher education was "essentially programmatic rather than systematic," focusing on individual teachers rather than addressing problems "within the school or district that impede the ability of teachers to teach in new ways" (Haycock, 1994, p. 19).

Haycock explains why there remains a "mismatch in perceptions" between higher education and K–12 schools regarding the role of higher education in school reform efforts:

First, though individual colleges and universities have mounted many programs of involvement with the schools, higher education as a whole has played little or no role in reform policy discussion to date. Second, although colleges and universities offer a great deal to schools, there is often a mismatch between what they offer and what schools need. Finally, as the nation gets further into K–12 reform efforts, it is becoming increasingly apparent to many observers who are looking at reform's future that all of the efforts will not make much of a difference without certain reforms in the way higher education goes about its own business. K–12 and higher education are in fundamental ways "all one system" [Haycock, 1994, p. 20].

Given this context, it in not surprising that K–12 schools are sometimes hesitant to enter into partnerships with colleges and universities, including those for service-learning. Nevertheless, the basic tenets of service-learning—mutuality, reciprocity, authenticity, and democratic collaboration—make service-learning a natural connector of the two educational systems.

Service-Learning Partnerships

As the chapters in this book make clear, partnership in service-learning is not an option but a necessary organizing principle. Partnerships allow independent entities to reach out beyond their own capacities as they meet their organizational objectives while enhancing their contribution to collaborative outcomes (Pickeral, 1996). In view of the limitations Haycock (1994) points out in the relationship between higher education and K–12 schools, Lawson and Hooper-Briar (1994) introduce the notion of *social morbidity* to describe how society has failed to identify, steward, and enforce the rights of children, youth, and families. They maintain that, by "neglecting our collective responsibilities, the systems we have designed . . . are not achieving their goals" (p. 9). Their suggestion is to "think differently about our collective responsibilities and service systems . . . and accept shared responsibility for solutions. . . . By themselves they [agencies] have been insufficient means to meet the challenges of the new morbidity. Heretofore separate, even competing, staff and their systems now must collaborate, seeking to integrate their services. By expanding partnerships, new models for service system design and implementation are appearing in neighborhoods, communities and schools" (pp. 9–10).

Service-learning partnerships have the potential to add value to each partner as well as to the collaboration and to provide needed efforts to address complex social issues. The chart in Exhibit 9.1 enumerates ways in which service-learning can help move K–12 partnerships toward becoming more balanced collaborations. It identifies partnerships between K–12 and higher education from two points of view, one without the application of the basic principles, or benchmarks, for service-learning partnerships, and one that incorporates them. See Chapter One for a discussion of the principles and benchmarks that underlie all authentic partnerships for service-learning. Although the descriptions in the chart do not equally characterize every partnership, they do offer general elements and an opportunity for critical analysis of partnerships.

Examples of High-Quality Partnerships Between K–12 Schools and Higher Education

As policy makers and practitioners in both K–12 and higher education seek to create sustained partnerships with the potential to address the issues related to social morbidity, the principles that guide service-learning offer tremendous promise. The following section describes in detail Project Connect in Bellingham, Washington, an outstanding example of a service-learning partnership. Brief sketches of two other notable partnership examples are also offered. All exhibit, in various ways and in varying degrees, the characteristics outlined in Exhibit 9.1.

Project Connect

Project Connect is a service-learning partnership that enables teacher education students to gain critical experience and skills, provides professional development and job enrichment for middle-school teachers, engages middle-school students in service-learning that complements the curriculum and allows them to make valuable contributions, and serves the community in multiple ways. Bellingham, Washington, a rural city with a population of sixty

Exhibit 9.1 Characteristics of Partnerships Between K–12 and Higher Education

Element of Partnership	*Without Principles of Service-Learning*	*With Principles of Service-Learning*
Leadership	Responsibility of leader or leaders of one organizational unit, usually adults	Shared responsibility for design, implementation, and assessment by all participants, including youth
Communication strategies	One way, ad hoc	Frequent, planned, and oriented to deliberation and decision making
Assessment of degree of success	Focus on impacts on select participants and institutions	Both process- and outcome-oriented, with emphasis on frequent reflection and commitment to continuous improvement
		All participants determine and contribute assessment criteria and measurement.
Decision-making processes	Decisions made in isolation	Decisions made by deliberation and agreement
Infrastructure	Capacity located primarily within one partner, usually higher education	All partners develop the infrastructure necessary to ensure full and highest quality collaboration.
Policy	Lack of focus on policies that encourage, support, and reward collaborative efforts	Focus by all partners to align partnership with existing policies and develop new policies to ensure sustainability
	Focus on practice over policy	
Sustainability	Efforts to sustain partnerships rest with individuals.	Systemic policies, practices, and infrastructure secure sustainability.
Commitment	Short-term commitments that usually end with particular project	Long-term organizational commitment to sustaining and enhancing partnership
		Partnership aligned with mission and priorities of each organization

thousand, offered a fertile environment for collaboration. It is home to Western Washington University, with a large college of education. Its K–12 schools serve students from widely diverse backgrounds. Several community agencies were willing partners, including the YWCA, Elder Care, Animal Care Centers, Nooksack Stream Enhancement Association, and the city and county Parks and Recreation Departments.

The project began in 1997 when a recent teacher education graduate who integrated service-learning into her middle-school curriculum joined with other district teachers interested in service-learning to share curriculum and service ideas, assessment strategies, and effective reflection activities. At the same time, the district developed its Middle Schools of the Future plan, which included service-learning. In 1999, the connection to Western Washington University's Woodring College of Education was formalized. Project Connect participants began to share responsibility for the creation of rich, developmentally appropriate curricular learning experiences for both college and middle-school students.

A university professor and a middle-school teacher involved in Project Connect comment: "Working together gives us—at both the K–12 and higher education levels—an opportunity to support one another in creating and implementing new curricular approaches at our respective levels" (Education Commission of the States, 2000, p. 1). They further acknowledge the benefits of service-learning collaborations for middle-school students: "Service-learning is a powerful way to enhance young adolescent learners' cognitive, social and moral development. Many standards set forth by the National Middle School Association's publication *This We Believe,* as well as emerging academic standards established by state departments of education and national teacher associations, can be effectively addressed through service-learning. Students' cognitive development is enhanced as they prepare for service. In conducting research about their projects, students develop and practice the skills of acquiring, analyzing and interpreting information—goals set forth by the National Council for the Social Studies" (p. 2).

Project outcomes include enabling middle-school students to feel more connected to their community, deepening their understanding of international and national issues through the study of local issues, encouraging them to become critical thinkers, establishing a sense of personal efficacy, and providing opportunities for them to interact with local policy makers and citizen advocates. Teacher education students gain valuable experience, knowledge, and skills as they work with both middle-school students and teachers. A key outcome at this level is for prospective teachers to learn about and practice working in authentic ways with youth and community agencies. Student teachers gain firsthand experience in, and develop an understanding of, how to create and sustain mutually beneficial and democratic service-learning partnerships.

Project Connect brings together students in both middle school and university teacher education classes in service-learning activities that meet local community needs and are related to specific course outcomes. In addition to providing high-quality service and learning opportunities for the two levels of students, the project offers models for community agencies to use as they engage students from other schools and colleges. Many of the youth continue to provide service to the agencies once they have completed their service-learning projects. Agency staff find they are energized by the enthusiasm of both the middle-school and college students for addressing the needs of the community and for the work of the community organization.

Project Connect secured its initial funding from a Washington statewide Contextual Teaching and Learning grant that paid for transportation, supplies, and reflection materials. As the project progressed and demonstrated positive outcomes for students, substantive community benefit, "fit" with K–12 and higher education missions, and strong interinstitutional support, additional resources were secured from the university's service-learning center to reduce faculty teaching load, cover attendance at state and national conferences, and enable faculty and teacher education students to increase collaboration with local service agencies. The school district provided staff support and money for professional and curriculum development. The school district and the university also combined resources to fund teacher training, project planning, and assessment.

The project's success is also a function of leadership at both education levels, ensuring sustainable systems and alignment with priorities. As a result of Project Connect, the school district has continued to support service-learning as a key component of its Middle Schools of the Future plan, and the university recognizes the role of service-learning in its institutional mission statement. The project offers a comprehensive model of what a service-learning partnership can be—a truly integrated, collaborative endeavor where university and K–12 partners work together with community agencies in a sustainable relationship that enhances education and the community in multiple ways.

Youth Empowered through Service

The University of San Diego, Mark Twain Junior and Senior High School, San Diego Parks and Recreation, Social Advocates for Youth (SAY), and the Linda Vista neighborhood's Partnership in Education, a school-community alliance, have developed a service-learning collaboration that manifests several of the characteristics of high-quality partnerships. Youth Empowered through Service (Y.E.S.) is a collaboration driven by a threefold vision: to empower youth, to provide tangible benefits to the community through the empowerment of youth, and to cultivate a "village approach" to raising *our* children (Campbell, 1998, p. 7). Students from both the school and the university join with community members to work in a local environmental center. The students help one another apply classroom concepts to the environment. They also come to understand the role of the community to foster students' learning and to improve the safety and health of its residents.

As far as the characteristics of excellent partnerships evident in Y.E.S., it is important to note that its leadership is provided by all its members, including youth. Its activities take place in various community locations. There is frequent communication and a focus on reflection and continuous improvement. In addition, each organization takes the lead on specified topics and areas. The partners have created a culture and expectation of reciprocity. Through their joint efforts, each partner adds value to the partnership and expects contributions in return.

It would have been very easy for the students and faculty from the university to descend on Twain School and provide services *to* the students and to feel good about doing it. Instead, through

Y.E.S., they work together *with* the students in service-learning projects in the community, demonstrating their commitment to mutual service and learning. This collaboration is based on the principle that *all* students have gifts to contribute to community improvement, rather than creating an artificial distinction between those who *have* and those who *have not*.

The university, school, and community participants consciously and intentionally value reciprocity and mutuality by modeling for students what it looks and feels like to work together, maximizing the assets of individuals and organizations. Thus, deep collaboration has become the norm—the university, the school, and the community find it difficult to strategize in isolation and to design service-learning programs without the assistance of their partners.

West Philadelphia Improvement Corporation

The West Philadelphia Improvement Corporation (WEPIC) began as a project by four University of Pennsylvania students who were interested in youth empowerment. They were enrolled in a course on urban university-community relationships taught by Penn's former president, Sheldon Hackney, and historians Lee Benson and Ira Harkavy. WEPIC is grounded in the concept that "schools can be the strategic and catalytic agents for community transformation" (Campbell, 1998, p. 9). The program is coordinated by the West Philadelphia Partnership, which includes the University of Pennsylvania, the Greater Philadelphia Urban Affairs coalition, the School District of Philadelphia, community organizations, churches, unions, job training agencies, and other city and state departments.

WEPIC has grown to become a neighborhood and school revitalization movement that is based in twelve public schools in the economically distressed area surrounding the University of Pennsylvania. Although it initially focused on youth, "WEPIC is now designed to produce staff-controlled, staff-managed, university-assisted, comprehensive community schools that involve, educate, and serve all members of the community" (Campbell, 1998, p. 9). It has also been very successful in acquiring grant funds to combat drug traffic around a local middle school; obtaining federal funds to establish a Head Start program; and partnering with the University of Pennsylvania Schools of Dentistry and Medicine to conduct neighborhood health fairs and screenings, provide individual consultations with doctors and nurses, and offer health education workshops in the community.

The University of Pennsylvania student group that founded WEPIC continues to assist WEPIC programs and to encourage student awareness of and involvement in local school and community issues. The members of the student organization take pride in their innovative programs that directly respond to needs identified by the schools, enable Penn students to apply their knowledge and skills in a real-world setting, and engage West Philadelphia students and teachers in dynamic service-learning experiences.

Challenges and Strategies

Service-learning partnerships across educational sectors face multiple challenges. Some of these challenges are shared by all partnerships between higher education and K–12, including a range of cultural, bureaucratic, and regulatory issues. In addition, service-learning partnerships must also grapple with the general "messiness" of service-learning and with the difficulties involved in starting and sustaining all cross-sector partnerships. This section highlights some key challenges and offers suggestions for dealing with them.

Among the initial challenges would-be partners in service-learning collaborations between colleges and K–12 schools will face are embedded in the culture, organization, and structure of both institutions. School and college terms are rarely synchronized, and class schedules of K–12 and college students often conflict. However, careful examination of schedules and willingness to compromise can result in workable solutions. Open communication and regular assessment enable changes to be made in a timely manner.

An unfortunate history of unbalanced relationships between institutions of higher education and K–12 schools often encumbers the development of service-learning partnerships. Many school system administrators and teachers complain of unilateral efforts by colleges and universities to "fix" problems or to "use" K–12 schools as learning laboratories for college students preparing to become teachers. This challenge can be addressed by acknowledging the history of previous attempts and focusing on reciprocity and mutuality as cornerstones of the partnership as it is formed and throughout its development.

Professional training of K–12 teachers and college faculty generally does not include the development of the knowledge and skills required to build service-learning partnerships or to overcome the challenges they present. As in the Project Connect example, educators on the college and K–12 levels can join together to demand professional development opportunities around service-learning collaboration from both colleges of education and school systems. In addition, teachers and faculty can create environments to learn together about integrating service-learning into courses, leading reflection activities, and articulating the benefits of service-learning to administrators and other stakeholders.

The reward systems in neither institution support service-learning pedagogy and practice. Increasingly, K–12 teachers are rewarded according to rising students' scores on standardized tests. As other chapters in this book indicate, the collegiate promotion and tenure process does not adequately recognize service-learning partnerships in the appraisal of teaching, research, and service. Although this is a formidable challenge, partners in service-learning collaborations can and should become advocates for appropriate recognition of service-learning as an effective teaching and learning strategy, academically rigorous research, and service to the community that is congruent with institutional mission.

The role of external regulatory agencies and processes such as school boards, boards of visitors, teacher certification, and testing programs also present challenges because they rarely recognize service-learning or the partnerships that support it. Addressing this challenge requires advocates to work on the policy level, locally, statewide, and federally. Advocates of service-learning partnerships should demonstrate how these partnerships align with higher education and school system priorities, goals, and initiatives. By identifying the specific ways in which service-learning advances mission-related objectives, assessment can be designed and implemented to provide evidence of these benefits. Some of the many potential outcomes of service-learning partnerships that are likely to align closely with outcomes sought by external agencies are increased opportunities for students to learn academic content and gain skills in critical thinking, creative problem solving, and teamwork; stimulating K–12 students' aspirations to attend college; and encouraging college students to seek careers in elementary or secondary education.

Another common challenge is simply knowing how to begin a service-learning partnership. The characteristics of effective partnerships listed in Exhibit 9.1 provide guidance, as do the benchmarks and principles highlighted in Chapter One. The lack of effective models of such partnerships in the literature is unfortunate. Although this chapter offers three successful examples, more case studies must be written and shared through journals and web-based resources. It is important that these descriptions include frank, honest accounts of obstacles encountered and strategies tried. In addition, reviewing the profiles of the other types of service-learning partnerships described in this book will provide strategies that are readily adaptable. As is true for all partnerships, essential elements include identification of shared expectations, clear definition of roles and responsibilities, establishment of implementation timelines, development of communication channels and mechanisms, and recognition that collaboration requires significant time and patience. Stakeholders also must anticipate and address challenges that occur as partnerships increase in size and scope. These include, but are not limited to, changes in leadership, shifting institutional priorities and politics, garnering resources, continuing communication, and assessment of progress. As these challenges are shared by all service-learning partnerships, useful methods for handling them may be found throughout the other chapters.

Over time, the mutual work of service-learning partnerships creates affinity among education professionals on all levels and begins to reframe institutional cultures to more readily accommodate collaborations. Working together for a common goal breaks down real and perceived barriers between educational sectors in the context of co-creating and sustaining service-learning partnerships.

Recommendations for Sustaining Partnerships

If we are committed to cross-sector partnerships for service-learning, it is important to develop support for sustainability at the national, state, and local levels. Advocates can work in multiple ways to propose and advance supportive policies, seek opportunities to connect service-learning partnerships to related priorities, and ensure that lawmakers and administrators understand the positive results of partnerships.

At the national level, advocates can encourage legislative support for K–12 and higher education service-learning partnerships through development of corresponding policies and priorities. For example, when guidelines for competitive federal grants or other funding are being designed, advocates can lobby that priority be given to collaborations between K–12 and higher education. Programs sponsored by the U.S. Department of Education, the Corporation for National and Community Service, and the National Science Foundation are prime advocacy targets. If policy makers seek to hold schools and colleges more and more accountable for student-learning outcomes and competencies, they can shape legislation to foster relationships across education systems by providing resources and rewards for partnerships.

Another useful strategy is to align service-learning partnerships with federal agendas or programs. Establishing linkages with an initiative like America Reads*America Counts can strengthen and add purpose to these tutoring programs, while taking advantage of the support of college students on Federal Work-Study (FWS) who serve as tutors. Colleges benefit in that the Higher Education Reauthorization Act of 1998 requires institutions that employ students using FWS funds to use at least 7 percent of those funds for students in community service positions and must operate a reading tutoring program (*Federal Register,* 1998). Advocates for service-learning partnerships between K–12 schools and higher education could lobby Congress to raise this percentage to increase the number of college student tutors.

In addition, members of national education and service-learning organizations can play a significant role in encouraging their associations to support K–12 and higher education service-learning partnerships. Some organizations are already leading the way. The American Association of Colleges for Teacher Education has developed two national service-learning initiatives that focus on preparing future teachers in service-learning pedagogy along with creating and sustaining effective school-college-community collaborations. The National Service-Learning In Teacher Education Partnership works with six regional centers to provide training and technical assistance to partners and creates issue briefs for education leaders and policy makers. Other national organizations are increasing their interest and focus on service-learning through theme-based journals, conference addresses and workshops, designing and implementing national initiatives, and demonstrating how service-learning is an effective strategy to fulfill their missions. The Education Commission of the States (ECS) has developed a National Center for Learning and Citizenship that focuses the attention of education leaders and policy makers on service-learning partnerships. In conjunction with Campus Compact, ECS conducted an Educational Leadership Colloquium on the Civic Mission of American Education in 2001. The colloquium encouraged service-learning partnerships around developing students' values, knowledge, skills, and commitment for citizenship.

In addition to influencing and using national policy agendas that support service-learning partnerships, advocates should establish standards of quality. To this end, they should develop a readily accessible set of models of successful (and less than successful) collaborations similar to the examples offered earlier in this chapter. A national research agenda should be developed to identify the state of current research on the impacts of service-learning partnerships and to propose research questions that need to be addressed to enhance their effectiveness. Possible research questions include:

- Are there specific content areas or service environments that yield the greatest student learning?
- What methods best enable faculty and teachers to collect and utilize data for continuous improvement?
- What program designs are most effective?
- What does it really take to sustain partnerships over time?

At the state level, advocates can also work to develop and implement policies supportive of service-learning partnerships. As on the federal level, alignment with state initiatives and desired student learning outcomes is effective. Proponents can develop and advance policy recommendations to state agencies and education governance boards that support and reward collaborations. For example, funding can be directed to service-learning partnerships that address established state priorities, such as school safety, dropout prevention, or drug and alcohol abuse. The leaders of K–12 systems and colleges involved in partnerships can host meetings to demonstrate the benefits of service-learning, to share supportive policies and models in other states, and to discuss how to leverage policies and resources to nurture existing or new partnerships.

At the local level, advocates can promote in local media the specific outcomes of service-learning partnerships for students, schools, colleges, and communities. Advocates can also encourage school districts, colleges, and community agencies to create recognition programs that showcase outstanding service-learning partnerships. It is useful to demonstrate congruence of local initiatives and projects with national and state agendas.

School districts can include service-learning partnerships in their professional development plans, ensuring that teachers have both the knowledge and the skills to effectively participate in collaborations and to engage students in service-learning. Both institutions of higher education and K–12 schools can create policies that support partnerships and hold key individuals accountable for their development and success. Teacher education colleges can integrate service-learning into their curricula, ensuring that future teachers understand why and how to employ service-learning pedagogy. Community agencies can deploy staff and develop processes to encourage and support service-learning activities of students of all ages. Civic leaders can develop programs that acknowledge and reward local service-learning partnerships.

Moving Toward the Future: P–16 Partnerships

Although the history of K–12 and higher education partnerships is rich, it is marred by many unbalanced, "in name only" partnerships that focus far more on outcomes for college students than on profound systemic impact. Embracing both the principles and practices of service-learning has the potential to address this critical issue in a variety of ways.

Recently, a sweeping new concept has emerged to represent a truly collaborative approach to a seamless educational system. The concept of P–16 refers to a system of education that ranges from preschool through baccalaureate: "Over the past two decades, legislators and educators have worked hard to update tried-and-true approaches to education in response to new demands—the increasing diversity of the population, technological advances, workforce changes, global competition and the need for active engagement in democratic processes. Bringing the three separate public education levels together into a seamless system is the logical step in the ongoing work of shaping the education system to fit the times" (Education Commission of the States, 2000, p. 19).

The National Conference of State Legislatures, the Education Commission of the States, and other national organizations that focus on education apply this concept. It is based on research that confirms the impact of neurological growth in infancy and early childhood on educational performance and achievement through the college experience. In fact, according to ECS, "Children who participate in high-quality early childhood and preschool programs outperform students who do not attend such programs in the following ways: higher rates of high school graduation and higher rates of enrollment in postsecondary institutions" (2000, p. 2).

In addition, P–16 systems purposefully align efforts at all levels, reinforce a logical progression, remove artificial barriers to coordination, and open the door to creative new ways of doing business. In 2000, the Education Commission of the States released *What Is P–16 Education? A Primer for Legislators,* which serves as a practical guide to moving toward an integrated educational system. It offers rationales, raises and responds to key questions, demonstrates the need for policy leadership, and provides valuable insights into the processes that are involved in creating P–16 systems.

Another recent publication goes a step further to highlight "P–16+" service-learning as a way to pass knowledge and understanding from one generation to another: "P–16+ service-learning brings connections across disciplines, grade and age levels, and across geographic, economic, racial and other 'people divides.' It connects students to other people across time through historical projects. But the most important connection is between a student and an enticing body of knowledge" (Greene, 2000, p. 9). Combining the concepts of P–16, or P–16+, education with service-learning offers tremendous opportunities to maximize connections among all sectors of education, reduce the imbalance in current K–12 and higher education partnerships, develop sustained and reciprocal collaborations, and engage students at all levels in service and learning.

References

Campbell, J. *K-H-Community Partnerships: Working Toward Deeper Collaboration Between Schools, Higher Education, and Communities.* Indianapolis: Indiana Campus Compact, 1998.

Campus Compact. *Annual Service Statistics 2000.* Providence, R.I.: Campus Compact, 2001.

Education Commission of the States. *Promising Practice for K–16 Project Connect: School-University Collaboration for Service-Learning.* Denver: Education Commission of the States, 2000.

Federal Register: Mar. 4, 1998 (Volume 63, Number 42), U.S. Department of Education, Office of Postsecondary Education, Federal Work-Study Programs Notice.

Greene, G. "P–16+ Service Learning: The Great Connector in Continuance: Knowledge and Understanding Passing from Generation to Generation." *Intergenerational Initiative,* Southern Illinois University, Fall–Winter 2000.

Haycock, K. "Higher Education and the Schools: A Call to Action and Strategy for Change." *Metropolitan Universities,* Fall 1994.

Jacoby, B. "Securing the Future of Service-Learning in Higher Education: A Mandate for Action." In B. Jacoby (ed.), *Service-Learning in Higher Education: Concepts and Practices.* San Francisco: Jossey-Bass, 1996.

Lawson, H. A., and Hooper-Briar, K. *Serving Children, Youth and Families Through Interprofessional Collaboration and Service Integration: A Framework for Action.* Oxford, Ohio: The Danforth Foundation and the Institute for Educational Renewal at Miami University, 1994.

Office of Educational Research and Improvement. "Statistics in Brief: Service-Learning and Community Service in K–12 Public Schools." Washington, D.C.: U.S. Department of Education, 1999.

Pickeral, T. "The Roots of Campus-Community Collaborations." In T. Pickeral and K. Peters (eds.), *Campus-Community Collaborations: Examples and Resources for Community Colleges.* Mesa, Ariz.: Campus Compact National Center for Community Colleges, 1996.

Chapter Ten

Empowering Residents and Students to Rebuild Neighborhoods: A Case Study

Janni Sorensen, Kenneth M. Reardon, and Cathy Klump

Since 1990, fifteen to twenty-five undergraduate and graduate students have regularly enrolled in the Neighborhood Planning Workshop at the University of Illinois at Urbana-Champaign (UIUC). This six-credit service-learning course provides students with an introduction to the theory, methods, and practice of citizen-led neighborhood planning. Why have students consistently sought entry into this course, which requires them to travel regularly more than three hours each way to complete their fieldwork in one of America's most distressed urban environments? Student evaluations indicate that this course enriches participants' education in both liberal arts and professional planning by offering them the opportunity to work with inspired civic leaders from East St. Louis to solve important social problems. Students and faculty involved in this ongoing course have worked with leaders from seven of the city's poorest residential neighborhoods to complete plans, designs, and proposals that have generated more than $40 million for new development in this struggling riverfront community. These planning and design activities use participatory action research methods that emphasize the critical contribution reciprocal learning makes to the success of community-university partnerships.

This chapter describes the origins and evolution of this community-based service-learning course from the perspective of three individuals who have taught it. We explain how residents, over time, have assumed an increasingly active role in the Neighborhood Planning Workshop and the impact their participation has had on student learning. It highlights lessons learned from the first iteration of this class in the fall of 1990 through the spring of 1999. The chapter concludes with several questions yet to be answered.

In this case study, we seek to convey the message that ongoing community-university partnerships offer unparalleled opportunities for students, faculty, and community residents to discover innovative solutions to the pressing problems confronting our poorest communities. We also make a strong argument in favor of training urban planners, designers, and policy makers in the use of empowerment planning methods, which seek to enhance the organizational capacity of community-based groups through the integration of participatory action research and direct action organizing.

Background

In 1987, State Representative Wyvetter H. Young (D–East St. Louis) became chairperson of the Higher Education Finance Committee of the Illinois State Legislature. From this influential legislative position, she challenged Stanley O. Ikenberry, who was president of the University of Illinois, to make a clear commitment to urban community service. Young pressed the university to demonstrate its civic engagement commitment by encouraging faculty to focus their research, teaching, and outreach activities on the critical problems confronting the residents of the once-thriving transportation, manufacturing, and retailing center of East St. Louis. This community was struggling to cope with the devastating effects of deindustrialization, suburbanization, disinvestment, and outmigration. Ikenberry responded to this request by reallocating $100,000 in campus funds to support student and faculty research to examine the environmental, economic, and social problems of East St. Louis. Between 1987 and 1990, architecture, landscape architecture, and urban and regional planning students completed more than three dozen reports, studies, and plans exploring the city's major economic and community development issues through a newly created urban outreach program called the Urban Extension and Minority Access Project (UEMAP).

The majority of these projects were carried out using the "professional-expert" model of planning practice in which university-trained planners selected the issues to be addressed, determined the research designs to be followed, analyzed the assembled data, and formulated the policy recommendations. The lack of interest that neighborhood residents and municipal officials showed in these campus-generated plans caused student and faculty interest in the project to wane. In 1990, Kenneth M. Reardon was recruited to join the department of urban and regional planning as a new assistant professor. Shortly after his arrival, the department chair asked him to assume responsibility for directing the university's stalled East St. Louis initiative. With this change in leadership came a new, more participatory, approach to working with the residents of East St. Louis and their elected officials.

Entering the Community

Following several years of serving as the subjects for various faculty-led research efforts, the majority of East St. Louis residents appeared disinterested in the university's UEMAP initiative. From the residents' perspective, university researchers were similar to those they called "ambulance chasers," who used distressing census data to justify public and private research grants that provided significant resources to their institution but few, if any, benefits to the East St. Louis residents whose lives and communities were being studied. Ceola Davis, a long-time community activist, expressed an opinion regarding the university's past outreach efforts shared by many East St. Louis residents: "The last thing East St. Louis needs is another university professor who looks just like you, telling us what any sixth grader in town already knows, and having the gall to charge us $100,000 in state funds for the privilege" (personal communication, 1990).

In 1990, William Kreeb became the executive director of the Lessie Bates Davis Neighborhood House, a one-hundred-year-old Methodist settlement house located in Emerson Park, a once vibrant working-class area that had become one of East St. Louis' poorest neighborhoods. At the time Reardon assumed responsibility for UIUC's East St. Louis project, Kreeb was one of the few local leaders who believed the university could make a meaningful contribution to the economic and community development efforts of local residents. Kreeb strongly encouraged Reardon to contact the leaders of the Emerson Park Development Corporation (EPDC), a recently organized neighborhood improvement organization, to see if they were interested in working with the university. The leaders of this group expressed their willingness, provided the faculty agreed to the following partnership conditions, which over time became known to the students and faculty participating in the project as the "Ceola Accords":

1. EPDC and its members—not the university or its funders—will choose the issues that the university will work on.
2. EPDC and its members will be actively involved with university students and faculty at every step of the planning process.
3. The university will make a minimum commitment of five years to EPDC beyond a one-year probationary period.
4. The university will assist EPDC to secure public and private funding to implement its revitalization plans.
5. The university will assist EPDC in establishing a 501(c)3 organization to enable neighborhood residents to carry on its revitalization efforts following the university's departure from the neighborhood.

With agreement on these basic operating rules, university students and faculty began working with Emerson Park residents to complete a five-year stabilization plan to improve the quality of life in their neighborhood. University faculty viewed the development of a comprehensive plan as an important vehicle to assist neighborhood residents, local institutional leaders, and city officials in formulating a clear vision for the revitalization of this neighborhood. They also believed that this effort would provide students with opportunities to apply their planning skills to the solution of critical urban problems, thus offering them invaluable professional experience unavailable within the protective walls of the university. Initially, the residents resisted the idea of preparing a comprehensive development plan on the grounds that they had been "studied to death." By emphasizing that most funders would resist investing in a severely distressed neighborhood like Emerson Park in the absence of a workable redevelopment plan, Reardon convinced EPDC's leaders to work with his students to create a plan during the fall semester of 1990. The leaders agreed to this proposal only when Reardon assured them that the university would assist their organization in securing the resources needed to implement this plan during the following semester.

The Emerson Park Neighborhood Improvement Plan

Nine graduate students and two undergraduate students enrolled in Reardon's Neighborhood Planning Workshop that fall. As the class began, Reardon informed them that they would be assisting Emerson Park's leaders to create a comprehensive stabilization plan. The students, who were eager to acquire hands-on experience before completing their professional planning degrees, appeared both excited by and fearful of this opportunity. In light of local leaders' criticism of the university's past "professional-expert" approach to planning in East St. Louis, Reardon recommended using participatory action research (PAR) methods to create the Emerson Park plan. This alternative approach to social science research seeks to involve community members as active co-investigators along with university-trained researchers at every step in the planning process. Chapter Eleven further describes this research methodology.

The students began the effort by inviting local residents to attend a preliminary planning meeting held at the Neighborhood House in September 1990. At this meeting, they worked in small groups using large-format base maps and color markers to identify their neighborhood's boundaries, subareas, landmarks, resources, and problem centers. As the residents completed this activity, students began collecting basic population, employment, income, poverty, and housing data from the 1960, 1970, and 1980 U.S. censuses. In mid-October, the students returned to Emerson Park to share the results of their census research with more than thirty residents who attended the second Emerson Park planning meeting.

As the students explained their final housing table, a young man complimented them on their work and then asked them why they had compared Emerson Park's demographic profile to those of the city of St. Louis and St. Clair County but not to the nearby suburban communities surrounding East St. Louis. By failing to do so, this young man argued, they had obscured the uneven pattern of development that was increasingly occurring in the St. Louis metropolitan region. The students looked to Reardon to provide a compelling professorial defense of their census analyses. He, however, agreed with the young man's critique of their report and pledged the students to modify the twenty-nine tables included in their document before the next community meeting.

During the students' return trip to Champaign, they voiced their displeasure with Reardon's decision to amend the census tables in response to the young man's comments. Their criticism gave Reardon the opportunity to remind them that such give-and-take between local residents and university researchers was one of the hallmarks of participatory action research. He argued that a failure to acknowledge the correctness of the young man's critique would have revealed arrogance on their part while expressing a lack of confidence in the ability of poor and working-class people to improve the quality of university-generated research.

In late October, following the completion of their census analyses, the students designed two survey instruments to evaluate the neighborhood's existing land uses, building conditions, site maintenance levels, and public infrastructure. When these instruments were completed, the students traveled to East St. Louis for a long weekend, at which time they joined local residents to form two-person teams to evaluate the condition of the neighborhood's 1,407 building lots and 220 street lengths. In November, the students returned to Emerson Park to discuss their preliminary research findings. Before they presented their newly collected data on physical conditions, the students took a few minutes to share several of the census tables they had modified in response to the comments offered by the young man at their previous meeting. Residents smiled as the students explained how this young man's suggestion had strengthened their analyses. The students' willingness to respond to this criticism of their work made a very positive impression on the residents. In the eyes of many residents, the class's humility in accepting the young man's critique demonstrated their understanding of the reciprocal nature of the learning process.

As the students discussed several areas of concentrated physical decline that they had discovered within the neighborhood, residents provided historical information that explained these patterns. Residents also helped the students acquire a deeper understanding of the role absentee landlords and real estate speculators were playing in destabilizing the neighborhood's residential housing and commercial building stocks. Following the completion of the physical conditions survey in early December, several Emerson Park residents volunteered to assist the workshop students in interviewing their neighbors as well as leaders of local institutions regarding their views of current neighborhood conditions and future development possibilities. During a four-day weekend in December, 20 students and 15 residents interviewed 140 community residents and 29 institutional leaders, using a six-page survey designed by the class with the assistance of EPDC.

The results of these interviews were subsequently used to create a preliminary outline for the Emerson Park Neighborhood Improvement Plan. Working with EPDC's leaders, 150 local residents and elected officials were recruited to attend a public hearing organized by EPDC in mid-December to elicit feedback on the draft of the plan. Residents responded enthusiastically to the plan, which sought to redevelop Emerson Park as a mixed-use, mixed-income, residential neighborhood attractive to a wide range of households. They strongly supported the plan's environmental, beautification, crime prevention, job generation, housing improvement, and municipal service objectives. They also appeared to be very pleased with the majority of the plan's fifty-five revitalization proposals. There were, however, several criticisms of the plan, including its failure to discuss problems related to the organization, operation, and management of the East St. Louis School District and its silence on the lack of civic engagement by churches located within the neighborhood. After considerable discussion, the residents attending the meeting voted overwhelmingly to endorse the plan and to work together, with the university's assistance, to press for its adoption and implementation.

Resident and student excitement regarding the plan rose dramatically in the days following the public hearing when the East St. Louis Public Housing Authority announced its intention to demolish several vacant structures where drugs were being illegally sold and to renovate thirty garden-style apartment units as recommended by the plan. When the U.S. Attorney for the Southern District initiated a major undercover effort to reduce illegal drug sales, resident support for the plan was further reinforced. Community and campus enthusiasm for the plan reached a high point when the American Institute of Certified Planners selected the Emerson Park Neighborhood Improvement Plan as the Best Project Plan in 1991.

Community and campus support for the plan was soon tested, however, when more than a dozen regional funding agencies refused to support the plan's most modest proposals. When students and faculty were unable to identify a single public or private funding agency willing to invest in their award-winning plan, university representatives dreaded attending EPDC's next meeting to share the disappointing news. Surprisingly, EPDC leaders were undaunted by the refusal of regional funders to support their neighborhood's improvement efforts. The leaders responded to the bad news by challenging the organization's members and neighborhood residents to work together to implement the plan with the resources at hand. EPDC subsequently organized a volunteer cleanup of the neighborhood's ten worst illegal dumping sites, which were located along 9th Street, one of the neighborhood's major through streets. For the next several weeks, EPDC leaders recruited local volunteers, collected hand tools, and gathered equipment for the proposed community cleanup, as the workshop students engaged in similar activities on campus.

In April, more than 125 community and campus volunteers removed illegally dumped trash from lots along 9th Street, where discarded tires were stacked knee-high. Everything proceeded smoothly until the residents and their student helpers realized that they had no legal way to dispose of the trash. At this point, Ceola Davis, the community activist, recommended that the volunteers solve this problem by stacking all the trash, which had been neatly packed into dozens of large black trash bags, on both sides of 9th Street. As 9th Street was a county-maintained road often traveled by local and county officials, Davis was optimistic that the St. Clair County Public Works Department would quickly remove the trash. As we placed the last of the trash bags along 9th Street, a St. Louis television crew mysteriously arrived to tape the activity.

Television, radio, and print coverage of the Emerson Park cleanup produced a $15,000 check from a St. Louis community foundation that the residents used to rent equipment and to pay the tipping fees at a local landfill so that the cleanup could continue. Despite the success of the neighborhood's initial planning effort and cleanup campaign, the local officials who managed East St. Louis' Community Development Block Grant Program refused to consider EPDC's numerous requests for assistance. Reflection upon their failure to secure local government support led EPDC's leaders and their university supporters to believe that although participatory action research methods were invaluable in gathering data, generating analysis, and producing innovative planning recommendations, these methods were, in and of themselves, incapable of eliciting the official support needed to guarantee the implementation of resident-generated plans. Over time, EPDC leaders and their university partners came to believe that participatory action research must be supplemented by direct-action organizing in order to generate sufficient pressure to encourage public and private investors to reinvest in low-income urban communities. By 1992, the partners were describing their approach to community planning as an "empowerment-oriented model" designed to enhance the capacity of community-based organizations to provide residents living in distressed neighborhoods a greater voice in local government affairs. Residents and university faculty celebrated this new approach by renaming their effort the East St. Louis Action Research Project (ESLARP).

Residents built upon the success of their initial volunteer cleanup activity with a long series of self-help improvement projects. With the assistance of a growing number of architecture, landscape architecture, and planning students from UIUC, EPDC initiated a housing rehabilitation program. More than twenty Emerson Park homes were improved through this volunteer effort that sometimes involved more than fifty residents and 150 students simultaneously working at more than a dozen sites. These activities, along with the ongoing outreach efforts of EPDC members and UIUC students, helped the organization establish an active membership base of more than seventy-five families.

The visual impact of these improvements on the physical appearance of Emerson Park brought the neighborhood's efforts to the attention of Peter Fitzgerald, former state senator and current U.S. senator from Illinois. Fitzgerald offered to place $5 million in locally collected state tax revenues in an East St. Louis bank where the difference between the interest rate demanded by the state and that offered by the local lender could be used to capitalize a no-interest home improvement fund. The success of this direct deposit program, along with EPDC's growing membership base and expanding list of external supporters, prompted the staff of the East St. Louis Community Development Block Grant Program to invite the organization to apply for federal housing rehabilitation funds. In the spring of 1995, UIUC students and faculty assisted EPDC to prepare an application for funds in the amount of $189,000 from the U.S. Department of Housing and Urban Development, which was approved. These resources enabled the organization to make major renovations to the homes of seven low-income families. The overhead provided by this and other federal grants enabled EPDC to hire its first full-time director, Vickie Forby, a graduate of UIUC's School of Architecture who had participated in the East St. Louis project since 1990. With Forby's assistance, EPDC developed a faith-based family housing program that built four 1,200-square-foot single-family homes in Emerson Park and nearby Olivette Park between 1997 and 1999. To complement these building projects, Forby secured more than $100,000 in funds from the U.S. Department of Agriculture's Urban Resources Partnership Act to implement a variety of open-space improvement projects that UIUC landscape architecture and horticulture students helped to design and install.

In addition to producing designs and proposals that led to the implementation of major portions of the Emerson Park plan, many of the students who participated in UIUC's Neighborhood Planning Workshop went on to join community development corporations (CDCs) serving low-income communities of color following their graduation. They did so, in large measure, because of their transformative experiences working with inspired civic leaders from East St. Louis like Ceola Davis. More recently, UIUC's East St.

Louis Action Research Project has gained a national reputation as a source of highly motivated and well-trained community development professionals. Major CDCs and intermediaries serving such communities as Chicago, Rochester, New York City, and Baltimore are now directed by graduates of ESLARP.

As UIUC's Neighborhood Planning Workshop students continued their community planning and development activities in East St. Louis, their approach became more and more participatory. Between 1992 and 1998, workshop students used this increasingly participatory planning approach to help neighborhood residents, business owners, and civic leaders create revitalization plans for East St. Louis' Lansdowne, Winstanley/Industry Park, Edgemont, and Olivette Park neighborhoods. The "bottom-up, bottom-sideways" planning approach used by workshop students generated significant new public and private investment within the city's older residential neighborhoods. This investment led to important new programs that reduced illegal drug activities, rehabilitated single-family homes, established a community-owned and operated farmers market, and reopened the Katherine Dunham Dynamic Museum. The insights gained from these experiences were applied by residents, students, and faculty participating in the 1999 Neighborhood Planning Workshop, which was organized to create a comprehensive revitalization plan for the Alta Sita neighborhood.

The Alta Sita Neighborhood Revitalization Plan

In the fall of 1998, Helen Hudlin, a well-known educator, respected community leader, and UIUC alumna, approached the university faculty to request help for residents of the Alta Sita neighborhood who wished to create a comprehensive revitalization plan. Hudlin made this request on behalf of Alta Sita Neighbors' Inc. (ANSI), a recently established community development corporation, whose leaders had observed how the work carried out by Neighborhood Planning Workshop students in other parts of the city had often resulted in significant levels of new public and private investment. Given that the basic methodology used in completing the Alta Sita neighborhood improvement plan was similar to that used in formulating the Emerson Park plan, we will not provide a detailed description of this process. Instead, we will highlight the refinements made in the process as a result of the experience residents, students, and faculty gained during Neighborhood Planning Workshops that took place between 1992 and 1998. Among these changes were the organization of a comprehensive community-based outreach and media campaign, the use of geographic information systems to make spatial data more easily available, the involvement of local residents in a broader array of participatory action research activities, the engagement of area youth in the planning process, and the hosting of a day-long Neighborhood Summit to provide residents with an opportunity to review and revise the basic substance of the plan.

As the students from the Neighborhood Planning Workshop began working with the leaders of the Alta Sita neighborhood association, it became clear that the organization had a very modest membership base and an even smaller leadership core. Because an empowerment-oriented approach to community planning requires the active involvement and support of the community to ensure its success, the students identified the need to promote a greater awareness of the neighborhood organization and its grassroots planning process as one of their priorities. This was achieved through the organization of an aggressive community-based outreach and media campaign that took place during the last week of January 1999. The campaign consisted of a series of press releases sent to the local news media, pulpit and bulletin announcements mailed to area religious institutions, delegation visits to all local faith-based organizations, and, most importantly, a door-to-door canvassing effort designed to reach every household in the study area. The latter activity involved teams of students and residents who knocked on every door in the neighborhood to distribute general information regarding ASNI and to invite members of each household to take an active role in the planning process. The teams collected the names, addresses, and phone numbers of interested residents and took notes regarding their interests, concerns, and suggestions. Attendance at ASNI's meetings increased from an average of six to eight people to twenty to thirty people as a result of the media and outreach campaign.

The students enrolled in the Neighborhood Planning Workshop also used their training in geographic information systems

(GIS) to create maps that effectively communicated data describing existing neighborhood conditions and provided residents with a flexible database upon which to base their future neighborhood improvement decisions. Through a Neighborhood Condition Survey designed by the students and ASNI leaders, parcel-level data were collected on current land uses, building occupancy, building conditions, construction materials, evidence of fire damage, and recent improvement efforts. The survey also gathered data on the exterior maintenance status of each building lot; the number of trees along the neighborhood's numerous rights of ways; street, sidewalk, and curb conditions; as well as general sewer system maintenance levels. Unlike previous workshop efforts in which such data were only made available during the latter stages of the planning process, the use of machine-readable data collection forms and GIS mapping software made this information available to residents and students throughout the process. The early availability of such information enabled residents to base their decisions on recent field surveys rather than on the selective memories of local leaders.

One of the hallmarks of participatory action research is the active participation of those most affected by particular planning or policy-making decisions in each step of the process. Although neighborhood residents had always been consulted in the design of the workshop's survey instruments and in the analysis of field data, students had rarely asked them to participate in data collection. During the Alta Sita planning process, the students sought to engage local residents in the data collection process in several important ways. First, they invited residents to document the assets, problems, and untapped resources of their neighborhood using disposable cameras. Every person who attended the first neighborhood planning meeting received a disposable camera and was asked to shoot nine images that captured what they most loved about their neighborhood, nine images that highlighted their greatest concerns regarding the area, and nine images that reflected their community's most significant untapped resources. Residents attending the second community meeting worked in small groups to examine the photographs and to place them in one of the following four categories: current strengths, current problems, future opportunities, and future threats. Once they placed all the photos into these four general categories, they organized the images by themes. For example, in the current strengths category, a set of photos might have depicted the neighborhood's solid building stock or its active church organizations. When the groups completed their strategic analysis of the neighborhood, they shared their work with the others as the facilitator recorded common themes.

When the participants finished this activity, the students sought the residents' assistance in interviewing other residents regarding their perceptions of the community, its future, and its development potential. In April 1999, ten two-person teams, each composed of an ASNI leader and a workshop student, completed nearly one hundred interviews. The involvement of local residents in the process increased the number of individuals willing to be interviewed. In addition, the residents' knowledge of the neighborhood's history improved the students' analysis of the interview data. For example, community volunteers provided detailed information about certain historical events that explained cryptic comments made in the interviews. At the neighborhood planning meeting following the interviews, students asked the leaders who had participated in the camera exercise and the interview effort to identify the key issues confronting the neighborhood. After a spirited discussion, they identified six major problems to be addressed in the Alta Sita Neighborhood Revitalization Plan: local economic development; housing rehabilitation and development; youth, family, and senior citizen development; improvement of infrastructure and municipal services; enhancement of the natural environment; and increased community organization. Prior to determining the exact scope of the plan, ASNI and the workshop students agreed that participation in the decision-making phase of the planning process should be broadened. They identified the young people of the neighborhood as a critical group that had not been given the opportunity to voice its opinions regarding the plan.

As a result, workshop students devised a creative way to involve the children who attended the Alta Sita Elementary School. The Children's Planning Exercise took place in March 1999. Fifty-one children from the Alta Sita Elementary School's after-school program were joined by a dozen UIUC students for an afternoon of neighborhood planning activities. The event was held in the school gymnasium and was attended by administrators, teachers, ASNI leaders and members, as well as several parents. The exercise began with the children enjoying pizza and juice as they informally met the university students. The students thanked the children, their teachers, and the school administrators for inviting them to participate in their after-school program. This was followed by a brief description of the planning activity. The students then divided the children into six groups according to their ages. Two students joined each group of eight to ten, hung a large sheet of white paper on a wall near each group, and asked the children to respond to three sentence stems: "My 3 Favorite Alta Sita Residents are. . .," "My 3 Favorite Alta Sita Places are. . .," and "My 3 Least Favorite Places in Alta Sita are. . . ."

As the children identified the positive and negative aspects of their neighborhood, the students rewarded them with chocolate candies. The children's long lists soon covered the walls of the gymnasium as they enthusiastically participated in this activity. In the next exercise, the children created large drawings of their neighborhood now and as it might look in the future. Younger children used crayons, while older ones used colored markers. The students asked the children to explain their drawings. Their explanations, along with Polaroid photos of the artists, were placed in small caption boxes at the bottoms of their drawings.

An exhibition of the children's artwork was subsequently hung around the perimeter of the gymnasium and displayed until the Neighborhood Summit was held there in April. In this way, the children's perceptions of the neighborhood surrounded the adults participating in the summit. Each child was given a letter inviting parents and family members to attend the meeting. Many parents and grandparents who might not otherwise have participated did so because the children's artwork was featured. In addition, approximately three hundred invitations were sent to neighborhood residents, area business owners, and local civic leaders. Personal phone calls were also made to each of these individuals. The Neighborhood Summit was designed to serve as the culmination of the neighborhood planning process. It was structured as an all day-planning and problem-solving session to address Alta Sita's most critical environmental, infrastructure, employment, housing, youth development, and municipal services problems.

Approximately seventy people attended the summit, including Alta Sita residents, City Hall representatives, merchants, UIUC faculty and students, area social service providers, regional funding agencies, other East St. Louis neighborhood leaders, and members of the press. The day began with a welcome from Helen Hudlin, president of Alta Sita Neighbors, Inc., and from Diane Bonner, director of the City of East St. Louis' Community Development Block Grant Operations Corporation. Darlene Lasley, a lifelong resident of Alta Sita, presented the goals of the summit and reviewed the day's agenda. Two university students then narrated a slide show summarizing the analysis of existing neighborhood conditions completed by residents at the previous neighborhood meeting. The attendees recommended a few changes to the analysis, and the students recorded these modifications. A member of ASNI offered the overall development goal and objectives that the organization had developed based on the analysis of existing conditions. Following a brief but spirited discussion, the participants approved the goal and objectives statement. At this point, the participants were asked to form small discussion groups organized around each of the six development objectives that had just been approved. Working in these teams, the participants were asked to brainstorm as many projects and programs ideas as possible that could be used to meet their group's objective. As the lunch hour approached, each team had generated more than twenty-five possible program ideas.

After lunch, the six teams got back together and prioritized their program ideas into current year, short-term, and long-term project categories. Area planners and policy makers with extensive program development experience in each issue area assisted them in this activity by sharing their assessment of the feasibility of each of the proposed projects. The teams placed their project proposals in order of importance. The final team activity was to select one of the prioritized programs and to develop it fully in term of tasks to be completed, staffing requirements, costs, possible funding sources, lead agency, and participating organizations. A spokesperson for each team presented its program development proposal to the larger group. The summit participants enthusiastically received these ideas. Among the programs proposed by the teams were a new community center, a three-pronged strategy for strengthening Alta Sita Neighbors, Inc., an elderly or disabled housing rehabilitation assistance program, and a comprehensive sewer improvement plan. Throughout the summit, the workshop students recorded changes, comments, suggestions, and positive and negative feedback offered by the residents. They then made every effort to incorporate this information into the final draft of the Alta Sita Neighborhood Revitalization Plan.

At their May meeting, ASNI's leaders and members rated the summit very highly. The majority believed that it had been beneficial to gather a broad group of residents, business owners, and public officials to discuss the neighborhood's future and to inspire better solutions for addressing its needs. The students presented their notes from the summit discussions together with their draft plan. At this point, the residents divided into issues teams to review the project proposals that had emerged from the summit. Working in these small groups, ASNI produced a final list of issue areas to be included: to improve ASNI's organizational capacity, to promote economic development in Alta Sita, to create new neighborhood housing solutions, to improve Alta Sita's environment and infrastructure, and to explore youth and senior services.

With strong group support of the overall structure of the plan and its list of proposed projects, the major task remaining was the further elaboration of the implementation strategy for each of the plan's major program elements. The university hired a research assistant to complete this work under the supervision of ASNI's executive committee during the summer of 1999. The research assistant prepared detailed implementation strategies for each of the six programs contained in the plan. At ASNI's June, July, and August meetings, members reviewed, discussed, and modified the implementation strategies developed by the research assistant. Postcard reminders were sent and telephone calls made to approximately 180 people who had participated in the planning process, encouraging them to attend these meetings. The research assistant incorporated the residents' changes into the final draft until the entire document had been revised to reflect their feedback. Prior to each meeting, drafts of the implementation strategies were shared with Hudlin and the ASNI block captains. The editing of the document continued throughout October, when the full plan was sent to Hudlin for review. At the November ASNI meeting, the

Alta Sita Neighborhood Revitalization Plan was presented to the residents for their final review and approval.

Lessons Learned

In this section we briefly summarize the most important lessons we have learned and would like to pass on to others wishing to do similar work. This section is largely based on an evaluation of our East St. Louis project by residents in 1998 and students' evaluations over the years.

The most powerful lesson learned relates to the corrosive effects of the legacy of uneven relationships between universities and communities on the development of future campus-community partnerships. Many community residents and leaders feel their communities have been used by scholars to justify research grants that have yielded important benefits for their home institutions but few, if any, benefits for the local communities that have been studied. Describing East St. Louis' history of engagement with colleges and universities, Richard Suttles, an Emerson Park leader, stated, "Our community hasn't even been the tail on the dog in these past partnerships, instead we have been the flea hoping to land on the tail of the dog" (personal communication, 1998). Given this history, we highlight the importance of using a highly participatory approach that offers local residents a significant degree of control over the research and planning processes. This type of power sharing appears to be one of the few ways to overcome residents' cynicism and alienation from campus-sponsored outreach and research efforts. We do not believe that our project would have successfully gotten off the ground if we had not used participatory action research methods.

Our experience also suggests that any university-based program that aspires to do participatory work must have a deep appreciation of the long-term commitment needed to overcome the decades of disinvestment and out-migration that has undermined the health and vitality of low-income urban communities. We believe that a campus can cause more harm than good if it engages in a series of short-term projects that repeatedly document existing problems without generating sufficient organizational momentum and commitment to address these problems. The gravity of the problems experienced by residents of severely distressed urban and rural communities requires us to go beyond positivist social science models that are satisfied to describe the world *as it is* to more participatory action research models that aim to *transform* conditions in low-income areas.

Our experience highlights the critical contribution that independent scholars can play in communities where political power is highly concentrated in the form of an entrenched political machine. Many of the research projects that our students completed could have been carried out by professionals working for local government agencies or nonprofit organizations. However, these professionals were strongly discouraged from undertaking this politically sensitive work by elected officials and party leaders who felt the results of such investigations could reflect badly upon them and their political allies. University planning, design, and policy students and faculty who are not controlled by local governmental organizations are in an excellent position to pursue advocacy and planning activities on behalf of the most marginalized groups in urban areas. In the short run, the information they develop and the resident mobilization that often results from their activities can have a dramatic impact on the discretionary spending of public and private institutions. In the longer run, these advocacy and planning experiences can provide students with the inspiration and values to pursue alternative career paths focused on social justice.

We came to recognize that young people can—and should be encouraged to—make valuable contributions to the neighborhood planning process. Introducing children to thoughtful and innovative planning helps them understand that the world and its problems can be improved through collective action. Children will be around to see both the intended and unintended consequences that "our" plans will have upon their quality of life, and should be equipped to critically assess such proposals when they assume positions of leadership. If we can assist children in identifying the elements of their surroundings that bring them joy as well as pain, then we should be able to teach them about smart planning practices that can avoid or address the effects of disinvestment, poverty, and violence on urban areas. Children, in contrast to some adults, spend a great deal of time in the neighborhoods where they live, which gives them a rich foundation of experiential knowledge of their surroundings that makes them particularly valuable participants in local neighborhood planning processes. Young people who learn the importance their actions can have upon conditions in their communities will grow up to be more informed, active, and empowered citizens. In addition, as children will be the nation's future planners, encouraging them to develop an appreciation of how intelligent planning and design can preserve the environment, promote equitable development, foster human diversity, and reduce health and safety threats should become an important objective of neighborhood planning.

We have also learned that participatory planning, regardless of how elegantly it is executed, can often be ineffectual if it is not linked to ongoing community-organizing activities. One of the early lessons student planners learned during their Emerson Park experience was the importance of generating broad-based political support when attempting to shift local government and private sector investment priorities. The students who worked on the award-winning plan learned that significant organizational capacity is needed to pressure public and private institutions to abandon policies that encourage investment within already privileged communities within metropolitan regions in order to move resources to areas facing serious economic and social problems.

Conclusion

We conclude our chapter by raising several important questions that we feel require further attention if we are to develop more democratic relationships between campus-based urban outreach projects and community-based planning and development organizations serving low-income urban and rural communities. We frame these issues in the form of questions because we do not pretend to have the answers.

- How do we reconcile the different schedules of busy community leaders and university students to facilitate closer cooperation throughout the research, planning, implementation, and evaluation phases of the development process?

- How do we sustain the planning process beyond a single semester? If it is a goal for us to support residents until projects are completed, how can universities support these activities? In our project, one or two students often get so involved with the residents of a single neighborhood that they continue to do their work independently beyond their initial semester commitment. However, the demands of the implementation phase of neighborhood planning require considerably more staff effort than one or two students can, without ongoing faculty engagement, provide.
- How do we better recognize and honor the critical contributions local civic leaders make to the development and implementation of successful neighborhood revitalization plans? Although students receive degrees based on the work they complete in these projects, there is no similar reward for the local civic leaders whose involvement is equally important.
- How do we overcome the differences between the lived experience, education, and training of community leaders who have often been denied the opportunity to pursue higher education and advanced training and the privileged status of students from prestigious research universities who have been afforded every educational and social opportunity?

We look forward to working with community leaders, university students, and urban scholars to discover meaningful answers to these and other questions related to neighborhood development and to the struggle to create a more just society.

Chapter Eleven

Partnerships for Collaborative Action Research

Philip Nyden

This chapter presents a collaborative university-community action research model that complements and supplements "traditional" research. In addition to distinguishing the collaborative research model from traditional, discipline-based research, it also draws finer distinctions between collaborative university-community action research and other participatory action research models. As a form of service-learning, collaborative action research can help students understand the connections among knowledge, service, and social change. Students involved in collaborative action research combined with reflection have the opportunity to view service as building community capacity rather than dependency and to learn about the dynamics of authentic partnerships. A case study of the Loyola University Chicago Center for Urban Research and Learning (CURL) will provide the foundation for a discussion of the challenges and opportunities of collaborative research.

The Traditional Research Culture of Higher Education

Most higher education research is aimed at expanding the knowledge base of the researcher's academic discipline. In typical university-based research, the disciplines control the research agenda in several ways. What gets published in top academic journals, what gets presented at national conferences, and what colleagues in one's department think about a faculty member's research topics shape the conventional research agenda. Faculty members, in turn, advise graduate students to select research topics based on this agenda. This is not an abstract system. Rewards are clear. Tenure, promotion, access to research grants, as well as status in the field, typically depend on how colleagues in the university and the broader discipline view both the quality of one's research and how it connects to major themes within the discipline. The status of a department in the university and in national rankings also depends on how much work its faculty members collectively publish in peer-refereed scholarly journals and how many prestigious research grants they receive.

In this traditional research culture, research on the global or national levels is more highly valued than research at the community level. "Pure," "objective," and/or theoretical research with broad implications is prized within the discipline-driven culture over practical, "applied" research with a local, community-based focus. The measure of successful research tends to be the numbers of books or articles published and grants received, rather than its effect on social change or the quality of life. Even when discipline-based research may be relevant to broader communities, it is often not accessible in its academic journal format and professional jargon-peppered language to those outside of academe. Research partners in the traditional paradigm do not include individuals outside the university. In fact, communities are frequently seen by scholars as laboratories where subjects can be found and theories tested. Even when some faculty do write reports of their research for local nonacademic audiences, the lack of community participation in shaping the research means that such products are not always useful to the community.

Participatory Action Research Models as Alternatives to Traditional Research

Participatory action research seeks to break down the barriers between the research enterprise and the process of social change.

The first barrier to be addressed is the distinction between the researcher and the researched. The "them and us" perspective that emerges from the objective scientist studying a subject population can obscure the reality that researchers are part of the broader society they are studying. Alternative models, on the other hand, explicitly recognize the interaction between the researcher and the community being researched. This alternative approach is grounded in the belief that the community not only contains knowledge to be mined through research but also has knowledge that is critical in identifying the research needs and in the design and implementation of the research itself, thus making the outcomes more meaningful and useful.

Second, participatory action research models approach research in the community with both an intellectual inquisitiveness and a sensitivity to community needs. These models use methodologies, protocols, and research designs that involve the community in all aspects of the research enterprise, including conceptualization, data collection, outcome analysis, and dissemination of results. Research is not necessarily community-driven. Academic researchers, in fact, often bring to the community research ideas based on work of other researchers or their own perceptions of community issues. These alternative research models involve a give-and-take in which researchers, service practitioners, community leaders, and community members compare and discuss the issues to be researched, as well as the resources that academic and community partners can bring to the project.

Third, positive social change aimed at furthering the interests of communities that have been denied access to opportunities enjoyed by the majority of our society is a primary desired outcome. Agreement on defining what positive social change means to all parties is a fundamental element of participatory action research, but sometimes it becomes a political and even contentious process. Leaders of community-based organizations, elected leaders, informal neighborhood leaders, and university researchers each may view the nature of desired social change differently.

Fourth, the research process gives voice to community members and builds their capacity to guide and participate in present and future change-oriented research. It also increases capacity by strengthening the community's voice in using research findings to influence governmental and other policies.

Among the many forms and variations of participatory action research, it is possible to distinguish three basic types: the community-only approach, independent (nonuniversity) research institutes, and university-community collaboratives. Because much has been written about the first two types of participatory research, only a brief description and references to further information are provided for these models. A more detailed description of the university-community collaborative model follows.

Going It Alone: Community-Only Models

The community-only approach presumes that partnerships between communities and powerful institutions such as universities are inherently unequal. As such, a strong community voice cannot emerge from this kind of relationship. Similarly, it assumes that if the community is to build and control its own research capacity, the community must direct the effort. Most notable among the intellectual leaders of the community-only model is Paulo Freire, the Brazilian social scientist and author of *Pedagogy of the Oppressed* (1970). Freire argues that it is not just the outcomes of research, but the democratization of the research process itself, that is important in finding solutions to social problems. Sociologist John Gaventa (1993), in his review of participatory action research models, adds that "to the extent that the research still remains in the hands of the researcher, a real transfer of ownership of knowledge may not have occurred" (p. 33).

Community-only models are particularly prevalent in Third World countries where extreme levels of social and economic inequity are also reflected in social and political gaps between universities and low-income (and other oppressed) communities. More information on these models can be found at [www.parnet.org]. Within the United States, centers such as the Highlander Center in Tennessee and the Applied Research Center in California represent similar approaches, although there is some contact with university-based researchers in both cases. More information on these centers can be found at their web sites [www.hrec.org] and [www.arc.org], respectively.

Independent (Nonuniversity-Based) Research Institutes

It is often difficult for community-based organizations, which must deal with a variety of pressing grassroots initiatives and are typically underfunded, to develop lasting research capacity. For example, although a community-based organization might engage in a certain level of housing research, it may find it difficult to keep on top of all the newly released data sets, develop specialized knowledge regarding affordable housing and banking, or sustain direct links to sources of new national policy developments that might be relevant to its community.

As a result, some community-based organizations have developed coalitions to support citywide, regional, and even national institutes to provide these and other research functions. One advantage to this approach is the institute's clear and sole purpose of serving the community. Unlike universities with priorities of teaching and discipline-guided research, these independent institutes can focus squarely on the community.

The Chicago Rehab Network (CRN) is an example of an institute that developed out of a coalition of neighborhood organizations. In 1976, representatives of neighborhood groups and citywide agencies started discussions about how to create housing opportunities for low-income families in Chicago. The representatives had common complaints that previous efforts at coalition building around issues of affordable housing had led to a propensity for the coalitions to become "downtown, staff-directed entities when it came to setting policies and programs for neighborhood groups to follow" (Chicago Rehab Network, 2001).

As a formal citywide organization, CRN has become a research and advocacy intermediary that links neighborhood housing development organizations to regional and statewide affordable housing initiatives. Through cooperation with local organizations, CRN has assisted in the prevention of the displacement of more than forty-one thousand Chicagoans living in fifteen thousand units of private, federally subsidized housing by successfully supporting legislation to prevent prepayment of U.S. Department of Housing and Urban Development (HUD) mortgages. It helped to create the (Illinois) Statewide Housing Action Coalition in addition to work with the (Chicago) Coalition for the Homeless to research the feasibility of, and successfully advocate for the creation of, Chicago's Housing Trust Fund, which sets aside approximately $750,000 annually to subsidize rent for low-income residents.

Local institutes are most likely to emerge in larger cities where they can be sustained by a critical mass of community organizations. Regional and national institutes have served a similar function, but distance from constituent communities is typically greater and makes regular connections with neighborhood-level organizations difficult. However, one can hope that information technology will facilitate regional and national coordination of decentralized community-based activities.

The University-Community Collaborative

A third model of participatory action research is the collaboration of universities with community-based organizations in conceptualizing, shaping, conducting, and using research. Collaborative research is distinct from research *on* the community; rather, it is research *with* the community. It does not treat the community as the "laboratory" for use by the university-based researchers to test discipline-driven hypotheses. Rather, this model is based on the conviction that knowledge generated by research is more complete when it incorporates community-based knowledge and experience.

University-community collaborations exist along a continuum ranging from shallow linkages of little substance that are overpromoted by the university's public relations department to genuine, deep, equal research partnerships. The following section addresses the characteristics, benefits, and challenges of the collaborative research model. Note that the terms *collaborative research* and *collaborative action research* are used interchangeably.

Building Collaborative University-Community Research Partnerships

University-community collaborative research recognizes that there is knowledge in both the university and the community. It challenges and eliminates false boundaries between the knowledge that resides in the academy and the knowledge that exists in the community—boundaries typically constructed to protect the illusion of the superiority of academic expertise. One knowledge set is not superior to the other. In fact, it is impossible to truly understand the world around us without combining both sets of knowledge. Moreover, community knowledge cannot simply be mined by academic "day laborers" who collect data through interviews, focus groups, surveys, and secondary data analysis. It is complex and dynamic and cannot be separated from those who live its realities.

An initial challenge for university-based researchers—as for others in the university who seek to engage with the community—is to decide just with whom one should work. There is no one correct representative of the community. It is well worth the time and effort to involve a range of people who live and work in the community and who know it in different ways. For example, in designing and administering a survey of the nature and sources of tensions between youth and adults in a community, are youth program leaders the best representatives of the parties? Are they sensitive to all the nuances of the issues? Do they understand all the nuances? Do they have the power to enlist the support of both youth and adults to complete the survey?

Collaborative researchers develop partnerships with a range of community members and leaders and involve them in the research process at the very beginning. By integrating community-based knowledge and guidance, collaborative research is more robust, providing a deeper, fuller picture. It is less likely to overlook vital community issues known to residents but not apparent to outsiders. Community partners can provide constant updates to guide ongoing research on matters that university-based researchers might otherwise miss. Adding multiple chairs for the community at the research table undoubtedly increases the complexity of the process, but it also contributes depth and brilliance to the result. Why settle for a black-and-white snapshot of the community when you can get a full-color, video-streaming, wide-screen version?

It is useful to note that the idea of collaboration in research is not new for universities. In fact, faculty often seek one another's perspectives in developing research ideas, conducting research, and analyzing the results. Academic researchers also regularly choose to engage in joint projects with colleagues in their own disciplines or across disciplines. What is new and different to the vast majority of university researchers is the notion of collaborating with individuals outside the academy.

University-community collaborative research requires that the partnership begin at the conceptualization stage. Cooperation at this initial phase creates built-in consumers for the research. It ensures that findings and reports will be of relevance to the community. Not surprisingly, it also increases the likelihood that elected officials and the media will find the outcomes to be of interest. Research conducted with the community and based on needs identified by the community garners more local attention than purely university-based research.

The collaboration must continue through all stages of the research process—designing the methodology, collecting data, analyzing data, writing reports, and disseminating research outcomes. Collaboration in methodology design and data collection can actually improve access to data. Community organizations are quite creative in figuring out ways to acquire data that university researchers may not even know exist. For example, the availability of survey data collected by food pantries ten years ago may be unknown to the university-based researcher. However, the data may provide valuable comparative data that can be used in documenting improvements in meeting community nutritional needs.

Similarly, involving community residents in various stages of the research can enhance the quality of the research. For example, prior to interviewing residents of an affordable senior housing development to better understand their needs, engaging them in the design of the questionnaire and in the interviewing process itself can ensure more focused questions, a better response rate, and greater credibility of the results.

Also, because access to government data can be a political issue, community organizations can sometimes obtain data that have been collected by government agencies more easily than can university researchers. Information is a valuable political commodity and is sometimes protected, hidden from the public eye, by government officials. However, these same officials often recognize the power of community organizations and regard their requests for access to data as more pressing and appropriate than requests by academic researchers.

Once the data are collected, community members may be very useful partners in analyzing it. Joining together the scope of a researcher with expertise in causes of poverty with the experience of a community agency director who works with low-income families every day creates a powerful frame for data analysis. Patterns overlooked by the researcher may be picked up by the practitioner and vice versa. In one case during our own research, the faculty and graduate students on the research team were puzzled by interview results showing a level of interfamily cooperation among residents of a multiracial, multiethnic subsidized-rent high-rise building that was unexplained by the data. It took the presence of a community organizer at the research table with knowledge of community dynamics to point out that the interracial and interethnic harmony in the building was at least partially produced by common fears that increased numbers of middle-class "gentrifiers" would take their building away from them. The conclusion that a significant cause of the racial and ethnic harmony was tenants' fears of an external threat of displacement became a major finding of the study.

Involvement of community leaders in a research project also gives them a better sense of the overall research process. This does not mean that they will then be able to complete research independently from trained researchers next time. However, it does give community leaders a better sense of the steps involved, the resources needed, and the time required to do credible research. Interestingly enough, although community capacity to understand and even complete elements of research projects has increased through our center's collaborative research efforts, it is even more significant that positive community experiences with research partnerships have generated additional opportunities for university-based researchers as community organizations gain greater comfort and find greater value in the research process.

Collaborative research also builds capacity for the university. Successful collaborative research projects increase trust between the university and community. Without trust, the door may be closed to future research opportunities, even for university researchers who were in no way connected to prior attempts at research collaborations. Community leaders who in the past have been involved in mutually beneficial collaborations may come back to the university with new research ideas. In some cases, they may already have funding in hand; in others, they may invite university partners to write joint grant proposals that are more likely to be funded based on the community's initiative and the established partnership.

Community involvement in the writing of reports or review of report drafts helps keep reports free of disciplinary jargon. Reports that are understandable by a broader audience increase the visibility and application of the results.

Faculty and students often find collaborative work in the community more exciting than traditional research projects. Knowing that their work will be used by community members and organizations is a source of motivation for students. University-community research collaborations epitomize the scholarship of engagement that Boyer (1994) encourages. He urges higher education to play an active role in addressing "the challenges that confront our children, our schools, and our cities, just as the land-grant colleges responded to the needs of agriculture and industry a century ago" (p. 48).

Students involved in collaborative research as service-learning can learn firsthand about the complexity of the research process and its relationship to social change. Collaborative action research underscores for both faculty and students that education in a rapidly changing society should not merely consist of learning discrete facts or past approaches to problems. Service-learning as research enables faculty and students to join with community colleagues to develop new information, ideas, and approaches. Students can actively engage in education as a process that teaches them to think, to question, and to innovate. Because university-community research partnerships are, by definition, immersed in social relationships, politics, and tensions of daily life, students gain awareness of the connections among knowledge, power, and social change. A closer look at the Loyola University Center for Urban Research and Learning provides an illustration of how collaborative research can help make these connections. Chapter Ten provides a detailed description of student involvement in service-learning through collaborative research.

Case Study of the Loyola University Chicago Center for Urban Research and Learning

The Center for Urban Research and Learning (CURL) was established in 1996 and grew out of the success of the Policy Research Action Group (PRAG), which had been created by a Chicago-area network of community leaders and activist faculty in 1989. With substantial funding from the John D. and Catherine T. MacArthur Foundation and the U.S. Department of Education, PRAG—now a network of four universities and more than thirty community-based and citywide organizations—has supported more than 175 collaborative action research projects.

PRAG emerged from the bottom up. It was not the brain-child of a university administrator. Rather, it grew out of the need felt by progressive researchers and community-based leaders for a more systematic connection between university and community resources in addressing policy issues ranging from gentrification and displacement of poor families to the negative impact of toxic wastes and emissions on low-income communities. PRAG was created by researchers and community leaders who were already working together on a variety of projects. Initially, however, the academics saw little support from their institutions for applied rather than pure research, and community organizers often felt pressure from their boards of directors not to waste time on research projects that may not have a direct and immediate impact.

Developing from a university-community planning process and pilot projects involving students as graduate and community interns as well as nonstudent community apprentices, PRAG eventually became a catalyst that created greater visibility for university-community collaboration. It gradually obtained more systematic support for collaborative research from universities, communities, and foundations. PRAG's success and ability to complete credible research products captured the attention of administrators at Loyola University, where it is based. Loyola was already serving as the fiscal agent for PRAG and providing some matching salary and space resources. However, the fact that PRAG had received more than $4 million in funding by the mid-1990s was no small factor in gaining early support for CURL. A description of the planning process along with final versions of state-of-the-art papers of community knowledge and needs in nine policy areas is provided in Nyden and Wiewel (1991). The development of PRAG is described in more detail in *Building Community: Social Science in Action* (Nyden, Figert, Shibley, and Burrows, 1997). Current information on PRAG activities and issues of its journal, *PRAGmatics,* are available at its website [www.luc.edu/depts/prag].

CURL was created with an operating grant of $600,000 and an endowment of $900,000 from the Robert R. McCormick Tribune Foundation. The endowment supported faculty, graduate students, and community fellowships. It is notable that the university's existing support for the collaborative research of PRAG as well as other community-engaged research was a significant factor in attracting the initial funding. Starting with three full-time staff and three graduate research assistants, CURL has grown to more than ten full-time staff and twenty-four funded graduate research assistants.

CURL uses a team-based approach in its collaborative research projects. To provide a full range of perspectives, each project team consists of faculty members, graduate and undergraduate students, and agency staff and/or community members. Teaching and learning occur in multiple directions and involve all members of the team. For example, faculty may learn from community leaders, and graduate students may learn from undergraduates who live in a particular community. Undergraduates have found the close guidance by graduate fellows to be particularly helpful in gaining an understanding of the substantive issues in the research as well as the nature of graduate and professional degree studies. Simply watching the process through which faculty learn from community leaders is an important learning experience for students. As one undergraduate commented, "I have never seen faculty ask questions before" (anonymous personal communication, 1997). Considering that a key aspect of service-learning is realizing that knowledge comes from a wide range of sources, the opportunity to view academics and community members in unexpected roles is valuable.

Fellowships, funded either through CURL's endowment or from current research grants, are provided for many of the team members. Faculty fellowships currently support a two-course reduction while faculty members participate in a project. Graduate fellowships currently provide $10,000 stipends and full tuition during the academic year with options for full-time summer work, depending on the project. In an average year, CURL involves graduate and professional students from more than ten departments, including the social sciences, the humanities, business, law, nursing, social work, and education. Undergraduate fellowships are available to a small number of students. About thirty students participating in the undergraduate urban life and policy studies program each year also work on projects as part of their core seminar. Finally, community fellowships of $10,000 per year are awarded to some community-based organization staff or community members who commit one or two days a week to a project. In other cases, grant funding provides direct support to community organizations for staff involvement.

At any one time, CURL has more than twenty projects in process. Although projects are always carried out by collaborative teams, they are developed in several ways. In most cases, community organizations come to CURL with needs and ideas. Opportunities for community initiation of project ideas are facilitated by CURL's participation in a variety of community-based or citywide organization meetings, hosting university-community working groups to develop research projects in particular areas, and scheduling informal breakfasts or lunches with community leaders to discuss community issues and potential assistance that CURL could provide.

CURL's outreach to the community often starts with a discussion of the resources that CURL can bring to the table and CURL's definition of research as a fully collaborative process. These initial discussions are critical because community leaders often have stereotypes of universities as money-hoarding institutions and an impression of research as a process that produces dry, irrelevant reports. Once community interest is secured, CURL organizes appropriate staff, faculty, and student support for the project. In other cases, faculty with existing community relationships come to CURL with a project idea. In addition, when CURL receives government and private foundation requests for proposals that have the potential to support community initiatives, staff initiate conversations with potential partners for the preparation of joint grant applications.

The topics of CURL's projects are as varied as the interests of community groups and the expertise of Loyola's faculty. For example, on one project, we worked with two different organizations to complete a three-year examination of the impact of welfare reform legislation on low-income families in the local area. One was an activist community umbrella organization that often puts direct political pressure on elected officials and business leaders to further the interests of low-income residents. The other partner was a traditional social service agency that provides child care, employment training, counseling, and some medical services to a similar population. Each of the three eight-page reports published in the course of this project attracted media attention, ensuring that low-income family needs were made visible in public coverage of welfare reform outcomes. One of the reports prompted a state legislator to sponsor legislation that restored cuts in benefits to elderly legal immigrants in the state. Although the work of a statewide coalition of advocacy organizations should be credited with the success, the project provided essential data for the effort. Another report was released a few days before President Clinton appeared in Chicago to celebrate the "success" of welfare reform. Media coverage helped to provide a more balanced view of welfare reform's successes and failures.

Another project focused on factors contributing to the creation of stable, racially and ethnically diverse urban communities. Recognizing that most of the work in this area has focused on segregated communities, CURL decided to investigate the factors that helped to produce a small but growing group of stable diverse communities—neighborhoods that have been diverse for more than twenty years. The research was funded by HUD and completed in cooperation with PRAG. Collaborative teams of university researchers and community leaders in nine cities studied fourteen stable diverse neighborhoods. Among the key findings were a number of factors that contributed to stable diversity, including the presence of strong community organization involvement in protecting the image of the community, the existence of a mixture of multiple-family rental buildings and single-family owner-occupied houses, and a desirable location in terms of transportation and recreational amenities. In some of the communities, we found a new kind of multiracial and multiethnic diversity, fueled by new immigrant groups. As a result, we recommended that new cooperative community leadership models needed to be developed to reflect this multifaceted diversity. These reports were ultimately published as a special issue of the HUD policy journal, *Cityscape* (Nyden, Lukehart, Maly, and Peterman, 1998).

The largest single group of CURL projects consists of participatory evaluation projects. Foundation and government funders typically require community organizations to provide evaluations to indicate the impact of projects they support. Many community organizations have felt threatened by outside evaluators who are seen as coming into their communities or organizations to complete "thumbs up" or "thumbs down" kinds of reports. Such reports have been of limited value to community organizations and social service agencies. However, by involving the community organizations in the planning, data collection, analysis, and writing of evaluation reports, CURL's participatory evaluations offer more complete documentation of successful new programs and are useful in organizational development and improvement of services. These evaluations have been completed in such areas as access to affordable housing, effectiveness of private high school education in a low-income community, tenant management, and quality of domestic violence prevention strategies in Asian immigrant communities. More information about CURL and a list of current and past projects can be obtained at its web site [www.luc.edu/dept/curl].

Opportunities and Challenges of Collaborative Research

Through work at CURL and PRAG, as well as through more than a decade of discussions and work with other university-community collaboratives around the country and the world, a number of issues have presented themselves and lessons have been learned that can provide guidance for others seeking to develop collaborative research initiatives. Several opportunities and challenges are presented here.

• *Lock in resources and commitment to collaborative action research while the "engaged campus" wave is still cresting.* The success of service-learning has led many institutions to seek more ways to connect teaching and research with community needs. National higher education organizations have made the engaged campus a central focus, as have foundations and federal government initiatives. As other funding patterns have indicated, support ebbs and flows depending on "hot" issues of the moment. Consequently, it is important to take advantage of current opportunities to institutionalize collaborative research now. It is critical to demonstrate how collaborative research helps universities fulfill their missions as socially responsible institutions.

• *Address the entrenched conservatism of discipline-defined research and the reticence to allow nonacademics into the research "club."* Collaborative researchers know that community participants bring to the table knowledge and experience that can more effectively shape and guide the research process itself and that serious involvement of community partners results in more reliable measures and, thus, in more valid research outcomes. It is important to take the time to explicitly demonstrate how collaborative research does not diminish the value of existing research approaches but rather opens up new, highly responsive, rigorous, and equally valid research processes. Presenting collaborative research findings at disciplinary conferences and publishing results in journals can help to legitimize this research in the eyes of traditional researchers. Do not overlook on-campus opportunities such as faculty meetings and research forums to highlight collaborative research projects.

• *Be ready to manage opposition.* Both the substance and style of collaborative action research challenge the status quo. Although this is part of its appeal and value, expect questions, doubts, discouragement, and downright opposition. Just as community leaders challenge elected officials or confront community institutions to bring about social change, change agents inside the academy need to engage in long-term organizing to win support and neutralize internal opposition to community-engaged work. It is not enough to feel holier than thou, believe in one's good work, or just complain about academic resistance. It is important to build a core of allies inside the university while establishing a record of successful research projects.

• *Tailor collaborative projects to the institution and the community.* There is no one-size-fits-all collaborative research model. Feel free to borrow aspects of existing models, combine them in new ways, and add innovative aspects. Several web sites provide information on collaborative research and research centers. One of the most comprehensive is HUD's Office of University Partnerships site at [www.oup.org/index.html]. Other useful sites include the Loka Institute [www.loka.org] and Comm-Org: The On-line Conference on Community Organizing and Development [comm-org.utoledo.edu]. Creating a unique model that meets institutional and community needs is part of the enjoyment of collaborative work.

• *Start small.* Large networks do not start overnight. Starting with limited collaborative projects, gradually building larger networks or centers, is the route that most established centers have taken. Do not think that you have to get a big grant before you can begin collaborative research work. The beauty of this kind of work is that it can start with one faculty member or one class working in partnership with one community organization. A well-run, successful initial project helps to establish a track record and build a cadre of supporters inside and outside the university. These are important elements in establishing the credibility and initial good-faith investment that most foundations and government agencies look for before funding more substantial projects.

• *Linear thinkers, beware.* Working on collaborative action research projects requires a high tolerance for complexity, ambiguity, chaos, and smashing into brick walls. The collaborative research road is not well-mapped or even completely built. As more perspectives appear around the research table, the process becomes both more interesting and more complex. This is very real and messy research; it is not a simple classroom exercise. During initial discussions with community organizations, it is common for multiple projects to be considered. Part of the discussion will revolve around what projects represent shared academic and community interests and are most appropriate given available community and university resources. In the course of the project, priorities and needs of community organizations are likely to change, delays in obtaining access to community data sources often occur, and other community needs emerge to compete for the attention of community leaders. All this plays out amid the normal complexity of coordinating faculty, undergraduate, and graduate student academic schedules with the real-world calendars of community partners. A flexible and adaptable project management style is required by all involved.

• *Remember, there is a constant need to define and redefine the bound-ary between the roles of researcher and political activist.* Although col-laborative research intentionally challenges the status quo to bring about positive social change, one's value as a researcher is directly related to one's credibility in conducting high-quality, reliable research. In some instances, a clear division between research and advocacy is advisable. For example, if researchers and students join community members at a sit-in at City Hall, some elected officials (possibly some with crucial swing votes) may begin to question the objectivity and value of the research team's results. In many cases, it is more appropriate for researchers to present research findings at a city council hearing or through an op-ed article. Research reports can lend legitimacy to a policy perspective. However, if the research and activism become too intertwined, some of the legit-imizing role of the research can be lost. Direct political action is the role of the community organization. The university re-searchers' credibility and scientific seal of approval are valuable commodities and should be protected.

The Future of Collaborative Action Research

The presence of an increasing number of research centers or net-works promoting links between university researchers and com-munity activists bodes well for the expansion of the collaborative research model and its ultimate institutionalization in university and community settings. University-community collaboratives are engaging in more face-to-face networking activities as a result of meetings organized and sponsored by federal agencies and foun-dations. For example, the U.S. Department of Education sup-ported interactions among more than fifty university-community partnerships through the Urban Community Service program in the 1990s. Although this program is now defunct, HUD continues such support and networking through its Office of University Part-nerships.

At the same time, major national educational associations are focusing on engaged scholarship. With funding from the Johnson Foundation, a group of national organizations including the Amer-ican Association for Higher Education (AAHE) and the American Council on Education held a pair of retreats at the Wingspread

Center to examine strategies for greater community engagement by research universities. The conferences discussed how the organization and culture of what are often called elite higher educational institutions can be changed to explore new avenues for community-university partnerships (O'Meara and Checkoway, 1999). The theme of AAHE's annual Conference on Faculty Roles and Rewards in January 2002 was "Knowledge for What? The Engaged Scholar." It is also very encouraging that academic disciplinary associations are exploring how to foster and facilitate networks of university-community research collaboratives. Formal or informal networks exist within the American Sociological Association, the Society for the Study of Social Problems, the American Psychological Association, and the interdisciplinary Urban Affairs Association.

However, further development of regional, national, and international networks of collaborative university and community researchers could occur by taking advantage of the powerful research and communications technologies that are now available. The domination that national research think tanks and elite universities have enjoyed in setting policy agendas and research protocols could be challenged by stronger grassroots-based coalitions of researchers and activists wielding powerful Internet-based communication tools.

Traditionally, much of the policy research developed in the United States has emerged from such "inside the beltway" think tanks or elite universities. It has been difficult, if not impossible, for local-level research and action projects to move beyond their immediate communities and to compare policies or strategies with similar organizations elsewhere in the country. However, information technology is eminently adaptable in facilitating complex networks of decentralized organizations. Not only can those involved in community-based projects communicate with one another directly, but effective coordination of large numbers of grassroots-based players is now more possible than ever before (Sclove, 1995). The more sophisticated and technologically savvy community organizations of today, plus the increased need to move beyond the local level in order to influence regional, national, and international policy, make it clear that the time is ripe to explore new avenues of policy research.

Using the ease of communication provided by the Internet, CURL is currently engaged in a local-to-local policy project linking university-community youth collaboratives in Chicago and Philadelphia. CURL is also developing project connections with universities and community organizations in Birmingham, U.K., as well as in Sydney and Brisbane, Australia. A January 2001 European Union–sponsored conference in Belgium marked strengthened interest in connecting collaborative research centers in eighteen countries. A new International Science Shop Network (ISSNET) was established at the conference. More information is available at [http://www.bio.uu.nl/living-knowledge/ISSNET.html].

At a time in our history when the decline in civic engagement has become the topic of numerous articles, books, and talk shows, there is a great need to demonstrate that we can make a difference in the world around us. Discussions of multinational corporations, big government, and the new global society can rob us, and particularly our students, of the resolve needed to continue to invest our time to improve our neighborhoods, our cities, our country, and our planet. The success of collaborative research and action initiatives, combined with the promise of new regional, national, and international connections, suggests that such efforts will not only continue to grow but will be a force to reckon with both inside and outside of academia in the years to come.

References

Boyer, E. L. "Creating the New American College." *Chronicle of Higher Education,* Mar. 9, 1994, p. 48

Chicago Rehab Network. "History of the Chicago Rehab Network." [http://tigger.uic.edu/~crn/History.htm]. April 2001.

Freire, P. *Pedagogy of the Oppressed.* New York, N.Y.: Seabury Press, 1970.

Gaventa, J. "The Powerful, the Powerless, and the Experts: Knowledge Struggles in an Information Age." In P. Park, M. Brydon-Miller, B. Hall, and T. Jackson (eds.), *Voices of Change.* Westport, Conn.: Bergin and Garvey, 1993.

Nyden, P., Figert, A., Shibley, M., and Burrows, D. (eds), *Building Community: Social Science in Action.* Thousand Oaks, Calif.: Pine Forge Press, 1997.

Nyden, P., Lukehart, J., Maly, M.T., and Peterman, W. (eds.), *Racially and Ethnically Diverse Urban Neighborhoods.* A special issue of the journal of the U.S. Department of Housing and Urban Development, *Cityscape*. 1998, *4*(2).

Nyden, P., and Wiewel, W. (eds.). *Challenging Uneven Development: An Urban Agenda for the 1990s*. New Brunswick, N.J.: Rutgers University Press, 1991.

O'Meara, K., and Checkoway, B. (eds.). *Strategies for Renewing the Civic Mission of the American Research University: Conference Proceedings*. Racine, Wis.: Johnson Foundation, 1999.

Sclove, R. E. *Democracy and Technology*. New York: Guilford Press, 1995.

Chapter Twelve

Involving Corporate Partners

Stacey Riemer and Joshua McKeown

Corporate partnerships with institutions of higher education have a long and varied history. They have supported important research and other endeavors and also drawn criticism from those who fear undue influence by the private sector on higher education's traditions of independence and academic freedom. As corporations of all sizes, like colleges and universities, are realizing that their well-being depends on the health and viability of their communities, corporate-university partnerships for service-learning are emerging. Both corporations and universities are engaging more and more in work to enhance the vitality of all levels of society. They know that they must assume the mantle of responsible citizenship or pay what Logan, Roy, and Regelbrugge (1997) term "the cost of inaction" (p. 28). Companies have human resources, expertise, technology, and knowledge of markets and market forces to contribute, in addition to financial resources. Universities can offer different expertise and technologies, access to facilities, respect as a community institution and asset, plus student and faculty involvement through service-learning.

Once universities and corporations genuinely commit to engagement with their communities, traditional, one-directional philanthropy and volunteerism seem paternalistic, of less value as an investment, and potentially even detrimental in the long run. In this chapter we discuss the concept of corporate citizenship, the benefits and challenges of corporate–higher education partnerships, characteristics of effective corporate-higher education-community partnerships for service-learning, examples of good practice, and future directions. Although the authors recognize that corporate citizenship, particularly for transnational corporations, is and must be global in scope, the focus of this chapter is on domestic, community-based partnerships.

Understanding Corporate Citizenship

Before any partnership can form between a university and a corporation, it is essential for each potential partner to understand the other's culture and motivations. This section addresses corporate culture and purpose for readers in higher education and the nonprofit sector. Other chapters in this volume describe these aspects of campuses and community organizations.

Although corporations are not monolithic, some basic concepts apply. By and large corporations are competitive, profit-oriented organizations. Profitability is an irrevocable concept (Logan, Roy, and Regelbrugge, 1997) for any company, and competition with other companies in some form is assumed (De Kluyver, 2000). Performing well enough to make money and stay in business is the primary goal of any corporation. However, several forces are redefining how corporations operate in the new millennium: globalization, the technology revolution, and deregulation (De Kluyver, 2000). *Globalization* is the concept that business is not limited by national boundaries. Trade agreements like the North America Free Trade Agreement and those that govern the European Union promote globalization. As the easy flow of products around the world increases, globalization also means that competition can come from almost any part of the world at any time. The *technology revolution* affects business in many ways because access to information and communication channels continues to grow dramatically. Companies that rely exclusively on controlled information and access are in danger. All must use the latest advances in information and other technologies to increase productivity, in turn, to ensure survival. *Deregulation* has forced predictable and stable industries like telephone and electric utilities to undergo huge adjustments from protected, monopolistic business models to a far more challenging and competitive environment. Government intervention in these industries has lessened, as the public seeks more choices and lower costs.

Increasingly, corporations of all sizes must actively anticipate how their markets are changing and will continue to change. Companies that were oblivious to the changes around them, or overconfident in their ability to withstand change, have fallen victim to new competitors (De Kluyver, 2000). Today, forward-looking companies seek deliberate, and sometimes unorthodox, ways to maximize long-term profit and success. Cooperative strategies in the form of joint ventures, alliances, and partnerships have emerged as one important way for companies to obtain the expertise, innovation, and market access needed for future success (De Kluyver, 2000).

Economist Milton Friedman's old belief that corporations have no social obligations beyond stockholders is not held by the most successful companies. It is not acceptable for corporations simply to be good stewards by leaving the community no worse off than how it was found (Tichy, McGill, and St. Clair, 1997). A new ethic of corporate responsibility is emerging in the more global, more technological, and less regulated milieu in which corporations now compete. With less government regulation and more global market opportunities, companies are increasingly aware that maintaining and enhancing the social infrastructure of the communities in which they do business must become part of their practice (Logan, Roy, and Regelbrugge, 1997).

Corporate citizenship is a comprehensive term that seeks to define what Tichy, McGill, and St. Clair (1997) call "a new era" in corporate-community relations. Beyond traditional corporate philanthropy, corporate citizenship enhances the quality of community life by mobilizing human, financial, and knowledge resources of successful companies through active, participative, and organized involvement in their communities (Tichy, McGill, and St. Clair, 1997). Although there is no single formula for effective corporate citizenship, there are a number of specific reasons for a company to embrace this concept. For some companies, it is enhanced reputation and public relations. For some, it is to establish contacts in the community to increase business or to safeguard against negative publicity. For others, it is to benefit their employees directly or indirectly. In this vein, more and more companies encourage their employees to volunteer during work hours in service projects such as neighborhood cleanup efforts in their own, or their coworkers', communities. For still others, it is an opportunity for direct marketing (Logan, Roy, and Regelbrugge, 1997).

Regardless of the motivation, looking at citizenship as a strategic concept for the company's long-term success means recognizing that the business of business is *still* business, but that meaningful partnerships for community enhancement are one of the ways corporations are using to *stay* in business. This combination of altruism and enlightened self-interest is shared by forward-looking institutions of higher education. For example, in a letter to the editor of *The New York Times,* Judith Rodin, president of the University of Pennsylvania, readily acknowledges that universities that engage with their communities do so from more than a desire to do good (2000). She recognizes, as have many other university leaders, that being surrounded by decaying neighborhoods is a competitive disadvantage that turns away prospective students and faculty. Like universities, corporations are concerned, again out of both social responsibility and self-interest, with national and worldwide issues. Among these issues are environmental decline, the increasing gap between wealth and poverty, civil wars, human rights violations, and disease.

This definition of corporate citizenship does not mean to suggest that traditional corporate philanthropy, totaling more than $7 billion annually (Logan, Roy, and Regelbrugge, 1997), is no longer valuable. In fact, the opposite is true. It recognizes that traditional, one-directional corporate philanthropy is increasingly leading to the development of reciprocal relationships. Reciprocity is the belief that all parties are partners endeavoring to enhance their situations in a structure of mutual respect and shared benefit (Jacoby, 1996). Eventually, reciprocal relationships lead to the community and the corporation becoming interrelated. The corporation works closely with the community to build on the community's assets and to address its needs; the community views the company as integral to its well-being and worthy of its support.

Kadushin (as cited in Tichy, McGill, and St. Clair, 1997) states that three beliefs are essential to shape a culture of citizenship in corporations. First, corporations must raise internal awareness that such activities and values not only are socially responsible but also contribute to the economic well-being of the organization and the sense of a positive work environment. Language and practices must support citizenship activities and encourage involvement in them. Even when citizenship partnerships are widely accepted within organizations, disagreement may exist about what issues to focus on or how to proceed. Ultimately, the challenge is to build awareness and understanding that community involvement and good business practice are connected.

The second belief is that one must be prepared for the messiness or uncertainty that accompanies cross-sector partnerships. There are different cultures not only among sectors but among departments within organizations. For example, in a corporation, the accounting, human resources, and risk management departments are likely to see issues in very different ways. Sustaining a relationship that does not appear to have immediate benefits might prove frustrating to some (Sagawa and Segal, 2000). Moreover, some partnership endeavors may have unintended consequences where social issues compete against one another, for instance, economic development versus environmental protection. This can result in ethical dilemmas for corporations (Tichy, McGill, and St. Clair, 1997). Tichy, McGill, and St. Clair give the following example: "Providing antibiotics for disease control will only be effective if the drugs are taken correctly. Failure by patients to complete their course of treatment may lead to the emergence of new strains of diseases that are more resistant to treatment. Thus it may be considered insufficient to provide the medication without providing sufficient support services to ensure that antibiotics are used appropriately. Such expanded responsibility is very costly and is also likely to take a company beyond its area of expertise" (p. 366).

A third major partnership belief is that one must overcome convictions held by skeptics within the corporation that citizenship activities are beyond its business focus or niche (Tichy, McGill, and St. Clair, 1997). Skeptics can point to the need to be focused on immediate sales, profits, and problems, not on long-term benefits of corporate citizenship, which are often harder to see and to account for. One famous CEO who specializes in turning around unprofitable companies reportedly eliminated *all* philanthropy and community service upon taking the helm, both to cut costs and to send the message to employees about what their singular focus should be.

Questions About University Partnerships with Corporations

A lively debate currently rages regarding the extent to which—and even whether—universities should become involved with corporations. Should higher education institutions with their proud history of nonprofit status, shared governance, and academic freedom partner with corporations that are profit-driven, hierarchical, and competitive? This question can be framed as part of the debate about the appropriate role of corporations in influencing university priorities, policies, and daily operations. Without doubt, corporations are already involved on campus through internship and placement opportunities for students, guest lectures and executives-in-residence programs, presence on governing boards and advisory councils, and especially financial support for research. Although many corporations make large and consistent donations to colleges and universities, their contributions may be viewed either as positive by the rankings-conscious public or as damaging by those who fear undue influence. What seems clear is that the traditional lines between higher education and the for-profit sector are blurring.

Among those who fear the advent of "the corporate university," corporate control of research and a corporate-traininglike approach to the undergraduate curriculum are key concerns. As a high-profile example of the growing influence of corporations on university research, in 1998 the University of California–Berkeley signed a $25 million agreement with Novartis, a Swiss pharmaceutical and bioengineering company. Although corporate contributions to research are common and total more than $14 billion annually, the Berkeley-Novartis deal is different in that the corporation's interest has been institutionalized. Novartis has the right to review faculty research and doctoral dissertations prior to publication or presentation. The company enjoys unprecedented corporate representation on the research committee that determines how its contribution is spent (Blumenstyk, 2001).

Some faculty and students at Berkeley have expressed deep concerns that Novartis-funded research could not possibly be free of bias, especially if researchers discover something potentially harmful to the company. Critics also believe that this level of partnership is a threat to campus departments that do not have as much profit potential. They fear that if the university seeks funding for research and programs with the greatest potential for corporate benefit, those that do not will be neglected or eliminated, as has happened at other universities. Most importantly, critics question whether the very independence and mission of the university are under siege because of deals like this one. They believe that teaching, learning, and serving the public good may take a backseat to technology transfer, patents, spin-off companies, and more control of research by corporations (Press and Washburn, 2000).

Concerns about corporate control of the undergraduate curriculum have also intensified in recent years as more universities strive to create curricula that make their graduates more marketable to private-sector employers. Although a program designed to increase the technological skills and practical experience of English majors at the University of Texas in Arlington has met with success ("A Glance at the Spring Issue . . .", 2001), a special program intended to link technology with cultural studies at Georgia Tech in Atlanta has been criticized by many of the humanities faculty members involved for being too focused on practical skill training and not theoretical enough. As a result, many faculty members have quit the program (McLemee and Smallwood, 2001).

In addition, technology-driven distance-learning programs operated both by traditional higher education institutions and by recently created entities like Western Governors University attempt to compete with for-profit corporations like the University of Phoenix. The American Federation of Teachers, a teacher's union affiliated with United University Professions, has warned colleges not to adopt a corporate approach to online programs that merely bundle together a standardized package of "cookie cutter" programs (Carnevale, 2001). In Canada, the Nova Scotia Teachers Union has challenged the province's department of education because of an excessive corporate role in developing and offering online programs ("Faculty Union in Nova Scotia," 2001).

This growth of corporate influence over what is taught and how it is learned has contributed to calls for the faculty to "recapture the curriculum" (Rhodes, 2001). Proponents believe that the undergraduate curriculum should be less focused on training skilled technicians in accordance with the interests of corporate leaders who often control boards of trustees and make large financial donations. They seek a return to the focus on broad-based learning that enhances students' ability to read, write, and engage in critical thinking.

Related questions revolve around whether contributions from certain types of corporations should be accepted. Although most universities do not accept sponsorship by companies that produce tobacco products, alcoholic beverages, or firearms, the issue becomes more controversial when the potential sponsors are those whose policies and practices are deemed by some to be exploitative of local workers or environments. A current example is protests by students against their institutions' contracting with overseas sweatshops to produce official-logo apparel. Another set of issues involves accusations that colleges and universities, including some of considerable wealth and reputation, have adopted a "corporate mentality" by failing to pay fair wages to custodial and food service staff as well as to teaching assistants. These concerns have their roots in the post–World War II years when booming enrollments caused many higher education administrators to adopt corporate models of institutional organization and management (Lucas, 1994). More recently, business practices such as total quality management, business process reengineering, and benchmarking became popular in the 1980s and are still in practice today. Critics posit that such corporate techniques are inappropriate in the academy and conflict with the core purposes of higher education.

Unfortunately, these issues create a climate of wariness for the development of university-corporate partnerships for service-learning from the university perspective. However, our review of successful and authentic partnerships that benefit higher education, corporations, and communities indicates that this climate need not be an impediment. It is improper to assume that corporate involvement somehow taints service-learning. At the same time, one should not simply brush aside the caution that service-learning and other endeavors could be harmed by excessive corporate control. Barber (1992) articulates a helpful distinction between the "university in service to the public and private sectors" and the "university in servitude to the public and private sectors" (p. 197). The service-learning partnerships we propose in this chapter go a step further, beyond simply service to the creation of reciprocal opportunities for both service and learning.

The "Learning Organization" at the Heart of Collaborative Partnerships for Service-Learning

The creation of partnerships for service-learning adds to this complex set of issues yet another dimension: the community. Without doubt, the cultures of higher education, corporate institutions, and community organizations are different. To ignore or minimize the differences would equal refusing to respect what is unique about what each organization brings to the partnership. In fact, this same conversation is present within the higher education literature regarding faculty and student affairs partnerships (Engstrom and Tinto, 2000) and throughout the service-learning literature regarding campus-community partnerships. Interestingly enough, the higher education literature, the service-learning literature, and the corporate literature suggest that more evolved or collaborative partnerships come together around the theme of shared learning. In fact, the concept of the "learning organization" comes from the corporate perspective (Senge, 1990). In learning organizations, according to Senge, systems are in place that support members in lifelong learning, challenge assumptions, build common vision, and facilitate collaborative learning among participants in a way that respects the voices of all involved. The cumulative effect on the organization is increased creativity and innovation, an enhanced environment of healthy entrepreneurialism, and a greater likelihood of being able to redefine itself for long-term success. These characteristics are present *within* organizations and shared *among* them in corporate-higher education-community partnerships.

The *Benchmarks for Campus/Community Partnerships* (Torres, 2000) that are featured in Chapter One may be readily broadened to include partnerships that involve corporate entities. Applying these benchmarks to corporate-university-community partnerships enables each partner to move toward becoming a learning organization. As with other service-learning partnerships, corporate-university-community partnerships must be based on a shared vision and clearly articulated values and beneficial to all partners (Torres, 2000). In corporate citizenship terms, all parties must view the partnership process as coming to understand what can be "usefully shared" (Tennyson and Zyszkowski, 1999, p. 85).

Similarly, corporate-university-community partnerships must be based on trust and mutual respect. The partners must draw on their own assets and their unique access to additional resources that can be leveraged to address mutual concerns. They need a clearly defined organizational structure and dynamic leadership (Torres, 2000). To sustain partnerships over time, they must become integrated into the missions and support systems of the partnering institutions; fueled by strong processes for communication, decision making, and response to change and growth; and evaluated regularly with a focus on both process and outcomes (Torres, 2000).

Examples of Developing Corporate-Higher Education-Community Partnerships

Although a wide range of partnerships involving corporations, universities, and community entities currently exists, this is still very much an area of growth and development. The following examples of such partnerships describe their genesis, opportunities, successes, challenges, and future possibilities. They may not at present exhibit all the characteristics of ideal reciprocal relationships among learning organizations; however, they are clear in their intent to keep moving in this direction.

JP Morgan Chase and the Community Development Competition

JP Morgan Chase, a leading financial institution, seeks to strengthen the communities in which it does business and works in many ways to set standards of corporate citizenship. Recently, JP Morgan Chase collaborated with the Center for Corporate Citizenship at Boston College's School of Business to develop a Standards of Excellence Curriculum. The curriculum delineates criteria for outstanding corporate citizens. Not only did the company help design the curriculum, it also required its community development officers to become certified by the program. They were the only financial institution to require the training for all its officers.

Chase espouses an ethic of citizenship and enacts it through daily business practice on multiple levels. First, on a lending level, they provide affordable loans for individuals with low to moderate incomes. They offer financial consulting and advice to nonprofit organizations and community groups. Second, as an employer, they foster community involvement of their employees through volunteer service and matching gift programs. For example, in October 2001, the firm hosted Global Days of Service, during which more than 18,000 employees participated in a wide variety of service activities with the community. Finally, the Community Development Group at JP Morgan Chase takes part in grant making and special projects in its tri-state region in the specific areas of community development, human services, pre-K through twelfth-grade education, and artistic development (JP Morgan Chase, 2001).

When developing its special projects, Chase acknowledges the "need for joint problem-solving and responsibility, coordination, collaboration, and a willingness to establish new bonds among partners" (Chase Community Development Competition brochure, n.d.). With this need in mind, the corporation created the Chase Community Development Competition based on the premise that its "legacy is an empowered community with increased capacity to foster sustainable change" (Chase Community Development Competition brochure, n.d.). Since 1994, this annual competition has brought together college and university students, community organizations, and JP Morgan Chase to support the economic revitalization of urban areas through real-world design projects. Students and community organizations are invited to apply as teams to the competition. The teams work along with professionals from JP Morgan Chase to develop complete financial real estate proposals. The ultimate goal is for each team to prepare a proposal that it could submit for funding and for students to gain project-design experience. As the competition brochure states, "For students of architecture, real estate and community development, opportunities to explore issues of community design are not as numerous as one would hope. Neighborhood groups that might benefit from the technical assistance of university programs are not always aware of the options open to them to frame, program and design a proposal tailored to their vision of what should happen in their community" (Chase Community Development Competition brochure, n.d.).

The competition has three stages, culminating in a presentation to a board of judges at the JP Morgan Chase corporate office in New York City. Although all teams walk away with a fully developed proposal, the top three teams receive financial awards ($25,000, $10,000, and $5,000, respectively) to help implement their designs. The example of Syracuse University and the Wilson Park Community Center chronicles one service-learning partnership developed for the 2001 Chase Competition.

The Wilson Park Community Center, built in 1938, serves the residents of the Pioneer Homes housing project. The Syracuse Housing Authority (SHA) currently holds the title to the Wilson Park Community Center, which is financed by the U.S. Department of Housing and Urban Development. The center offers educational and recreational programs in conjunction with various groups, such as Concerned Urban Parents (CUP) and Syracuse University students. CUP is a group of Pioneer Homes community members who work on projects to promote quality education programs for neighborhood youth. Over time, the demand for programs has grown, but space restrictions and a lack of resources have left these needs unmet. In addition, the Pioneer Homes Community has been physically marginalized over the years by city expansion around its perimeter, including a major interstate highway and a steam plant. The need for an expanded community center and enhanced educational programs is also demonstrated by various demographic statistics. The "near Westside" is the twelfth poorest predominantly white neighborhood in the United States based on 1990 census figures, and the 2000 census does not promise improvements (Wilson Park Community Center Team, 2001). Moreover, 85 percent of the schools in the city district scored below the statewide sixth-grade reading-level standard ("Poverty and Achievement Statistics," 1998).

Stemming from an already established relationship with the Wilson Park Community Center, the Community Design Center (CDC), located in the School of Architecture at Syracuse University, partnered with CUP and SHA to develop designs and strategies for the Wilson Park Community Center expansion. The Community Design Center provides service-learning experiences for students studying design and community development in conjunction with community members and nonprofit organizations: "In an effort to build upon the traditional, academic atmosphere of the design studio where students work on individual projects, the CDC course—or workshop as it is known—complements the design experience. The CDC workshop fosters an environment where undergraduates and graduates from multiple departments work together in teams addressing issues related to the physical environment. The goal of the collaboration is to expose the students to the multi-disciplinary nature of the real world" (Gamble, 2001, p. 3). The 2000–2001 team included students from the university's schools of law, management, architecture, and public affairs and administration. David Gamble, assistant professor in the school of architecture, was the primary adviser for the project. Other advisers included faculty from each of the represented schools as well as the director of the Center for Public and Community Service.

During the fall of 2000, the Wilson Park Community Center team held a variety of planning meetings involving community members, where the needs for the center were articulated. The CDC team then developed designs that not only maximized the use of the space but also took into account other factors such as costs and desired benefits. The team worked on the project throughout the academic year and reached the final round of the JP Morgan Chase Community Development Competition. In May 2001, the CDC team plus representatives from CUP and SHA traveled to New York to present their designs and strategies to a panel of experts. As a result of their collaborative spirit, thorough designs, and strong research, the team won first place and $25,000 toward the implementation of their plan (JP Morgan Chase, 2001).

Through seven years of developing, facilitating, and funding the competition, JP Morgan Chase has learned much about successful collaborations for community development. Jean Smith, vice president in the Chase Community Development Group and competition organizer, states that it is essential for teams to have key leadership across constituent groups, including faculty advisers who can spearhead the effort on campus. She also iterates the need for Chase, at the early stages of the program, to ascertain that projects meet "real" needs and that relationships are sound so that projects do not backfire (personal communication, December 2001).

The Massena Learning Consortium

The people of Massena, New York, like those in many small, rural communities, face the simultaneous challenges of educating children for diverse social and economic realities while seeking ways to keep the regional economy strong enough to maintain adequate employment. This is not always easy to accomplish. Young people often leave the area for better jobs out of state, and employers work continually to improve their prospects for short- and long-term business success in a relatively remote rural environment. A unique service-learning partnership between local industries, colleges, and the school district was purposefully developed to address these concerns.

The Massena Learning Consortium is an effort to create more interactive, effective educational experiences for high school students, while providing service-learning opportunities for college students and business benefits for the corporate partners. The partners include the Massena Central School District, five area businesses ranging from the multinational aluminum giant Alcoa to the local natural gas distributor, St. Lawrence Gas, and two local colleges (Clarkson University, a private research university, and Canton College, a public two-year college). Two additional partners are the St. Lawrence Seaway Development Corporation, a federal entity, and the New York State Power Authority, a state agency (Deforge, 1998).

This successful partnership began with a conversation in 1995 among Massena high school teachers from the English, math, and business/technology departments about whether they were providing a meaningful education for all students. They quickly agreed that they were not and that those students not going to college were particularly at risk of dropping out. One of the teachers recalled visiting the local General Motors plant, an eventual corporate partner, where he learned that the math he had been teaching for years was virtually irrelevant to the work that his non-college-bound students were likely to aspire to do at GM. What could the teachers do to make the high school curriculum more relevant to students not on the traditional college-bound track? They began to build a curriculum that would center on three key academic areas—English and communications, business and technology, and mathematics—with an approach specifically geared to students who preferred hands-on or contextual learning rather than merely mastering concepts. To implement the new plan that included teaching all three subjects together in blocks of two and one-half hours rather than the standard forty-two-minute periods, the teachers quickly realized that they needed assistance and support. Fortunately, at the same time, Congress had just funded the federal School-to-Work Act, which sought to link schools with business and industry to develop high academic standards plus workplace skills and competencies. In addition, the federal Perkins Vocational and Technical Act made money available for developing technical high school curricula that focused on the same content areas and that connected high school curricula to postsecondary education and the workplace.

Clarkson University agreed to oversee the new partnership, drafted the strategic plan, developed means for acquisition of resources, and committed its students to guide the high school students as they tackled the new curriculum. For Clarkson, the partnership offered its students a unique service-learning opportunity that would also benefit the institution through enhanced corporate and community relationships (Zuhlsdorf, 2001). The school district and the university sought initial corporate partners from companies where they had contacts or ones they expected to be supportive. The language that the partners adopted to define their partnership embodies the concepts of community-defined need and reciprocity. Although the school district was viewed as the self-proclaimed customer, all parties must benefit. Other principles included the requirement that all partners participate in the development of the goals; that frequent, conscientious communication is essential; and that concern for the external and internal welfare of all must be maintained. By fall 1996, the first group of eighteen high school juniors had signed up for the new program (Deforge, 1998).

In 1997, seventeen Massena high school students and three teachers took part in visits to local employers and engaged in challenging yearlong, real-world case studies of business problems of participating corporate partners. The school provided time during the school day for these activities, as well as for transportation, facilities, and teachers' time and expertise. The corporations organized the site visits, provided staff time and expertise to create the case studies, offered job-shadowing opportunities, and contributed direct financial support. Graduate business students from Clarkson University and undergraduates from Canton College managed the case-study projects, helped the high school students navigate the complexities of the work sites, and provided training in technical skills, communication, teamwork, public speaking, conflict resolution, management, time management, and goal setting (Deforge, 1998).

The program has become institutionalized because all partners have needs that it helps to meet: the school desires enhanced student achievement, the business partners seek qualified workers and to be involved in their communities, and the colleges want to give their students opportunities to develop better management, communication, and interpersonal skills. All partners have seen positive results.

The school district benefits from being able to offer this alternative educational opportunity. The teachers also receive professional development, and the school has forged links with local industry. The companies, both large and small, gain outside insights into their business problems, bolster the educational system's ability to prepare their future work force, and acquire valuable understanding of the next generation of employees. The colleges acquire increased learning opportunities for their students, while building important community and industry links for faculty research and job placement. As a result, the Massena Learning Consortium received the New York State Tech Prep Partnership Award in 1998. Of the eighteen original students who were considered to be noncollege-bound in the fall of 1996, all but one eventually graduated from college.

Among the challenges the partners have faced, the most onerous have involved acceptance by, and institutionalization within, some of the partnering organizations. This has forced several corporate partners to terminate their involvement. As far as the student teams are concerned, some anger and confusion have resulted when their work was not accepted by their teachers or corporate sponsors.

Despite these challenges, this partnership is entering its seventh successful year and has become a fixture in the community. In part, its success is a result of the willingness of the business partners to provide funding in addition to the project opportunities for the students each year. The faculty at the colleges have granted approval for the service-learning program. Further, the Office of

Educational Partnerships of the local Board of Cooperative Educational Services (BOCES) has played a vital role in institutionalizing the partnership by establishing appropriate educational and vocational goals; convening community meetings of partners, students, and parents; and using its public relations means to generate enthusiasm for the partnership. The Massena Learning Consortium has expanded to include one high school class each of junior and senior students, or approximately thirty-six students each year.

Although there is no additional major expansion planned, it is interesting to note that approximately one hundred other school districts have traveled to Massena to see this unique partnership in action or have attended conferences that highlighted the Consortium's work. The BOCES Office of Educational Partnerships has developed a statewide network of contacts that make it easy for other districts to visit and replicate the program in their communities. At least six have already done so.

New Century Councils

In 1991, East Tennessee State University (ETSU) formalized relationships with several rural Appalachian counties to create and sustain new relationships while promoting community-based student learning and the sharing of faculty, student, and community resources to address community-identified issues. The initiative, funded by the W. K. Kellogg Foundation as part of its Community Partnerships Program, formed New Century Councils in two rural counties and later expanded to four within eighty miles of the university. The councils provide a means for identifying, prioritizing, communicating, and working on community issues.

The New Century Councils were intentionally established to involve a diverse group of local stakeholders. This became a challenge, as the councils initially attracted mostly political leaders, educators, and community organization representatives. Ultimately, small-business operators emerged as the leaders. Currently, an assortment of country store owners, car dealers, newspaper editors, artists, craftspersons, bankers, and the more traditional corporate officers of larger firms located in the four counties serve on the councils. Participants view the councils as a vehicle to bolster community engagement by "opening the door from both sides." Involvement has led to communication, communication to understanding, understanding to cooperation, and cooperation to active collaboration in designing and conducting community-based learning and projects that meet community needs. The celebration of the one-hundredth meeting of two separate councils in April 2001, chaired by two small-business operators, a manufactured-home dealer and a local-branch banker, provide evidence of a sustained commitment to the model (B. Behringer, personal communication, December 2001).

Two examples illustrate how the councils have assisted businesses, enhanced university programs, and developed the greater community. The projects described below are the result of a request for proposal process designed and promoted by the New Century Councils and ETSU. Funds from the Kellogg Foundation are allocated to selected proposals generated by community-university teams. The councils hold countywide meetings to foster team development by introducing the communities to university academic leaders, faculty, and students. The proposal process requires a description of each partner's contributions to the project and their expected benefits. This allows community partners to elucidate the issue to be addressed and faculty to be explicit about desired student learning outcomes.

The first example concerns preserving local heritage and promoting tourism. The central Appalachian mountain region is noted for its natural beauty, and tourism plays a major role in the East Tennessee economy. However, small towns share the frustrations of attracting travelers off the interstate. The ETSU theater and English departments transformed their respective curricula and collaborated with the towns' arts councils to develop and present plays based on local history. Students in composition classes collected the oral histories of local citizens, conducted additional historical research, and presented their stories in class. The theater department then worked with rural arts councils and county museums to create new plays based on the oral histories. The plays, which have been produced at preexisting county festivals, have been hugely popular. Three small museums have been acclaimed for their community support and tourism development. Students noted the intensity and satisfaction of performing a community's own stories to the hometown audience (East Tennessee State University Office of Rural and Community Health and Community Partnerships, 2001).

Because of the natural assets of the East Tennessee mountains, a large number of artists and craftspersons reside and work in the area. They generally sell their goods through county festivals and regional arts fairs, which is not conducive to regularity of cash flow. Artists and craftspersons asked faculty members in ETSU's marketing and technology departments to build into their courses an assignment to design a web-based mechanism that would advertise their products year-round. To complete the assignment, students interviewed these clients, helped to digitally photograph their works, designed a web site, and organized the ordering and distribution processes. Engaging in reflection as part of the service-learning experience helped the students better understand the issues small-business operators face as well as the joys and limitations of working in rural communities (B. Behringer, personal communication, December 2001).

The success of these community partnership projects is based on the strongly held operating philosophy that all partners both teach and learn. It was an initial challenge for the business owners and operators to feel confident that they, as well as the students, possessed much knowledge and expertise to share. Frequently in initial negotiations, the small-town residents doubted their ability to teach anything to college students while citing the many "business lessons" that recent college graduates they have encountered never learned. For the students, the learning in and about the rural community is an important outcome. Observing businesses in small towns firsthand allows students to grasp the pivotal role that local owners and operators play in community life. Students also come to realize that they can learn something about their academic discipline from anyone. Faculty recognize the value of partnering with community members in the teaching process and report learning much from their community colleagues. They also note the increased complexity of their students' thinking as a result of their work in this broader experiential context (B. Behringer, personal communication, December 2001).

The university and local businesspeople believe that the New Century Councils will be sustained over time. The specific partnerships represented by the councils have opened up further avenues for collaboration (Cohen, 1999). Businesses interested in a specific project have become involved in addressing broader community issues, thus engaging in additional forms of corporate citizenship. Similarly, the councils' relationships with the university have led communities to seek its expertise and assistance in other ways. Also, business leaders now view the service-learning students from various disciplines with whom they work as potential future employees (White and Taylor, 2001).

Future Directions

Without doubt, cross-sector partnerships for service-learning that feature deep engagement by corporations of any size are only just beginning to emerge. This section suggests issues that must be addressed if such partnerships are to become more plentiful, more mutually beneficial, and more sustainable.

Sagawa and Segal (2000) define "long-term, high-yielding alliances between business and social sector organizations" with the moniker "new value partnerships" (p. 213). Their examination of numerous cross-sector partnerships and review of the literature from both the corporate world and social sectors led them to characterize new value partnerships by elements that form the acronym COMMON (communication, opportunity, mutuality, multiple levels, open-endedness, and new value) (Sagawa and Segal, 2000). Although Sagawa and Segal do not directly address the role of higher education institutions in their partnership equation, the COMMON elements apply well to a discussion of the future of corporate-university-community partnerships.

Effective *communication* is a cornerstone in new value partnerships because it is inherent in all other COMMON elements. For any partnership to be successful and sustainable over time, information and ideas must be shared honestly and frequently throughout the relationship. This exchange should begin at the early stages of the partnership and involve all stakeholders. Such interaction should occur both between partnering organizations and within them. Fundamental to the success of the New Century Councils are the networking meetings attended by university students and faculty, community members, and small-business owners.

As partnerships evolve, participants must recognize the dynamic nature of such relationships and be prepared to welcome *opportunities* as they present themselves. Logan, Roy, and Regelbrugge (1997) suggested that partners think strategically about new and different ways constituent groups can work together for common and individual interests. Conceptualizing partners' roles as multipurpose, rather than monolithic, fosters sustainability. For example, viewing a corporation's role as only providing financial resources could potentially limit the involvement of its employees in partnership projects. For new value partnerships, the initial need is the issue that brings partners together, but the relationship eventually becomes synergistic, developing into a web of opportunities.

Closely related to opportunity is the extent to which partnerships are marked by *mutuality*. Participants must maximize opportunities for shared learning. Students, corporate employees, and clients and staff of community agencies can learn from each other through both intentional and serendipitous cross-sector communication. From this perspective, as students gain skills for jobs, corporations and community organizations gain experienced present and future employees. In the spirit of mutuality, each stakeholder should respect the unique and potential contributions of the other and minimize potential power differentials by viewing each other as learners. The Massena Learning Consortium demonstrated the importance of the value of mutuality by incorporating this concept into the language the group uses to describe itself. Moreover, shared learning between small-business owners and students has become fundamental to New Century Councils.

Engaging participants from *multiple levels* within partnering organizations "brings structural integrity to the partnership" (Sagawa and Segal, 2000, p. 223). Involving several individuals within each organization helps ensure that a project will continue even if one or more key individuals leave the organizations. Multilevel participation in a partnership also enables its work to occur on several levels of an issue, including direct service or action, community organizing, fund-raising, leveraging resources, goal setting, strategic planning, and policy formation. As such, participants can include community agency clients and staff, students, faculty, administrators, workers, midlevel managers, key leaders, and members of governing boards. As with any sustainable endeavor, "new value partnerships often have multiple centers of interaction" (Sagawa and Segal, 2000, p. 226).

In new value partnerships, all partners view the relationship as *open-ended*. Partnerships have cycles, and when the community changes, so must the goals of the relationship. Viewing the partnership as a continual learning process fosters the development of new projects as current projects are completed. For example, the New Century Councils continue to identify and communicate new issues and to extend the call for proposal process, even as projects are still under way or are nearing completion.

The final COMMON element is *new value*. Sustainable partnerships for service-learning continually explore new opportunities to add value to each partner by assessing the status of the partnership, reviewing each partner's needs, and revisiting why the partnership endeavor is important. Because of their ethic of reciprocity, each party appreciates the successes of all partners. Finally, partners celebrate and reward their successes as individual organizations and as a partnership. As a result, new value partnerships have tremendous potential to contradict the fears and bad images of corporate involvement in higher education.

Conclusion

More creative ways to involve corporate partners in service-learning are emerging. The traditional corporate business model that stressed almost exclusive accountability to stockholders is giving way to a new sense of accountability to a broader definition of community stakeholders. Although corporations are embracing a new sense of social responsibility based on a concern for the social infrastructure in which they operate, challenges still remain to building effective corporate-university-community partnerships. These include significant differences in values, motives, organizational cultures, attitudes, and work styles. One of the most powerful concepts that organizations of all types are embracing is that of learning-centeredness. When learning-centered organizations join one another in mutually beneficial partnerships, entrepreneurialism, innovation, creativity, and redefinition result. This makes corporate involvement with community and higher-education partners not only a philanthropic and ethical decision but also a strategic one.

Potential benefits for colleges and universities are also great. As institutions of higher education seek to become engaged with their communities for reasons of both altruism and self-interest, they are realizing more and more that involving corporate partners helps to reduce the burden on their own resources while increasing benefits to the community. Although purists fear that corporate involvement can taint service-learning, creating reciprocal, democratic partnerships helps to avoid this unnecessary pitfall.

Intentionally designed, actively pursued, and creatively sustained corporate-university-community partnerships for service-learning, like the ones highlighted in this chapter, can lead partners away from more passive, paternalistic, one-way models of involvement to new value partnerships that constantly create possibilities for growth for all participants and true mutual interest in each party's success (Sagawa and Segal, 2000). Such partnerships break down traditional barriers between organizations and sectors and help move partners toward socially responsible citizenship. As Rodin (2000) has similarly asserted for universities, the late chief executive officer of the Coca-Cola Company, Roberto Goizueta, argued that businesses must support the communities that support them because business itself is a stakeholder in the larger community (Carroll, 1998). As corporations and communities become more engaged, colleges and universities can continue to play a pivotal role in forging and sustaining authentic partnerships for the common good.

References

"A Glance at the Spring Issue of the Association of Departments of English Bulletin: Making English Majors Marketable." *Chronicle of Higher Education,* [http://chronicle.com]. April 23, 2001.

Barber, B. *An Aristocracy of Everyone: The Politics of Education and the Future of America.* New York: Ballantine Books, 1992.

Blumenstyk, G. "A Vilified Corporate Partnership Produces Little Change (Except Better Facilities)." *Chronicle of Higher Education,* June 22, 2001, p. A24.

Carnevale, D. "Teachers Union Report Criticizes Businesslike Approach to Distance Education." *Chronicle of Higher Education,* [http://www.chronicle.com]. August 31, 2001.

Carroll, A. "The Four Faces of Corporate Citizenship." *Business and Society Review,* 1998, *100–101,* 1–7.

Chase Community Development Competition brochure. New York: JP Morgan Chase, n.d.

Cohen, M. "Health Model Expanded to Connect University with Communities." *W. K. Kellogg Foundation International Journal,* 1999, *1*(10), 14–15.

Deforge, N. *The Massena Learning Consortium—Helping Today's Student Become Tomorrow's Employee.* Potsdam, N.Y.: Clarkson University School of Business, 1998.

De Kluyver, C. *Strategic Thinking: An Executive Perspective.* Upper Saddle River, N.J.: Prentice-Hall, 2000.

East Tennessee State University Office of Rural and Community Health and Community Partnerships. *Year Three Expanding Community Partnerships Report to the Kellogg Foundation.* Johnson City, Tenn.: East Tennessee State University, 2001.

Engstrom, C., and Tinto, V. "Working with Academic Affairs to Enhance Student Learning." In M. Barr and M. Desler (eds.), *Handbook of Student Affairs Administration.* San Francisco: Jossey-Bass, 2000.

"Faculty Union in Nova Scotia Takes Hard Line on Distance Learning." *Chronicle of Higher Education,* June 15, 2001, p. A29.

Gamble, D. *Syracuse University Community Design Center, 1998–2000.* Syracuse, N.Y.: School of Architecture, 2001.

Jacoby, B. *Service-Learning in Higher Education: Concepts and Practices.* San Francisco: Jossey-Bass, 1996.

JP Morgan Chase. [http://www.chase.com/chase/gx.cgi]. May 2001.

Logan, D., Roy, D., and Regelbrugge, L. *Global Corporate Citizenship: Rationale and Strategies.* Washington, D.C.: Hitachi Foundation, 1997.

Lucas, C. *American Higher Education: A History.* New York: St. Martin's Griffin, 1994.

McLemee, S., and Smallwood, S. "Harvard Removes Head of Arts Program: Georgia Tech Sees Exodus of Humanities Programs." *Chronicle of Higher Education,* May 25, 2001, p. A10.

"Poverty and Achievement Statistics from the NYS Department of Education." *Syracuse Post Standard,* March 17, 1998, p. B8.

Press, E., and Washburn, J. "The Kept University." *Atlantic Monthly,* 2000, *285*(3), 39–54.

Rhodes, F. "A Battle Plan for Professor to Recapture the Curriculum." *Chronicle of Higher Education,* September 14, 2001, pp. B7–10.

Rodin, J. "Working with the Neighbors." *New York Times,* December 30, 2000, p. A15.

Sagawa, S., and Segal, E. *Common Interest Common Good: Creating Value Through Business and Social Sector Partnerships.* Boston: Harvard Business School Press, 2000.

Senge, P. *The Fifth Discipline: The Art and Practice of the Learning Organization.* New York: Currency Doubleday, 1990.

Tennyson, R., and Zyszkowski, A. "The Learning and Sharing Process: Why Is Partnership Between Sectors Such a Challenge?" In L. Regelbrugge (ed.), *Promoting Corporate Citizenship: Opportunities for Business and Civil Society Engagement.* Washington, D.C.: CIVICUS World Alliance for Citizen Participation, 1999.

Tichy, N., McGill, A., and St. Clair, L. (eds.). *Corporate Global Citizenship: Doing Business in the Public Eye.* San Francisco: New Lexington Press, 1997.

Torres, J. (ed.). *Benchmarks for Campus/Community Partnerships.* Providence, R. I.: Campus Compact, 2000.

White, D., and Taylor, T. *East Tennessee State University Office of Service Learning Outcomes Assessment Report.* Johnson City, Tenn.: East Tennessee State University, 2001.

Wilson Park Community Center Team. *Chase Community Development Competition.* Syracuse, N.Y.: School of Architecture, 2001.

Zuhlsdorf, S. "The Clarkson University School of Business, Business/Educational Partnership Program." Memorandum to J. McKeown, April 2001.

Chapter Thirteen

Partnerships for International Service-Learning

Linda A. Chisholm

Once you have studied and implemented successful partnerships for service-learning on or near your campus, your thoughts may turn to the opportunities for service-learning abroad. You imagine all that your students might learn from immersing themselves in a nation and culture other than their own. You imagine the needs around the world that they might address. You know the richness of service-learning experiences, and so you would likely agree with Chantal Thery, director of languages and service-learning at the University of Montpellier in France, that "service-learning goes beyond mere academic tourism" (personal communication, May 1998). You sympathize fully with the student who wrote, "It is one thing to study abroad, learn about a culture and see the sights. It is quite another thing to go beyond that temporary, visiting tourist status, and collaborate with a community that will welcome and receive you as one of their own. The breadth of this type of experience is just so much more fulfilling and rewarding" (D. Del Pozo, personal communication, December 1999).

But, quite correctly, you are apprehensive. You have traveled and perhaps even lived abroad, but you know that establishing working partnerships and putting your students' well-being into the hands of others is another matter. In order to establish and sustain a program of academic quality and truly useful service, you will need the full cooperation of your college's faculty, administration, and students, as well as trustworthy and responsible partners abroad. You must negotiate the program goals, design, and budget so that the expectations of all parties are met. How to go about designing and implementing service-learning in an international setting with international partners is the subject of this chapter.

Why Service-Learning Abroad?

As you begin to raise the possibilities with colleagues, you are certain to hear the argument that with so many needs to address at home and so much to learn from the local community, there is no need to send students abroad for service-learning. However, we live in an increasingly international society and a global economy in which social problems and issues cross national borders. The destruction of the environment, the spread of communicable diseases, including AIDS, and drug trafficking are but three such issues. Further, local problems such as hunger and homelessness, unequal educational opportunity, and insufficient care of the elderly and the disabled are repeated in city after city around the world. Creative approaches to resolution of a problem in one place may be well worth replicating in another. If solutions to these problems are to be found for our interdependent world, they will come from the cross-fertilization of ideas of one culture with another and from cooperative efforts between and among nations. Training students in their formative years to think globally and to work cross-culturally prepares them for the leadership we hope they will one day assume in addressing local and international problems.

Even if your colleagues argue that in the future your students are likely to be involved only in local issues within the United States, you may want to counter with the reminder that the United States is now itself an international culture. Virtually no U.S. city or town is without an immigrant population, and our country is constantly being called upon to embrace people of varying cultures and beliefs. As students enter professions, they will be required to interact frequently with those different from themselves. The experience of studying and serving abroad highlights cultural differences, making students aware that their own values and realities are not necessarily those of others. Experiencing a culture at its roots makes teachers, doctors, nurses, businesspeople, lawyers, and engineers more aware of and sensitive to the needs and values of those with whom they will surely deal. They will come to understand the necessity of crafting policies and programs that incorporate the values and meet the needs of the population whose concerns they are trying to address. They will learn the importance of balancing conflicting agendas and negotiating to the advantage of all parties.

As you promote the case for international service-learning on your campus, you will find students to be ready allies. Today's students are seeking opportunities for international education. Many have traveled abroad already and are sophisticated enough to realize that programs that allow them to be immersed in a foreign culture will bring them greater rewards than superficial travel or study-only programs. You can help them think more deeply about this. Traditional study abroad, which sends students from a U.S. college or university to a similar institution overseas without the concomitant experience of service, limits students' encounters with the host culture. Further, higher education is a privilege to which few around the world are privy. Therefore, to go from a college "here" to a college "there" is perforce to go from a middle-class culture to a middle- or upper-class culture and to make contacts almost exclusively within the same age group. In contrast, most service assignments expose students to other socioeconomic strata as well as other age groups, giving them a wider range of experiences from which to gain an understanding of the host country.

You may well ask why overseas partners would be interested in having young, untrained, and inexperienced American college students come to their countries to participate in service-learning. Rest assured that around the world there are college and university faculty and administrators and service agency professionals who share the same concerns that have stimulated the service-learning movement in the United States. Many would agree with Colin Bundy, vice-chancellor of the University of Witwatersrand in South Africa that "no university is an ivory tower—even if it wishes to be. Universities are deeply implicated in the modern state and are key agents of modern society. This means that they should be conscious of, and make choices about, the *terms* of that involvement. . . .

Higher education *must* be critically engaged in the needs of communities, nation and the world" (Berry and Chisholm, 1999, p. 10).

There are educators in virtually every nation who are deeply distressed that too often higher education is directed toward its own advancement, without a sense of responsibility to the larger society. Rance Lee, principal of Chung Chi College of the Chinese University of Hong Kong, has declared, "Most students have become individualist as well as materialistic. From my contacts with major universities in the Chinese mainland, similar changes to student culture have taken place there. . . . Perhaps this is a world-wide trend. . . . I want to find ways to reshape the student orientations. I hope that all institutions of higher education around the world come to join forces in building up humanitarian values among leaders of future generations" (Berry and Chisholm, 1999, p. 5).

Instead of becoming the leaders Dr. Lee seeks, that is, graduates who will remain in their own communities working in one way or another to address social needs, graduates of universities around the world often use the privilege of higher education to move "up and out," thereby divorcing themselves from the social issues of their communities and countries. Educational reform directed toward connecting campus and community, the development of young leaders with humane values and cross-cultural communication skills, the promotion of active citizenship, the connection of theory and practice, and the fulfillment of institutional mission has motivated educators around the world to initiate and develop service-learning, just as these reasons have inspired service-learning in the United States (Berry and Chisholm, 1999).

Similarly, service providers are anxious to involve young people, including those from overseas, in their work. Mithra Augustine of India, who serves as trustee of an organization of social service agencies throughout Asia, expressed concern for developing caring leaders: "The role and function of universities and colleges were earlier seen as integral to the processes of social engineering, developing in students critical faculties, creative potential and initiative towards applying these to the tasks of freeing people from material and intellectual deprivation. Amidst current trends of modernisation and globalisation the culture of self-interest is growing dominant in centres of higher education. The interest is in training for lucrative careers at the expense of all else once supportive of social concerns of justice, peace, and the integrity of creation" (Berry and Chisholm, 1999, p. 12).

Because many service agencies already rely on both volunteers from their own culture and foreign volunteers or interns, they welcome the help of energetic and intelligent students and realize the role they may later play in promoting and supporting the mission of the agency. In addition, these agencies frequently have only a few trained professionals on staff and therefore seek opportunities for meaningful interaction with students.

Finally, you may add to your argument for service-learning abroad that your students have so very much to give. Like it or not, chosen or thrust upon us, the fact is that the United States, its young people, and their popular culture are a source of fascination around the world. With a twinkle in his eye, one service-learning student described his appeal to the children of Mexico: "Because I'm so tall and black, the children I worked with thought I was the basketball star, Michael Jordan. Despite my disclaimer, they hung on me and did everything I told them to—including coming to school every day and working hard at their lessons!" (R. Miller, personal communication, April 1997). Young Americans who go abroad as learners and willingly apply their energy, skills, intelligence, and imagination for the benefit of others act as goodwill ambassadors for their nation and for their college or university, serving to correct the less favorable impressions that U.S. tourists and businesspeople sometimes leave behind.

Three Options for International Service-Learning

Congratulations! You have convinced your colleagues that providing service-learning opportunities abroad for your students is important. Now you must ask how best to provide them. There are three possible options. One is utilizing the programs of other institutions and organizations. A second is for you and your colleagues to design, develop, and manage a program yourselves. A third is to use a combination of the first two approaches, developing one or two programs yourself and using other programs to provide a wider array of locations, types of service, and program designs.

Should you decide on the first option—utilizing already existing programs—you might, for example, encourage your students to enroll in the programs of other colleges and universities. Many college-sponsored programs of international service-learning accept students from other institutions. For example, the Center for Global Education of Augsburg College in Minneapolis offers a service-learning option in its study-abroad programs in Central America and Namibia. At Arcadia University (formerly Beaver College) in Glenside, Pennsylvania, the Center for Education Abroad has a program in Greece that includes a service component. Or you might make known to your students the programs of Lafayette College in Easton, Pennsylvania, in which students, accompanied by a Lafayette professor, engage in a common project for two to four weeks.

In addition to college-sponsored programs, organizations such as the International Partnership for Service-Learning offer programs that enable students to join students from other U.S. colleges for a semester or a year in studying at an affiliated overseas university, learning from local professors in classes especially designed to integrate the service with learning about the culture, and working twenty hours per week in a service agency to which students are individually assigned on the basis of interest and skills (International Partnership for Service-Learning, 2001). Since its founding in 1982, the International Partnership for Service-Learning has offered undergraduate programs that combine rigorous academic study with substantive service. Partnership programs vary in length from summer to yearlong and exist in twelve countries. A master's degree in international service, inaugurated in 1997, prepares students for careers in international relief and development work. The year of study begins with a semester of study and service at either Universidad Autonoma de Guadalajara in Mexico or the University of Technology in Jamaica. In the second semester, all of the students come together in London for service in an agency and for continued studies and the preparation of the thesis at the University of Surrey Roehampton, which awards the degree (International Partnership for Service-Learning, 2001).

The Higher Education Consortium for Urban Affairs (HECUA) offers courses combined with internships and other types of experiential learning around the world, with a focus on urban affairs and social justice issues. Founded in 1971, HECUA examines the systems that create inequality and the systems through which change can be made (HECUA, 2001).

In using already existing programs, you do not have to reinvent the wheel but rather can rely on the experience and structures already in place. You will not need to have a minimum number of students to make the program viable, as the sponsoring organization will involve students from several colleges. This means that you can soon be up and running with international service-learning opportunities for your students and begin to see results as the first one or two students enroll. Because the range of possibilities is great not only in location but in program design, you will find that in advising your students you can consider not only their academic and personal goals but also their individual levels of maturity and independence.

A possible disadvantage of this approach is that a college's faculty and study-abroad advisers are likely to be less knowledgeable about a program that is not of their own creation and management. They may therefore be less able to assist students in selecting the program that best meets their particular needs. For students, using a program that does not emanate from their own college may have either advantages or disadvantages. They may welcome a time away from their home campus and their classmates, especially if they have been in a close-knit and insulated group. Leaving the secure and familiar is for many an important step to the independence of adulthood. A disadvantage of this option is that students may view the experience of study and service abroad as an interlude rather than an integral part of their college education.

A second option is that of designing and managing a program yourself for your own students. The program may be targeted to specific academic goals, such as those of Pace University's campus in White Plains, New York, and the University of Pittsburgh in Pennsylvania, whose students engage in service-learning in Latin America in order to improve their Spanish-language skills. Other examples of discipline-specific programs are those of the University of the South in Sewanee, Tennessee, whose environmental studies students work to preserve rain forests in Costa Rica, and Hobart/William Smith Colleges in Geneva, New York, whose Third

World studies majors serve and learn in the Dominican Republic. Directors of these programs speak of the bonding that occurs among students and between themselves and the students. When a program is designed especially for the curriculum of a particular institution, it can include pre- and postprogram studies that allow students to experience their study and service abroad as an integral part of their college education. In addition, a proprietary program is readily adaptable over time to accommodate both lessons learned and shifting institutional and student interests and priorities. One disadvantage may be that the students may spend most of their time as a group, thereby failing to develop the autonomy and independence that are among the great benefits of service-learning abroad. When asked why he chose the program he did, one student reported, "I was ready to separate myself from my fraternity brothers and other college friends. I like them and look forward to returning to campus for my senior year, but I also needed a time apart, to do my own thing, and find out who I am" (T. Fergueson, personal communication, October 1994). Two other related disadvantages should be noted. If the program is to be well-designed, the startup time necessary to identify appropriate locations and partners and to work out all the arrangements is significant. Many institutions would find it difficult to dedicate the time and resources that program development demands. Once the program is operational, the communication, management, and constant vigilance required are similarly demanding.

The third option is that of combining the first two plans, creating and managing a service-learning program of your own plus recommending programs of other organizations and institutions as appropriate for individual students. Pacific Lutheran University (PLU) in Tacoma, Washington, is only one of many colleges selecting this approach. PLU-specific programs engage both faculty and students, reinforcing for the campus community the value of service-learning. At the same time, PLU students have access to the many locations of the International Partnership for Service-Learning, allowing each student to decide whether he or she needs the support of familiar friends and faculty or wants to move to greater independence, responsibility, and individual identity. Bard College in Annandale-on-Hudson, New York, offers its own programs and then relies on an array of other programs for those students who, in a year of study abroad, wish a traditional study-only semester followed by a semester of service-learning. The combination of locations can be of enormous benefit to meet students' varied educational levels and goals. For example, a student might select his or her own college's program of intermediate language study in Mexico and then, after mastering sufficient language skills to be of service to a local agency abroad, participate in service-learning in either Mexico or Ecuador through the International Partnership for Service-Learning.

The combined approach to international service-learning programs limits the institution's commitment while offering the widest range of opportunities for students. It is most successful when advisers know both the students and the programs and are willing to help the students explore the choices and select the one most suited to their needs and goals. This approach also involves both the advantages and disadvantages described above for the other two options.

Issues to Consider in Selecting an Approach

The process for deciding the best route for you, your students, and your institution begins with an honest examination of your own ability to follow through. Are you prepared to make the long-term commitment that is necessary for the program to be effective, in terms of both the learning and the service, and one that is fair to your overseas partners? The question to be asked at the outset—one that goes to the very heart of service-learning—is, Are you truly dedicated to providing service in response to needs identified by the host community? Or are you and your institution primarily (or only) concerned with what the students will learn from the experience? If you are committed to service, then in the very beginning of your planning, you must model the values that you are purporting to teach students through service-learning.

It is important to recognize that the professional time needed for planning and developing a quality service-learning program is a commodity in short supply everywhere, especially in the developing world. This truth is exemplified in the rueful statement made by the president of a college in the Caribbean who said, "Sometimes I wonder for whom I work, the United States or

Jamaica. I am besieged with visitors from the U.S. who take my time discussing possible partnerships but disappear before anything substantial comes of it" (A. Sangster, personal communication, June 1984).

It is unfair to claim the time of potential overseas partners unless you are prepared to be a long-distance runner in the endeavor. A five-year agreement is reasonable in order to make the planning time worth the effort of everyone involved. Overseas partners sometimes complain that just as a program is running effectively and efficiently, the sponsoring U.S. institution may drop the program. As you look forward to your next few years, will you have the time and interest to commit to an ongoing international service-learning program?

Having answered the questions about your own commitment, ask the same questions of your institution. Do you expect that your president and key administrators will remain in place for the foreseeable future? If not, what is the likely effect on your program? Does experience indicate that you can count on administrators' continued support if they give initial assent? To what degree are your plans dependent on "soft" money? If so, what are the plans for sustaining the program? Are there decision-making bodies, such as a county or state legislature or board of trustees, that might veto your plans or withdraw their support mid-stream? You do not want to be in the position of explaining to enthusiastic partners abroad that your support has collapsed and the program must be canceled.

Next you must look at your student body. Students can be your greatest ally, but remember that the student body changes every few years and that student interest in service-learning waxes and wanes like other student interests. Moreover, students may enthusiastically endorse the idea of service-learning abroad without fully considering the limiting factors. For example, they may be enrolled in academic programs that allow for few electives, making it impossible to participate without delaying graduation. Many students need part-time and summer jobs to finance their education. Sports, theater, and other extracurricular activities pose competition for international service-learning. In some cases, parents veto plans for study and service abroad because they are fearful for their child's safety, because they believe that time could be better invested in another activity such as a business internship, or because in-depth international experiences are outside their own realm of experience.

Sophisticated organizations such as the School for International Training in Brattleboro, Vermont, and the International Partnership for Service-Learning find that colleges with enrollments comprised mainly of nontraditional students or of those who are the first in their families to go to college pose a particular challenge. Work, family responsibilities, and economic circumstances are often obstacles to participation in international service-learning. Minority students tend to participate in study-abroad experiences at a lower rate than do others. It is often not sufficient to make available the opportunity for international study and service; some students are likely to require extra encouragement in the form of advising, mentoring, and financial aid. As you consider your student body, be realistic in assessing their interest, life circumstances, and commitment, however enthusiastic their initial response. Assess, as well, the job you will have to do with regard to publicizing, recruiting, and advising for your international service-learning program. You will want to talk with the study-abroad officer at your college as well as the service-learning coordinator to get a realistic picture of what majors are most closely related to your program and of how many students are likely to actually sign up for a program you may develop.

It is important to determine early on whether students will be able to afford to participate in service-learning abroad. Federal financial aid—Pell grants and student loans—may be used for programs of service when academic credit is earned. Institutional policies governing their own scholarships vary. Some allow students to apply all scholarships to service-learning abroad; others are more restrictive. It is advisable to work with your study-abroad and financial aid officers to understand your institution's policies and, if appropriate, to develop support for seeking policy changes to enable more flexibility in the use of financial aid for international service-learning.

A useful exercise is to compare the process and finances of mounting and sponsoring your own international service-learning program with the cost of outsourcing to another sponsoring college or organization. Most legitimate programs realize no more than 5 percent of the cost of the program for administrative fees. The other charges go to pay direct costs overseas, such as room and board, instruction (whether by a faculty member of your college or by an overseas university), supervision of service, field trips, liability insurance, publicity, and the salaries of home-campus personnel who recruit, register, and advise students. The International Partnership for Service-Learning estimates that it takes a minimum of one year to arrange a program and another year to publicize before the first students enter the program. The cost ranges from $60,000 to $100,000 for the professional time and travel to research locations and establish the needed partnerships.

Should you conclude that using existing programs of other institutions and/or organizations is the preferred method for offering international service-learning for your college or university, you may nonetheless make these opportunities integral to your own academic programs and campus community. By offering predeparture courses and postprogram seminars, you can extend the experience for students and their reflection upon it. For example, students enrolled in Project Citizen at the University of Florida–Gainesville take a course together on campus in the spring semester and then participate in summer service abroad. The course includes such topics as philanthropy, volunteerism, service-learning, and global cultures, highlighting the differences between U.S. culture and the culture the students will encounter in their service. St. Augustine's College in Raleigh, North Carolina, requires students returning from service-learning abroad to give talks to campus and community groups as a means of reflection on their experiences by communicating to others what they have learned from international service-learning. Pacific Lutheran University encourages its students who have participated in service-learning abroad to volunteer in the city of Tacoma during their senior year in the hope and expectation that they will continue their service after they graduate. The key to developing successful campus predeparture and postservice programs lies in cultivating a close working relationship with the program sponsor so you understand the program and can design sequential experiences for students.

Three Principles for International Partnerships

If, after examining your ability and that of your institution to make a serious and sustained effort, you decide to move forward with creating your own program of service-learning abroad, you will then begin the process of selecting the right location and identifying possible overseas partners who are interested in collaborating with you on the design and management of a program. Throughout the process of developing and managing a program, you must constantly remind yourself of the three cardinal virtues that make for a good and lasting relationship: trust, mutuality of benefit, and open communication.

The basis for a trusting international relationship lies, as it does in any good relationship, in the confidence that you and your partners are truthful with each other. Being clear and open about your own goals, budget, and limitations encourages your partners to share the same information. Do not engage in the "hard sell" or make promises you may not be able to keep. Sometimes, for example, a college may overstate the ability of its students to perform service, and agency personnel end up disappointed because they believed they were getting students capable of complex social science research or with advanced technical skills. Or the agency may be led to expect a group of fifteen or twenty students, only to find that the enrollment is three or four. Be forthright about the experimental nature of what you are proposing and acknowledge that you cannot predict the results. Such honesty need not be an obstacle. Overseas partners are often willing to take a risk on a program that may prove to be worthwhile to them in the long run.

Conversely, you need to feel confidence in commitments made to you. You will look for signs in the investigation and planning process that give you an indication of the reliability of your potential partners. Is the overseas university or agency respected locally? Has the leadership been in place long enough to deliver what they promise? Are you convinced that their interest in receiving your students goes beyond financial gain? Do they have the resources and skills to use your students effectively? Are they willing to teach and learn with your students? If you answer such questions affirmatively, you will likely have found a trustworthy partner.

The second characteristic of a lasting partnership is mutuality of benefit. Service-learning partnerships should be negotiated as are any good business agreements. You should begin by stating that your students want and need to learn about the host culture and that the learning will come from structured experiences that include a supervised service project combined with formal classes, guest lectures, field trips, and, possibly, home stays. In exchange for the overseas partners' providing these services, you are offering both financial payment and the volunteer service of the students. The host culture may ask for other compensation, such as a scholarship for one of their students to attend your university. Both you and your potential partners must be realistic about what is required, what is offered, and what is negotiable.

When you enter into an agreement, you must be willing to accept the values and cultural patterns of the host culture, however different they may be from what you and your students may envision. As a result, what the students learn may differ from originally established learning objectives. For example, you may anticipate that students will learn how an exemplary community-based organization operates. The actual learning may be considerably different but equally or more valuable. As one student recorded in his journal: "[My] agency is an institution with many faults. A lack of administrative organization causes a great deal of confusion at times. . . . There is, however, a different side . . . [for my agency] serves an important and necessary function. . . . [It] provides services that do help the people of the community . . . [making] the administrative problems (and the irritable nature of the gringos) seem unimportant" (Hathaway, 1990).

A third characteristic of a healthy and lasting partnership is that of open and complete communication. You and your partners must agree on how communication, ranging from formal evaluation procedures to informal "checking in," will occur. Your partners must inform you on matters relating to each student's adjustment, health, and performance. Agencies, overseas universities, and host families should be given the opportunity to raise issues about individual students as well as about the program as a whole. In the beginning of the relationship, courtesy and formality will prevail. With time and frequent meetings, the partnership will hopefully become collegial, with the familiarity that leads to greater openness.

As you consider the issues of communication, remember to include students. They, like you and your overseas partners, should have the opportunity to give both formal and informal feedback during and after the experience. You will want to take the opinions of students seriously, but remember that each student responds uniquely to an experience and program. "My supervisor was really super. She took the time to show me what to do, and advise me how to do it," wrote one student (Berry and Chisholm, 1992, p. 30). Another reported, "My supervisor was O.K. She knew what she was doing, but she expected me just to get on with it, and didn't have a lot of time to give me direction" (Berry and Chisholm, 1992, p. 30). Both comments were written about the same supervisor! By all means, fine-tune the programs as you go, but not in response to the comments of a single student. Recognize that service-learning is a very human situation to which each party will have a somewhat different response.

Developing International Partnerships

Many decisions are required during the process of developing international partnerships. You will need to consider the location; the program design; the length of the program; the kind of service to be performed; the content of academic studies; how the study and service will be linked; how you will provide support services including housing, health care, orientation, and field trips; ongoing supervision; and costs. You will need to determine how academic credit will be awarded and by whom, and by what criteria the learning will be judged. The most satisfactory programs grow out of extensive discussion among the partners on all these matters, rather than through a priori decisions. Of course, you will begin with some ideas, but be prepared to adjust as potential partners describe their goals, resources, expectations, and limitations.

Very early in the process, before any decisions are made, you will become aware that all parties are, in effect, learning a new language. Even if the language of the country is English, you will quickly recognize that cultural norms, systems of education, and definitions of service are different. First, you may find that common terms have radically divergent meanings. For example, *course* in U.S. educational terms means a small unit (generally 1/40th) of the overall degree program. In British systems, *course* refers to the three-year program of studies leading to the degree. Similarly, *social concerns* or *social responsibility* may have serious political connotations in some countries and cultures. In Korea, selecting the appropriate language to refer to service is critical: some phrases recall days of student protests that once threatened its universities. Similarly, in Latin America, certain expressions are code words for the radical political left. In former Soviet republics, *service* was once enforced and therefore recalls an experience that was anything but voluntary and, for some people, deeply resented.

Beyond the issues of semantics are differing purposes and methods. The respective roles of teacher and student vary widely between cultures and educational systems. Failure to recognize and explain important differences to students and international partners can result in serious misunderstandings and ill feelings. When unaware of these differences, faculty members, especially in Asia, may judge U.S. students as arrogant and rude because they often question the teachers' conclusions. Conversely, U.S. students may perceive the teaching as authoritarian in cultures where the professor is revered and honored for greater knowledge and wisdom. Or, in British or British-derived systems, they may believe that the teachers come to class unprepared when, in fact, the teacher's role is that of tutor and facilitator, not lecturer.

Similarly, U.S. students, especially those who have participated in service-learning in a U.S. college or university, may define the goals of service through the lens of advocacy for social change and find any other purpose trivial. Partner service agencies, on the other hand, may see their mission solely as the alleviation of immediate suffering and do not speak of social change. Mother Teresa, for example, believed that she was not called to the task of creating a new health care system and standard for India, but rather to give dignity to dying individuals. Learning about the different definitions of what constitutes service and the controversy surrounding the work of Mother Teresa, one student serving at the Home for the Destitute and Dying in Calcutta wrote, "As the world strives at an alarming pace for a progress defined as material wealth and quality of life based on material comforts . . ., the Missionaries of Charity give people a peaceful way to die" (M. Beasley, personal communication, April 2001). You can expect that not all of the issues related to the language of learning and service will come to the surface in the planning of a program but will emerge as the program develops over time and you become more familiar with the subtleties of your partners' culture and programs.

Selecting a Location and Local Partners

Location is probably the first decision to be made. Too often the country is selected because a faculty member has a contact in the government, a university, or a service agency there. Although personal connections can be most useful, it is critical that they not limit your search or lead to a premature conclusion. In determining the country in which to develop your program, you will want to consider its political stability, the likelihood of war or terrorism, issues of health and environmental safety, access to adequate medical facilities, and the availability of reputable service agencies and academic institutions. Become familiar with the academic calendar—which varies widely around the world—as well as weather patterns. Any of these factors may make a program impossible or at least unwise. Recognizing that all institutions may undergo change, you will want to select a place where you are not entirely dependent on one academic institution or a narrow range of service agencies. Should one of your overseas partners become incompatible with your program needs, you will want to have other options available.

Once you have done your research and selected a location, you will set about the task of choosing partners. As is true for the domestic service-learning programs described in previous chapters, a range of partnerships is required. In addition to local service organizations, you may want to be linked to an overseas college or university. You will undoubtedly need others to provide housing and support services. You will want to investigate a number of possible partners until you find those with whom you share the greatest potential for long-term compatibility. Far too many U.S. institutions do not give adequate time and attention to this critical step. Failure to do adequate background research early on can lead to entering into relationships while remaining ignorant of key issues. For example, the partnership between an elite British university and a U.S. community college failed because the U.S.

students who went abroad were unprepared for the level of study and service expected of them.

By far the best approach to selecting partners, one that will help you avoid countless problems, is to seek a qualified native informant, someone who is familiar with the past and present conditions in the country you have chosen, who knows the inside story of the country's service agencies and institutions of higher education, and who has a large network of connections on which to draw. Locating the right person may require considerable effort. Begin by soliciting suggestions from anyone familiar with the country you have chosen. If, for example, your institution is religiously affiliated, the church's national headquarters will likely have staff members who work overseas. Organizations such as Rotary International, sister-city programs, and perhaps service agencies with whom you work locally may have useful connections. International faculty members and students on your campus may have contacts in their home countries. The Returned Peace Corps has area and country committees.

You may need to talk with many people before you find the right person. The International Partnership for Service-Learning has found that the best native informants have lived in both the country in question and the United States and have experience in both the social service sector and in higher education. Your native informant should provide names and addresses of potential partners and permit you to use his or her name. If at all possible, one of the most useful investments you can make is to compensate your native informant for making the initial contacts, arranging visits for you, and accompanying you to first meetings, as described below.

As you begin to make contacts through correspondence, your native informant can help you assess the realism of the responses you receive. Almost everyone who hears of service-learning is enthusiastic about participating. Occasionally, the lure of the U.S. dollar is the motive, or prospective partners may be enticed by idealized visions of what service-learning can accomplish. But much more often, the willingness to partner indicates a shared understanding and appreciation of service-learning. The ability of potential overseas partners to deliver may be another matter. For example, service agencies may not have the personnel to supervise American undergraduates. They may have experience working with highly trained professional volunteers—doctors, teachers, or computer programmers, for example—and expect the same level of skill and maturity from your students. Overseas universities may not have enough housing facilities or faculty with sufficient English-language skills.

In some countries, it is important to inform the local and/or national government officials about your plans. Your native informant can be very helpful here. But remember that politicians all over the world seek to make themselves and their parties look good in the eyes of their constituencies. It may be wise to gain their cooperation by speaking publicly of their support. Generally, it is highly desirable to establish the service-learning program through what one native informant for the International Partnership called "the untouchables" (H. Beckford, personal communication, April 1984). He was referring to those people in his society such as college presidents, nongovernmental organization directors, and religious leaders who will remain in their roles regardless of which political party wins the next election.

When you have enough information to believe that you will find the right agency, university, and other partners in your chosen location, you will want to set up a visit. Rely on the advice of your native informant and, if at all possible, arrange for him or her to accompany you. A delegation of two or three is preferable to a visit by just one person, because overseas institutions interpret a delegation as having more authority and greater seriousness of purpose than an individual. Moreover, it is useful for one person to take notes while the other converses. Both may hear what is said differently, so comparing what has been heard and understood may avoid later misunderstandings. Remember that your hosts in such situations will be courteous to a fault. In many cultures, the pattern of communication is indirect. That is, you will not be told no, so you must interpret the nuances to see if your proposals are being well-received. Again, the native informant will be able to tell you what was *really* communicated. Just as you will be assessing in your initial meetings whether your expectations can be met, so also you will need to listen carefully to the expectations of your potential partners and ask yourself if you can meet them. To avoid disappointment, do not make promises that you are unlikely to be able to keep. Disappointed overseas partners may conclude that we in the United States are not serious about service or learning about another country and that they have been exploited without regard for their time and interests. Anger and resentment add up to bad feelings about your institution that may be generalized to the United States as a whole.

Making Decisions About Service and Learning

Several key decisions are required in designing the service and academic components of the program and how they will complement one another. As with other service-learning partnerships, the desired outcomes for both students and community partners must guide your decisions.

The length of a program and the amount of time devoted to service are critical issues. Understandably, agencies are eager to obtain the maximum amount of time from the volunteers. Service that is truly useful to an agency and a community cannot be performed in a few weeks or in a few hours a week. In fact, it may be said that short-cycle service-learning programs or those requiring only four or five hours of service a week are not only of little help but may be disruptive to the schedule and work of an agency. The amount of time and effort required to orient, train, and supervise student volunteers new to the culture may outweigh the benefits of their service. It is also counterproductive to convey the wrong message to students, leading them to believe that valuable service can be accomplished with a minimum commitment. Service of fifteen hours or more each week for a minimum of three to four months allows students to become more like staff members and to accomplish important tasks.

Short-term and summer programs may be useful to the communities and agencies involved, but only if the service to be performed is carefully fitted into the available time frame and the time of year. For example, summer camps that operate for only a few weeks may match up well with summer service-learning programs. In such situations, students must be trained in advance of arrival in the host country and prepared to step into their roles immediately. Some environmental projects such as tree planting, stream cleanups, or trail clearing can be done in short periods of time.

If your service plan calls for construction work, take your cue from the University of the South in Sewanee, Tennessee, whose service-learning coordinator is the former owner of a construction company. He teaches the students building skills well in advance of their overseas departure, assembles all the needed materials and tools, and then, as a professional builder, supervises their work on-site. "I was skeptical of the plan to bring American college students to lay the foundation for our new wing," said the director of a children's home, "but it has stood the test of time. No cracks, no problems" (C. Parris, personal communication, September 1997). The outcome of such well-planned and executed service will not be another of the half-finished and then abandoned service projects that one sadly sees throughout the developing world.

If the service is to be direct human care, the task is more demanding. Orientation to the mission, philosophy, clients, staff and culture of a school, health care facility or community development project takes a minimum of two weeks. Programs of at least three months and preferably a year ensure that the time spent orienting the students will be worth the investment to the agency. It also gives students the chance to grow in the job, assuming more responsibility as time goes on and learning the complexities of the issues and culture.

Another factor to consider in designing service-learning abroad is whether to link to an overseas college or university for the delivery of the academic component. There is no doubt that is easier to send a teacher from the U.S. home university to accompany the students and direct the academic studies. No time is required for developing a partnership with an overseas university. No negotiations to arrive at an agreed-upon curriculum, teaching methods, and costs are needed. No special skills of cross-cultural negotiation are necessary, and no one will seek return favors. However, in selecting this model, it must be acknowledged that the students' learning will be limited. First, such a plan wrongly suggests to students, albeit unwittingly, that the country has no teachers capable of delivering a quality academic program. It denies students the opportunity to learn about the host country's methods of education that both reflect and shape cultural patterns. It limits their opportunity to meet college students of another culture and to become familiar with how the more privileged people of the host society think and what they value.

In-country academics are likely to be more knowledgeable, sophisticated, and current about their own culture than is a foreigner, however well-educated. Service-learning in an international setting can and should be the impetus for asking the most demanding questions. It should be a time of uncertainty, as the student faces a wholly new set of values and assumptions about human life. Too often, students are encouraged to reach conclusions with little knowledge, no research, and minimal contact with the host culture. Conclusions may be presented even before the program has begun, and sometimes by the home institution teacher. To avoid these pitfalls, more and more U.S. programs rely on in-country faculty. In addition, overseas university partners are likely to have other support services, including housing, library and computer facilities, buses, counseling, and health care, in place for their own students. You may generally make arrangements to use these services for your visiting U.S. students.

Partnering with an overseas institution is easier if the institution is itself engaged in service-learning. More and more universities have service programs for their own students and are linking the service to academic study. If the faculty are new to service-learning, it will take a considerable amount of time to introduce them to the idea of linking academic study and volunteer service, just as you and your colleagues had to learn and experiment when you developed service-learning on your home campus. You may wish to provide your overseas colleagues with some of the service-learning resources you use and inform them of upcoming service-learning conferences.

Other questions of design that you and your overseas partners will need to address include whether the service and study will be held concurrently or in a "sandwich" pattern. When the service sites are located near the university, you may arrange, for example, mornings in service and afternoons in class and study, or three days of service and two days on campus each week. You will need to know the schedule of both the university and the service agencies to make this determination. If the service site is removed from the university, a pattern based on several weeks of full-time study followed by full-time service and concluding with a period for the writing of final papers, class presentations, and examinations may be appropriate.

Another consideration related to the service is whether students will work as a group, with one or two other students, or as individuals. Although the latter involves more service agency partners and hence is more complicated to arrange and supervise, the benefit to both the students and the agencies is greater. Working alone or in groups of two or three, students tend to assume more responsibility and to interact to a greater degree with staff and clients of the agency than they do in large-group projects. Additional learning can be facilitated by engaging students in structured opportunities to compare the mission, philosophy, and management of their various agencies. Such comparisons deepen and extend students' understanding of the issues facing the host nation as they see the different ways in which agencies approach the issues.

As you negotiate with your partners, you will need to be clear about the role each partner will play. What is the agency's role in orienting and teaching? Who determines the placement for each student? Who determines if a change in placement is advisable? Does the home institution or the overseas university award the credit and on what basis? Walk through the program with your partners step by step, agree on who takes responsibility for each piece, and ensure that students will have ongoing support and supervision.

The final task in designing a program is building a realistic budget. In addition to issues to be considered in budgeting for any university program, several further issues related to overseas programs in general and to overseas service-learning programs in particular must be considered. First, it is essential to become familiar with the economy of the host country and how it fluctuates based on global and internal market factors. The relative costs of food, housing, and gasoline may or may not be greater than at home. Understanding the subtleties of the host country's economy allows you to judge if the costs quoted to you are reasonable. Program budgets should contain funds necessary to compensate service agencies for any costs they may incur related to preparing for and engaging your students in service, including transportation, food, equipment, materials, and perhaps even staff supervision. Faculty at overseas universities should be compensated for teaching in your program according to the local institution's scale. Paying them by U.S. standards may seem an appropriate and generous move on your part, but doing so may cause severe inequities that can result in resentment on the part of faculty not involved in your program. This may also create problems for host institution administrators.

Although numerous issues are bound to arise once the program is in operation, the solid foundation outlined in this section will enable you and your international partners to work through them and to sustain the partnership. Partnerships based on trusting relationships, mutual benefits, and open and frequent communication are most likely to survive the inevitable ups and downs. Regular reviews of details and budgets are essential and should lead to changes as needed. Most critical is to make changes *only* in conjunction or consultation with your partners. Do not impose by asking for excessive favors. One otherwise laudable program came to an abrupt end when the in-country director quit. As she explains, "I was chauffeuring a U.S. director around for shopping and personal business. We do have taxis and he can afford to use them! I got tired of being his personal handmaid" (V. Lewis, personal communication, 1997).

Selecting and Preparing Students

Once the program design is complete and arrangements have been finalized with your overseas partners, it is time to make the opportunity known to students by printing a brochure, listing the program in your college catalogue, mounting a web site, and promoting the program through appropriate academic departments and student services offices. It is important that your materials describe the program accurately and honestly, including the academic and service requirements. If the program involves hard physical labor or if the living conditions will not be what the students are accustomed to at home, explain just what they will encounter. The most satisfied students will be those who anticipate and accept the challenges before signing on for the program.

In selecting students, you should require an application and an essay that enables students to describe themselves, their learning objectives, and their degree of preparedness for study and service abroad. Interviews are also useful in determining students' motivations, skills, and maturity. Including students with a variety of interests enriches the program, but certain levels of responsibility, readiness to learn, and instrumental autonomy are necessary.

As students are selected, you will want to provide them and their parents with more detailed information about the program; options for study, service, and other opportunities; required standards of behavior; and contacts in case of emergency. Above all, emphasize that students are guests in the country they are visiting and that the burden of adaptation rests with them rather than with their hosts. For example, as has been mentioned, the respective roles of teacher and student vary widely among different cultures and educational systems. Orientation programs should teach students how they will be expected to behave in the classroom. The proper ways to address faculty members, service agency supervisors, and even the mother and father in a host family also vary from culture to culture, and students should be told of these formalities so that they do not offend. The director of the Mexico program of the International Partnership for Service-Learning related this reaction to a U.S. student: "He called the professor by his first name and put his feet on the desk. We were shocked! Later we discovered that he is really a very nice person" (G. Delgadillo, personal communication, February 1999).

Except in very short-term programs, you do not need to teach students all the host country's customs and cultural patterns in advance. Take your cue from the Peace Corps, which once did extensive predeparture training in the United States and now conducts its training in the host country and on-site. Learning about a country and its customs is best done as the student encounters the realities. Like the Peace Corps, the International Partnership for Service-Learning believes that orientation is best handled by in-country people who are knowledgeable about customs and current conditions.

In addition, in-country orientation should enable students to acquire the requisite life and coping skills. They must learn how to use the telephone and local transportation, how to exchange money, and how to get help if needed. They should be shown the location of the nearest hospital and the police station and be briefed on the areas and activities that are off-limits for reasons of safety and security. Students must understand that customs regarding relationships between men and women vary in different cultures. Behavior and dress acceptable in the United States may convey an entirely different—and unwanted—message abroad. Above all, your students should become acquainted with the people to whom they can turn for advice and then be encouraged to do so as situations and questions arise.

Similarly, the service agency will orient students to their expectations about dress and behavior. Knowing these expectations is especially important if the service-learning student is working with children or adolescents because the agency will want the student to serve as a role model. Schools, health clinics, and other service agencies will require that their records, whether of an individual client, donor, or the operation of the agency, are confidential. Agency personnel must tell service-learning students not to delve into these records without permission, nor are they to divulge confidential information. In your orientation, you should only caution students to move slowly in these matters during their first days in the agency. By offering to do simple tasks that enable agency personnel to get to know them, students will both learn the rules and earn the trust that leads to greater accessibility and responsibility.

New Directions for International Service-Learning

New opportunities and directions for international service-learning are constantly emerging. One of these is the introduction and promulgation of volunteerism and service-learning itself. Alec Dickson, founder of Voluntary Service Overseas, called this the cascade effect (1994). One of the ways Americans serve abroad lies in the very example of organized volunteer service. People in less mobile and more rural cultures have traditionally and informally helped family, clan, and community in time of need. However, in response to dramatically increased migration between and within nations, nongovernmental agencies and volunteer programs are springing up, organized by local people to address a specific issue in their communities and to meet the needs of those separated from family. International service-learning programs can be designed to introduce or expand the practice of volunteerism. For example, U.S. students assisting in schools may organize local children in the "game" of clearing this neighborhood of trash and with the intent of leaving a structure in place so that the effort continues when students leave. They may teach a skill and ask that their pupils teach it to others. They may help newly created local agencies to develop volunteer programs.

In addition to spreading the concept and practice of volunteerism, it is encouraging that universities that have served as partner institutions for international service-learning programs have begun to implement service-learning for their own students. Universities in Jamaica, Ecuador, France, England, Scotland, and the Philippines have made service-learning an integral part of their curriculum as a direct result of working with the International Partnership. U.S. universities and organizations should share service-learning information with their overseas partners, invite them to participate in professional development opportunities, and conduct workshops in host countries (see Chapter Three for a description of innovative service-learning partnerships being developed in South Africa).

Another opportunity for international service-learning lies in creating new ways for students from many nations to learn and serve together. Under the sponsorship of the Henry Luce Foundation, the International Partnership for Service-Learning offers a program in the Philippines for students from the United States and nine Asian nations. Together they study at the host college, Trinity College of Quezon City; serve in agencies in Manila; and live together on the college campus. They take two academic courses: Contemporary Social Issues of the Philippines and Major Asian Religions: Theologies of Service. The service they perform is intense and often disturbing because of the extent of the need the students encounter. To process their questions and give them a chance to explore their reactions, faculty provide both highly structured and informal opportunities for the students to discuss their varying cultural assumptions, as well as to discover the ideas and values they have in common. They gain knowledge not only of their host nation and of themselves but about their fellow students and their nations, thereby making it an even richer experience. By the end of the program, they have proved that they can work collaboratively with others of widely different backgrounds and cultures, and they correctly view themselves as internationalists.

Yet another new direction, perhaps even more difficult than creating programs for students from many nations, is organizing programs that require the cooperation of institutions of higher education in more than two nations. Bilateral international agreements abound in higher education, as two universities agree to exchange students for study, and sometimes for service-learning. Just as corporations and international relief and development organizations have learned to move goods and people around the world, so higher education must follow suit if it is to educate students about our global society. Colleges and universities must prepare their students to work in, manage, and develop multinational programs whether they plan careers in business, government, education, or the helping professions. Thus, institutions of higher education must themselves model what it means to work in and with those from many nations. One example of such a program is the master's degree in international service designed and organized by the International Partnership for Service-Learning, in which three universities in three different nations cooperate, giving one another full faith and recognition of the academic work. In this program, students select for the first semester either Mexico or Jamaica. There they engage in community service and academic studies. For the second semester, the students go to England, where they continue their studies at the partner university, serve in a London agency, complete the thesis that was begun in the first semester, and receive their degree. All parties have agreed upon the coherent and coordinated curriculum, recognize the academic qualifications of the other partners, and have approved the degree program at their institutions.

Conclusion

Is international service-learning worth the effort? No matter who administers the program, significant amounts of energy, time, and resources are required. As in any all service-learning partnership, harm rather than good can result if all parties involved do not act in the spirit of equality, reciprocity, and mutuality. This is even more true of international partnerships because partners are often viewed as representatives of their nation and culture.

However, when programs are conceived and implemented as advised in this chapter, the benefits are often profound. If the program is of sufficient length and depth and if the students move beyond the circle of their peers to interact substantially with the staff and clients of the agency, over time they inevitably gain an enormous respect for the people with whom they are living and serving and from whom they are learning. They ask themselves if they would have the strength of character to cope with the problems faced by the host culture, the agency, and its clients. The people served are affirmed and ennobled as these university students convey day by day, in small but unmistakable ways, the respect that comes not from an abstract ideology but from genuine encounters.

International service-learning, then, is more than just another program. It validates the reality that there are valuable epistemologies beyond those found in the traditional academic disciplines. It makes concrete the mission of higher education to widen our horizons and to lead us beyond ourselves toward actively addressing human needs and the pressing issues faced by communities, nations, and the world. At its best, international service-learning demonstrates that it is possible to be at one with others in a common task despite apparent and real differences. As the director of Children International of Ecuador wrote of the service-learning students whom he has directed for more than a decade, "These one hundred young men and women worked directly, sometimes in a one on one relationship, with children that could be correctly considered to be the poorest of the poor. Soon after this encounter, we found that they became one unit of friendship and love, one unit no longer of a first world volunteer and a third world needy child; they became a unit of partners with trust between them, with credibility in their sincerity. They, both service-learning students and the children, were really the new members of a world anew" (Mariduena, 1998, p. 17).

References

Berry, H. A., and Chisholm, L. A. *How to Serve and Learn Abroad Effectively: Students Tell Students.* New York: International Partnership for Service-Learning, 1992.

Berry, H. A., and Chisholm, L. A. *Service-Learning in Higher Education Around the World: An Initial Look.* New York: International Partnership for Service-Learning, 1999.

Dickson, A. "Education for Real." Presentation at the International Partnership for Service-Learning Conference, Washington, D.C., Mar. 1994.

Hathaway, J. "Esperar: v.1. To hope 2. To wait (for)." *Action/Reflection* (Fall 1990), 6–7.

Higher Education Consortium for Urban Affairs. *Learning for Life: Off-Campus Study Program Catalog 2001–2002.* St. Paul, Minn.: HECUA, 2001.

International Partnership for Service-Learning. [www.ipsl.org]. 2001.

Mariduena, V. "International Service-Learning: Constructing the World Anew." *Papers and Proceedings from Wingspread.* New York: International Partnership for Service-Learning, May 1998.

Chapter Fourteen

Civic Renewal

A Powerful Framework for Advancing Service-Learning

Elizabeth Hollander and Matthew Hartley

Anyone who has championed change at a college or university understands that powerful dynamics sustain the status quo in these complex organizations. The diffusion of power stymies any one group attempting to unilaterally advance a broad-based initiative. The diffusion of attention—the multiplicity of interests that compete for the time and energy of various internal constituents—inhibit consensus building and often slow change to a glacial pace.

Given this context, the sweep of service-learning across the landscape of higher education must be recognized as a triumph. The success of service-learning is, in our view, testament to the extraordinary ability of its proponents to build partnerships. We have forged partnerships across disciplinary and divisional lines on our own campuses. We have also reached out beyond local contexts and linked our efforts, forging a wider movement. Finally, we have found many allies outside the academy. National associations, foundations, and the government have all been key partners in this effort. They have disseminated information, provided resources, engaged us in critical conversations, and made visible the magnitude of our efforts. These external partnerships are vital to the long-term survival and growth of service-learning.

More recently, a new, broader agenda—civic renewal—has captured the attention of these partners. We contend that many of our future opportunities for partnering will rest on our ability to link our efforts to the civic renewal agenda. Of course, the aims of civic renewal and service-learning are not identical. Civic renewal aspires to the wholesale revitalization of our democracy through the re-animation of the citizenry to participate with increased vigor in our democratic institutions. While many service-learning programs emphasize civic responsibility and democratic participation, others are appropriately grounded in missions such as spirituality, social justice, leadership development, multicultural education, practical application of academic course content, or enhancing critical thinking and problem-solving abilities (Jacoby, 1996).

Nevertheless, service-learning is positioned to play a major role in advancing civic renewal in higher education, and affiliation with civic renewal can significantly strengthen service-learning. In this chapter we describe the history, status, and future of partnerships among the networks supporting civic renewal (including service-learning) and argue that together these reform efforts can refocus the academy's attention on its highest purpose—the nurturing of our democracy and the renewing of our communities. In particular, we also examine the relationship between service-learning and the civic renewal movement in higher education and the potential of this relationship to advance service-learning on our campuses.

Civic Renewal as a Social Movement

Before we describe how service-learning might fit into a broader civic renewal movement, it will be useful to briefly discuss civic renewal as a social movement. Movements are sustained efforts made by a loose alliance of people whose purpose is either to promote or to block social change. Mario Diani of Milan's Bocconi University identifies three characteristics common to all such collective efforts: social movements arise to address societal problems, members are bound by a "shared set of beliefs and a sense of belongingness," and movements consist of "networks of informal interaction" (Diani, 1992, p. 7). In our view, the collective civic renewal efforts possess all these characteristics and clearly constitute a movement (Hollander and Hartley, 2000). Although each of the above elements is important, we will focus most of our attention on the third: defining the informal networks. It is by examining the nature of these networks, or partnerships, that service-learning's special role in the civic renewal movement becomes most evident.

Need to Address Societal Problems

Discontent is the oxygen that feeds the fires of change. The recognition and articulation of a pressing problem animates change on the organizational level (Kotter, 1996) and in societies (Wallace, 1956). Problems can be framed in various ways. For example, a movement may arise to remedy a particular social ill or political problem. Or a movement may represent the wholesale rejection of an entire sociocultural system (Wallace, 1956). Similar concerns animated civic renewal and service-learning in the 1980s, both of which grew out of a pervasive sense that individualism had trumped community. Personal success, usually defined in terms of wealth, was exalted to unprecedented and dizzying heights. The media pointed to the self-absorption and materialism of youth. Indeed, the evidence suggests that the faith of both youth and adults in our political system had ebbed substantially (Pitkin, 1981). In a study of college freshmen, one in four indicated that community involvement was "very important," while eight in ten identified financial success as a priority (Astin and others, 1988). Government's capacity to address social problems was under widespread attack. Low voting rates cheapened our elections (Delli Carpini and Keeter, 1996). Putnam's research showed that participation in voluntary associations declined dangerously during this decade, and even beyond (1995). Many measures of collective political participation revealed deep declines, including attending a rally or speech (off 36 percent between 1973 and 1993), attending a meeting on town or school affairs (off 39 percent), or working for a political party (off 56 percent) (Putnam, 1996). Putnam concluded that "the weight of available evidence confirms that Americans today are less significantly engaged with their communities than was true a generation ago" (1996, p. 360). These symptoms pointed to a deep-seated malaise that could threaten the health and vitality of our democracy. In response, some called for efforts to renew those "habits of the heart" that link individuals with the community (Bellah and others, 1985, p. 275).

Higher education was seen as an important potential agent of change. A Carnegie report published in 1985 concluded: "If there is a crisis in education in the United States today, it is less that test scores have declined than it is that we have failed to provide the education for citizenship that is still the most important responsibility of the nation's schools and colleges" (Ehrlich, 2000, p. 3). It was in this environment, and partly in response to these concerns, that higher education's civic renewal efforts began to emerge. Both Campus Compact and the Campus Outreach Opportunity League (COOL) were founded in 1985. Each stressed the importance of student volunteer engagement. Campus Compact sought to involve college presidents in addressing the need to develop the skills and habits of citizenship; COOL targeted students and gave them opportunities to express their interest in community service.

Shared Set of Beliefs and a Sense of Belongingness

Common interests form the basis for coalition building among disparate groups, but shared goals and values must be present to produce the "belongingness" endemic to a movement. Indeed, they are the very glue that holds a movement together. As Melucci points out, "The true bulk of social movement experience has to be found in the cultural sphere: what is challenged is not only the uneven distribution of power and/or economic goods, but socially shared meanings as well, that is the ways of defining and interpreting reality" (Diani, 1992, p. 10).

Fundamentally, what binds civic renewal proponents together is the desire to increase our national capacity to build the commonwealth. It is, quite simply, a resurgence of a potent strain of idealism that has been so central to our experiment in democracy—an attempt to realize the radical vision of an America shaped and governed by an informed and active citizenry. Citizens should know, and be willing and able, to act upon their responsibilities by serving on a jury, debating public policies with rigor but without rancor, holding their elected officials accountable, and even running for office themselves. The civic renewal movement is based on the understanding promulgated by de Tocqueville in *Democracy in America,* originally published in 1831, that the government is not "them" but "us" and functions best when citizens "guide and assist" in determining and carrying out public policy (de Tocqueville, 1956). The latter can be seen in acts such as community policing, serving on a school or planning board or block association, or working to sustain the myriad nonprofit associations that improve the quality of American life and seek to influence public policy.

As discussed earlier, mounting concern about disengagement and the decline in civic participation has animated the movement. A number of sociologists, political scientists, and other scholars—notably, Benjamin Barber, Robert Bellah, Michael Delli Carpini, Jean Elshtain, and Amitai Etzioni—have focused on various aspects of social capital, including associational life, habits of citizenship, the strength of the third sector, degrees of civility, and levels of direct participation in voting. All have arrived at the conclusion, eloquently stated in the Nunn-Bennett Commission report, that we have become a "nation of spectators" (National Commission on Civic Renewal, 1999, p. 6).

An integral shared belief of the civic renewal picture is that diverse voices must be intentionally engaged in building our democracy. The United States in the twenty-first century is the great proving ground for the possibility of sustaining a democracy made up of the most disparate groups—by race, ethnicity, country of origin, length of time in the United States—of any nation in the world. A healthy civic life will require citizens who can relate to people different from themselves in part because they have a secure sense of their own ethnic and social identity (Knefelkamp and Schneider, 1997). Thus, the civic renewal movement asks the question, Can our nation reflect our diversity in every aspect of our commonwealth and encourage both minority and immigrant populations to assume their democratic rights and responsibilities?

The great educator John Dewey said that democracy needs to be born in every generation and that education is its midwife (1916). Citizens are not born to know their democratic responsibilities; these responsibilities must be taught to, and learned by, each new generation. Hence, any discussion of civic renewal among its proponents soon turns to education. How does the civic renewal effort, then, reflect itself in higher education? It has expressed itself in a number of movements, which we argue are beginning to coalesce.

Movements as Networks of Informal Interaction

In order to form a movement, likeminded groups or networks must find one another and band together. Diani (1992) notes that elements of a movement often initially operate in isolation, unaware of one another. Only as common interests and ideals bring networks into contact is a movement born. The movement grows to the extent that new partners are identified and coordination is maintained across the disparate networks. The civic renewal movement in higher education is built around several key networks, each of which has its own proponents and a somewhat distinct agenda. Service-learning constitutes but one of these. However, as we shall see, it has the potential of playing a critical role in the overall movement and stands to reap significant benefits from its involvement. The five networks contributing to the civic renewal movement are efforts to promote diversity, campus/community partnerships, student voter registration and public policy engagement, character education and moral development, and service-learning. Each of these networks, in turn, consists of coalitions of higher education institutions, national associations, government, and foundations.

Starting in the 1960s, efforts to promote diversity have become an increasingly influential catalyst for change on college campuses. Building on the impetus provided by the civil rights movement, the academy has sought to increase diversity in its students, its faculty, and its curricular offerings. Much of that effort has taken place on individual campuses and has not had a particularly civic framework. However, since 1989 the Association of American Colleges and Universities (AAC&U) has championed diversity in higher education as an essential dimension of all students' learning in a democratic society. In 1992, AAC&U launched a multiproject initiative, "American Commitments: Diversity, Democracy and Liberal Learning." Supported by major grants from the Ford Foundation, the National Endowment for the Humanities, and the William and Flora Hewlett Foundation, this initiative addresses fundamental questions about effective preparation for a diverse democracy and provides resources for colleges and universities willing to engage those questions as dimensions of institutional mission, campus climate, and curricular focus. Through American

Commitments, AAC&U has three times sponsored Boundaries and Borderlands: The Search for Recognition and Community in America. This intensive ten-day summer institute assists institutions in developing curricula aimed at helping students develop new capacities for democratic citizenship and skills to negotiate multiple communities and commitments in a diverse democracy. In addition, Diversity Web [www.diversityweb.org], an AAC&U- and University of Maryland–sponsored web site designed to share information and highlight best practices in diversity and civic engagement, averages more than 167,000 hits each month. AAC&U also produces *Diversity Digest*, a quarterly that highlights the best institutional practices and research on diversity, civic engagement, and learning, and coaches higher education leaders on ways to help the public understand the significance of campus work on diversity. It is sent without charge to fourteen thousand faculty and administrators. Specifically linking diversity to service-learning, *Integrating Service-Learning and Multicultural Education in Colleges and Universities* by Carolyn O'Grady was published in 2000.

The second network contributing to the civic renewal movement consists of colleges and universities engaged in community partnerships. These institutions are putting into practice the civic purpose articulated in almost every college and university mission statement. They acknowledge that as institutions with vast intellectual resources, their civic responsibility requires that they use these resources on behalf of the communities in which they reside. Ernest Boyer describes this responsibility as the scholarship of engagement: "The scholarship of engagement means connecting the rich resources of the university to our most pressing social, civic, and ethical problems . . . [and] creating a special climate in which the academic and civic culture communicate more creatively with each other" (Thomas, 2000, p. 64). Thomas notes that colleges and universities fulfill Boyer's vision when they use "an integrated approach to fostering students' citizenship skills through both educational and co-curricular programs and activities and conscious modeling of good institutional citizenship through external partnerships and activities" (p. 66). Other institutional indicators of an engaged campus include a civic mission, committed leadership, engaged pedagogies, and infrastructure to support faculty and student engagement and community partnerships (Hollander, Saltmarsh, and Zlotkowski, 2001). There are now many campus-community partnerships across the length and breadth of American higher education (Thomas, 2000). The U.S. Department of Housing and Urban Development and associations including the Council of Independent Colleges, the National Society for Experiential Education, the National Association of State Universities and Land-Grant Colleges, the New England Resource Center for Higher Education, the American Association of State Colleges and Universities, and Campus Compact have developed networks of institutions that have partnered with communities.

The third network consists of initiatives to sharpen the political skills of students and to encourage that most fundamental of civic acts, voting. The National Association of Independent Colleges and Universities (NAICU), under the leadership of David Warren, has been the lead organizer of higher education efforts to promote student voter registration. To accomplish this aim, they have provided a tool kit for campuses during the last two national elections regarding student voter registration and voting. They also caused a regulation to be added to the last federal bill supporting higher education that requires institutions to provide voter registration forms to all enrolled students.

In the 2000 national election, there was a major effort on the part of many higher education associations, in partnership with other organizations such as Project Vote Smart and the Youth Vote Coalition, to increase the participation of college students in the election. Campus Compact mounted a web site, shared the NAICU tool kit with all of its member campuses, and regularly urged its presidential members to emphasize voter participation.

A related effort has been undertaken by the Council on Public Policy Education, supported by the Kettering Foundation and the Pew Charitable Trusts. The project involves a network of approximately thirty universities and is aimed at helping students express their political will. Groups engage in discussion about matters of public policy, in a way that is reminiscent of the traditional New England town meeting, to cultivate students' skills in public debate and deliberation (Matthews, 1998).

Character education and moral-ethical development is the focus of the fourth network. A new online publication, the *Journal of College and Character* edited by Jon Dalton of Florida State University, is a visible outlet for this network, which is supported by the Templeton Foundation [http://collegevalues.org/]. It is no accident that two vocal proponents of civic education and service-learning, Thomas Ehrlich and Elizabeth Hollander, have been asked to serve on the journal's board of advisers. The Templeton Foundation also publishes a directory of colleges that have been selected for notable activities promoting student character development. These colleges are selected on the basis of their ability to "inspire students to develop and strengthen their moral reasoning skills . . . encourage their spiritual growth and moral values . . . and provide community-building experiences" (Templeton Foundation, 1997). The link to civic renewal is in the emphasis on the development of moral leadership skills on behalf of the common good. The Templeton guide cites the following quote from Benjamin Franklin: "Nothing is more important for the public wealth than to form and train youth in wisdom and virtue. Only a virtuous people are capable of freedom" (p. xi).

Finally, we turn to service-learning. Service-learning has greatly contributed to civic renewal efforts. In part this is because of the shared goals, values, and beliefs of those pursuing civic renewal and service-learning, including engagement in the community, concern for others, and individual and collective efforts on behalf of the common good. Stanton, Giles, and Cruz point out that from its inception, service-learning's proponents have pursued three agendas: service to society, social justice, and democratic education (1999). One of the founding purposes of Campus Compact was to promote student engagement in public issues and community service to "develop the skills and habits of citizenship" [http://www.compact.org/about/#Anchor-Our-6640]. In the late 1980s and early 1990s the National Society for Experiential Education gathered educational leaders to define principles and research needs of service-learning. The first of the ten *Principles of Good Practice for Combining Service and Learning* speaks directly to engaging people in "responsible and challenging actions for the common good" (Porter Honnet and Poulsen, 1989). The *Research Agenda for Combining Service and Learning in the 1990s* includes questions on the effects of service-learning on participants as citizens, how service-learning contributes to the development of democratic community, and the extent to which service-learning results in long-term habits of participation in the community (Giles, Porter Honnet, and Migliore, 1991). This focus on civic engagement has remained prominent. Howard (1993) points out that one of the most important aspects of service-learning is that it "engages students in service to the community and contributes to the development of students' civic ethic" (p. 3).

The service-learning network is extensive and highly organized. The variety and volume of its initiatives are considerable. A number of national organizations, including Campus Compact, the American Association of Community Colleges, the American Association of Higher Education, the Council of Independent Colleges, and the National Society for Experiential Education support service-learning by sponsoring hundreds of training and development opportunities each year. The Campus Compact and AAHE web sites list a plethora of these opportunities. AAHE and Campus Compact have also formed a trained cadre of tenured faculty from a variety of disciplines who serve as a consulting corps to institutions seeking to develop their service-learning programs.

Increasingly sophisticated training is now being offered as service-learning programs initiate more and more complex community initiatives. Campus Compact, its twenty-seven affiliated state offices, and its center for community colleges use a service-learning pyramid to categorize campuses at introductory, intermediate, and advanced levels so that appropriate assistance can be targeted for them [www.compact.org]. The New England Resource Center for Higher Education (NERCHE) has also identified twenty-six campuses that are altering tenure and promotion guidelines to recognize service-learning and civic engagement (see [http://www.compact.org/advancedtoolkit/faculty.html] for details).

Service-learning proponents have made inroads with a number of disciplinary associations in encouraging them to promote service-learning (Zlotkowski, 2000). The Community-Campus Partnerships for Health is a particularly active group committed to community activism around issues of health. The National Communications Association has partnered with the Southern Poverty Law Center in promoting a "teaching tolerance" curriculum. The American Political Science Association (APSA) included a special section in its journal, *P.S.*, with articles on the practice of service-learning and the declines in college student civic engagement.

But how exactly can the service-learning network integrate its efforts with the civic renewal movement? Before we answer that we must first describe the state of the civic renewal movement itself.

The State of the Civic Renewal Movement

In surveying the landscape of civic renewal in 1999, we described it as a "prairie with a lot of unconnected silos which could, if brought together, produce a rich feed for the civic renewal movement" (Hollander and Hartley, 2000, p. 351). Since that time, considerable progress has been made in linking efforts within higher education. Indeed, with the advantage of hindsight, we see that much of the current momentum for civic renewal stems from the creation of the Forum on Higher Education and Democracy in 1998 under the leadership of Thomas Ehrlich and Zelda Gamson. On June 18–20, 1998, the forum sponsored a leadership conference at Florida State University on the subject of civic renewal. Attached to the annual Florida State conference on college and character, it gathered several hundred leaders. It became clear that literally hundreds of disparate programs aimed at civic renewal were under way, but, although widespread, they were also largely uncoordinated. It was clear that the contours of this movement needed to be explored and its guiding principles defined. This consensus set in motion a number of efforts.

To describe the current state of affairs, *Civic Responsibility and Higher Education* (Ehrlich, 2000) describes civic renewal efforts in every sector of higher education. In 1999, Campus Compact began gathering information on civic education initiatives as well. Its web site [www.compact.org/mapping] offers a detailed listing including nineteen distinct civic renewal efforts sponsored by associations, twenty-six curricular reform efforts, and ten partnerships between K–12 and higher education.

To begin the process of framing a common understanding of what these efforts aim to achieve, two manifestoes were written and widely circulated. The *Wingspread Declaration on the Civic Responsibility of Research Universities* (Boyte and Hollander, 1999) was the outcome of several meetings convened by Barry Checkoway of the University of Michigan during 1998–99. The declaration calls upon higher education to help revitalize American democracy by encouraging students to become engaged in their communities, supporting the scholarship of engagement, and involving the academy in community building. In ringing terms, it set out the following challenge:

> As agents of the democracy, colleges and universities will consciously prepare a next generation of involved citizens reflecting the full and immensely varied cultural and economic mix of America, by creating innumerable opportunities for them to be in college and to do the work of citizenship. This means conceiving of institutions of higher learning as vital, living cultures, not simply an aggregation of discrete units in competition with each other. The public dimensions of our common cultures require intense and self-conscious attention. Opportunities for students, faculty, staff, and administrators to use their many talents for the greater good must once again pervade every aspect of our work [Boyte and Hollander, 1999].

The second manifesto was the *Presidents' Declaration on the Civic Responsibility of Higher Education,* put forth at a joint meeting of the American Council on Education (ACE) and Campus Compact at the Aspen Institute in July 1999 (Campus Compact, 1999). The document asked college and university presidents to commit themselves publicly to the idea that higher education is a primary architect and agent of our democracy. As such, colleges and universities need to educate students for active citizenship and to be active institutional citizens within their own communities. By the spring of 2001, more than four hundred college and university presidents had joined the effort as signatories of the declaration.

After the issuing of these manifestos, efforts were made to form a collaborative of national higher education associations. The leaders were ACE, AAHE, Campus Compact, AAC&U, and APSA. However, after several meetings devoted to exchanging information and agreeing to a title, the Higher Education Collaborative for Democratic Engagement, little was accomplished beyond mounting a web site at AAC&U [http://www.aacu-edu.org/KnowNet/civic. htm]. The strands of the movement have been woven together more informally by the efforts of national leaders like Thomas Ehrlich, who is consistently issuing the call for the civic engagement of higher education through his roles as senior fellow at the Carnegie

Foundation for the Advancement of Teaching, chair of the board of AAHE, and member of the policy committee of Campus Compact and of the board of the Center for Civic Education in California. Other faculty leaders who are present in multiple networks include Harry Boyte of the University of Minnesota, Barry Checkoway of the University of Michigan, Alexander Astin of the Higher Education Research Institute (HERI) at the University of California–Los Angeles, Ira Harkavy of the University of Pennsylvania, David Cox of the University of Dayton, and William A. Galston and Benjamin Barber of the University of Maryland. Galston and Barber, together with University of Maryland colleagues, have created the Democracy Collaborative, which seeks to become a global nonprofit institute committed to strengthening democracy and civil society locally, nationally, and globally. In the association and government worlds, Elizabeth Hollander, Judith Ramaley of the National Science Foundation and current board chair of Campus Compact, Barbara Holland of the U.S. Department of Housing and Urban Development's Office of Community-University Partnerships, Deborah Hirsch of NERCHE, Carol Schneider of AAC&U, and Yolanda Moses of AAHE also constantly connect disparate efforts related to civic renewal.

Service-Learning in the Context of Civic Renewal

We believe that both service-learning and civic renewal stand to benefit from a close association. Service-learning encourages behaviors that are consonant with civic renewal. A longitudinal study conducted by HERI compared students who were engaged in service with those who were not, using thirty-five outcome measures, including civic values. In describing the study, Astin noted, "What was especially remarkable about the findings was that every one of the thirty-five student outcomes was positively influenced by service participation" (1997, p. 10). Service-learning promotes students' ability and willingness to act on behalf of the common good, advances multicultural understanding, and promotes willingness to work with others (Astin, Sax, and Avalos, 1996). It also improves students' academic performance and skills acquisition (Astin, Vogelgesang, Ikeda, and Yee, 2000; Billig, 2000; Eyler and Giles, 1999). It is a powerful shaper of students' lives, particularly when the service is coupled with purposeful reflection and closely related to course content (Eyler and Giles, 1999).

Indeed, very recently, Lori Vogelgesang at HERI has discovered a correlation between college student engagement in service-learning and voting. "In plain language, even after taking into account many student and some institutional characteristics, those students who participated in community service were more likely than non-service participants to say they voted in a state or national election during college. Service-learning participants were even more likely than community service participants to have voted" (2001).

Despite these positive indicators, service-learning, at least as it is practiced now, has *not* resulted in a more robust interest in public affairs in college students (Sax, Astin, Korn, and Mahoney, 2000; Mellman Group, 2000; National Association of Secretaries of State, 1999; Roper Starch Worldwide, 2000; Institute of Politics, 2000). Among many college students, there is rampant cynicism about whether systemic change is possible and a deep distaste for national politics. Thus, increasing numbers of students turn to direct action through community service where they believe they can get a more tangible, immediate return for their efforts. But we are not, and should not be, satisfied with that response.

It must be said that many service-learning programs came into existence primarily to promote direct service, which was often framed as encouraging acts of charity and expanding students' capacity for compassion. Although the civic renewal movement has led to many exemplary service-learning programs that educate students about the political elements of social problems and how to effect systematic change through democratic participation and policy making, service-learning continues to encourage the performance of individual ameliorative acts (Stanton, Giles, and Cruz, 1999). Promoting compassion is therefore a distinct, and in our view, critically important element of service-learning—one that is perhaps less emphasized in civic education. Indeed, young people would never have encountered "the other America" had they not done so through service-learning. These personal encounters across socioeconomic lines are essential to those who aspire to build American democracy.

We believe that the twenty-first-century challenge confronting service-learning is whether service-learning can enable students to overcome their cynicism and distaste for politics about systematic change *and* to respond directly to particular community needs. The honest answer is that we do not yet know. We do know that without political involvement and national policy development there is little hope that substantive, lasting change will be possible. Finding the answer requires a shift in service-learning research. Walker (2000) points out that most service-learning research does not define citizenship in these terms and, as a result, we cannot determine its impact in these areas.

It has become clear that service-learning advocates have powerful reasons to embrace civic renewal and to become more deeply involved in the movement. The ability of civic renewal to catch the attention of a broad array of leaders of higher education institutions has been clearly demonstrated. The *Presidents' Declaration on the Civic Responsibility of Higher Education* touched a deep chord among college presidents. Their enthusiasm is reflected not only in the numbers who have signed on but also in their willingness to attend public signing ceremonies organized by the state Compacts and by the extraordinary growth in Campus Compact membership since the declaration was issued. Presidents are excited by its lofty aims. The declaration put their leadership to support civic engagement and service-learning in the context of addressing our most pressing national needs. The signatories no longer view service-learning as simply an experimental pedagogy but rather as a building block of democracy.

The civic renewal framework also provides an opportunity to link college and university service-learning programs with civic education at the K–12 level. William Galston, staff director of the Nunn-Bennett Commission, has started a new organization called the National Association for Civic Education, which   promotes lifelong civic education. In July 2001, Campus Compact and the Compact for Learning and Citizenship organized an Educational Leadership Colloquium. Fueled by a general concern about the need to reassert the civic mission of education, this meeting brought together teams of college presidents, chief state school officers, school superintendents, and state Compact directors to develop a statement of shared responsibility for providing lifelong civic education. Teams also developed action plans for realizing this responsibility in their states.

Civic renewal also provides a powerful opportunity for service-learning educators to embed service-learning in the extensive work going on to "reinvent" democracy at the local level. Leaders in the local government and nonprofit sectors, such as those involved with the National Civic League, are promoting and documenting the widespread interest in, and power of, citizen engagement at the local level (Sirianni and Friedland, 2001). Examples are community policing, the sustainable communities movement, locally based environmental efforts, and parental involvement in school governance. The grass-roots movement to reengage citizens in community building has been going on for at least two decades. We believe that when successful, such efforts serve as a powerful antidote to the cynicism about national politics and the possibilities for citizen influence. Because most students involved in service-learning provide their service at the most local level, educators can consciously expose them to local democracy building and then help them to think more positively about both political engagement and policy making at higher levels.

On a merely pragmatic level, foundation and government supporters of service-learning are shifting their focus to advancing civic engagement. Their concern is the result of a series of studies over the last few years that document the extensive interest of college students in volunteer service combined with their deep distaste for national politics, disinterest in public affairs, and apathy toward exercising their right to vote (Astin, Vogelgesang, Ikeda, and Yee, 2000; Mellman Group, 2000; National Association of Secretaries of State, 1999; Roper Starch Worldwide, 2000; Institute of Politics, 2000). Examples of foundation interest include new youth civic engagement initiatives at the Pew Charitable Trusts and the Carnegie Corporation of New York. In addition, the Grantmaker Forum on Community and National Service initiated a series of dialogues on the relationship of service to civic engagement at their 2000 annual meeting and continue to address the issue in their strategic plan and subsequent meetings.

In 2000, the Corporation for National and Community Service's Learn and Serve America grant program began to look with particular favor upon those proposals that emphasized civic education in addition to service-learning. This is a notable and even surprising development in an agency that prohibits AmeriCorps members from engaging in voter registration activities.

A major potential benefit of embracing civic renewal is the influence it is likely to have on sustaining and increasing the quality and impact of service-learning. In our view, the future of service-learning depends upon demonstrating significant measurable positive outcomes for students and communities. The civic renewal frame helps us to do that because it demands outcomes greater and more significant than student compassion and is not satisfied with simply counting student hours spent in the community. Education for civic engagement provides structured, intentional ways to encourage students to think more systemically about how social policy is made and how to bring about social change. It also reinforces the importance of not merely *serving* the community but *working with* the community to develop its own capacity to improve itself. The democracy-building skills promoted by civic renewal are also closely aligned with many desired outcomes of undergraduate education: critical thinking, ability to articulate a point of view in written and oral form, exercising moral and ethical judgment, and leadership development. Although many of these goals may already be shared by service-learning proponents, the civic framework reinforces them and may help us to document them more systematically.

Although college faculty are as adverse to politics as any other profession, faculty in some institutions have a long and deep tradition of educating students for civic leadership (Hollander, Saltmarsh, and Zlotkowski, 2001). There is also current evidence of growing faculty interest in the civic education agenda. According to the 1998–99 *Chronicle of Higher Education* Survey of the Attitudes and Activities of Full-Time Faculty Members, the respondents noted four goals for undergraduate students as essential or very important: "prepare students for responsible citizenship" (60.0 percent), "enhance students' knowledge of and appreciation for other racial/ethnic groups" (57.8 percent), "develop moral character" (57.5 percent), and "instill in students a commitment to community service" (36.2 percent) *(Chronicle of Higher Education, 2001, p. A29)*. Galston and his colleagues at the University of Maryland received a $4.57 million grant from the Pew Charitable Trusts in 2001 to create the Center for Information and Research on Civic Learning and Engagement, a new center that will explore the causes of civic disengagement among youth as well as factors and initiatives that can encourage their civic engagement. There are faculty who are concerned that they do not know how to serve the community and are afraid that service-learning may devolve into second-rate social work but are, indeed, comfortable with, and even enthusiastic about, using their knowledge to effect public policy (Heffernan, 2001). Faculty in some faith-based institutions have pushed service-learning into the more politically active agenda of social justice.

Service-learning advocates hope that placing service-learning in the civic renewal framework will attract more faculty to service-learning. Campus Compact provides additional technical assistance to faculty through a series of activities, including a new book, *Fundamentals of Service-Learning Course Construction*, that contains examples of course syllabi with a civic dimension (Heffernan, 2001). Recently published is another book by Richard Battistoni of Providence College and the Pew Charitable Trusts, entitled *Civic Engagement Across the Curriculum: A Resource Book for Service-Learning Faculty in All Disciplines* (Battistoni, 2002). These volumes are disseminated through faculty workshops conducted by national and state Compacts and the Campus Compact–AAHE consulting corps. In addition, the American Association of University Professors recently published an entire issue of *Academe* on the civic responsibility of higher education (July–August 2000).

Service-learning has much to bring to the civic renewal movement. There is a well-articulated body of knowledge about service-learning pedagogy and practice. An outstanding example is the AAHE-sponsored series on service-learning in the disciplines, eighteen monographs developed under the editorial leadership of Edward Zlotkowski. Campus Compact's *Introduction to Service-Learning Toolkit* (2000) is a respected and widely used reference. A rich body of literature supports our work and provides thoughtful explanations of how responsibility to community can be expressed programmatically (Jacoby, 1996; Eyler and Giles, 1999; Heffernan, 2001). The *Michigan Journal of Community Service Learning* recently expanded from one to two issues per year. A new publication, the *Compact Reader*, disseminates thoughtful articles about the intersection of service-learning and civic engagement. Journals such as *Academe* and *About Campus* regularly feature articles on service-learning.

Service-learning provides the clearest example of how students can "practice" civic engagement. Campus Compact has identified service-learning courses that act consciously as "civic bridges" and teach the skills of advocacy, public policy development, and the importance of civic acts like responding to the census and voter registration (Heffernan, 2001, p. 111). There are countless courses embedded in a variety of disciplines that make clear to students how academic knowledge can be used to address serious social problems. More and more courses focus specifically on the knowledge and skills required for active participation in a democratic society. Heffernan (2001) provides descriptions of several outstanding examples, including The Individual and Community in Democratic America, Northeastern University; The Civic Community: Theory and Practice, Rutgers University; The Democracy Seminar: The Politics of Community Action, Swarthmore College; and Multiculturalism and Ethnicity in Education, Trinity College.

Of course, there are potential dangers that come with linking service-learning and civic renewal. The service-learning movement has clear bipartisan support. That support has allowed the Corporation for National and Community Service to survive changes in political leadership and to continue to provide significant funding to colleges and universities. However, if civic renewal were to be viewed as tied to one political agenda over another, service-learning's bipartisan approval could be threatened. In addition, certain goals of service-learning may not be directly related to civic renewal. As we have mentioned, the goals of service-learning may appropriately focus primarily on academic, interpersonal, or spiritual—even religious—development in certain institutional settings. The challenge is to value what each movement can bring to the other without insisting that their aims be identical.

Practical Suggestions for Using the Civic Frame to Advance Service-Learning

Aligning service-learning with civic renewal provides opportunities to advance service-learning both within institutions and beyond. Several practical suggestions are offered here.

Tying service-learning to the civic renewal agenda can help secure the support of presidents for service-learning. One indication of the extent of presidential interest in, and commitment to, civic renewal is the signing of the *President's Declaration on the Civic Responsibility of Higher Education* (Campus Compact, 1999) by 430 presidents of all types of institutions. Its comprehensive list of questions regarding institutional civic responsibility has prompted many campuswide conversations and assessments. Such activities offer excellent means for raising the visibility and understanding of service-learning. Presidents and other institutional leaders are constantly queried by external constituents about how their institutions are addressing the needs of the community. Service-learning activities represent a concrete and visible example of civic engagement. However, it is critical that service-learning proponents regularly convey information about the process and impacts of service-learning to the president and his or her key advisers. By framing service-learning as civic engagement, service-learning advocates can help presidents understand that service-learning is much more than a classroom or cocurricular activity that enhances student learning and development.

Legislators, government officials, foundation officers, and community leaders share widespread concern over the diminishing level of civic engagement. Like academic leaders, these important higher-education stakeholders may not understand what service-learning is or how it can positively affect students' understanding of, and participation in, civic activities. It is important to seize this opportunity to help these crucial stakeholders appreciate service-learning as a force for civic renewal. Similarly, trustees, alumni, and funders should be included in efforts to showcase the benefits of service-learning and its role in civic education.

Another powerful use of the civic framework is to increase faculty awareness of, and involvement in, service-learning. Faculty using service-learning pedagogy are often key participants in institutional conversations about and self-assessments of civic engagement. Through their participation, their academic and community leadership is often recognized in new ways. In addition, placing service-learning in the civic frame may open the thinking of other faculty about how they might add a civic dimension to their own work. Using the language of civic engagement rather than the language of service-learning is helpful to faculty in disciplines other than the social sciences in conceptualizing, for example, the potential civic dimensions of their courses. For some faculty, service-learning may simply conjure up images of students working in soup kitchens. Using the civic framework in faculty development workshops can introduce faculty to service-learning in ways that seem more logical for their disciplines.

The civic framework is also useful in faculty development for those already engaged in service-learning. Campus Compact's *Fundamentals of Service-Learning Course Construction* (Heffernan, 2001) encourages faculty to consider their intended outcomes from service-learning, including their students' development of civic skills. This has proved to be the basis for very rich conversations about the aims of service-learning programs and courses. Faculty are intrigued with working with students to enable them to see connections between their service and their roles as citizens. For example, organizing opportunities for students to reflect on their service-learning experiences with the community leaders and members with whom they have worked can increase their understanding of the relationship of their service to larger public issues.

Sharing the studies about the disengagement of young people with students involved in service-learning can provide the basis for a very lively and useful dialogue. Service-learning educators are concerned that students may view participation in service activities as an appropriate and effective substitution for civic or political engagement. Encouraging students to consider to what extent and why this is the case and the potential ramifications is an important topic for reflection. Campus Compact did this with a nationally gathered group of students in April 2001 and learned a lot about how students see their own civic development and how they define engagement. One very interesting finding was that these students saw their service as *alternative politics,* not as an alternative *to* politics: "Participation in public and community service work is a form of *unconventional* political activity that can lead to social change, in which participants work outside of (primarily government) institutions; and service politics is the means through which students can move from engaged service to political engagement" (Campus Compact, 2001, p. 1).

Conclusion

Service-learning's growth has in no small part been a result of its ability to build partnerships. Building partnerships within the concept of the civic renewal movement in higher education presents an exciting opportunity for service-learning to grow in quality, impact, and longevity. Recent calls by proponents of service-learning to move beyond individual acts of charity to systemically working for social justice are consonant with civic renewal. The challenge will be to seize this opportunity and to use it both to improve our own practice and to drive notions of community and civic engagement deeper into the heart of higher education.

Service-learning is already one of the most important strategies for realizing the ideal of an engaged campus. As we embark on efforts to frame service-learning as civic renewal, we will need to carefully consider the implications of our work. For example, when does education about a social issue become lobbying for a particular point of view or political stance? Administrators who seek to promote service-learning as civic engagement will also be called upon to express the civic behaviors they seek to instill in their students through the policies and structures of their own institutions. We must welcome these challenges. Indeed, this kind of critical reflection can serve to reinvigorate our movements. What better way of reasserting the role of service-learning in higher education than by dedicating it to the purpose of renewing our democracy?

References

Academe, 2000, *86*(4).

Astin, A. W. "Liberal Education and Democracy: The Case for Pragmatism." *Liberal Education*, 1997, *83*(4), 4–15.

Astin, A. W., Sax, L. J., and Avalos, J. *Long-Term Effects of Volunteerism During the Undergraduate Years.* Los Angeles: University of California–Los Angeles, Higher Education Research Institute, 1996.

Astin, A. W., Vogelgesang, L., Ikeda, E., and Yee, J. *How Service Learning Affects Students.* Los Angeles: University of California–Los Angeles, Higher Education Research Institute, 2000.

Astin, A. W., and others. *The American Freshmen: National Norms for 1988.* Los Angeles: University of California–Los Angeles, Higher Education Research Institute, 1988.

Battistoni, R. M. *Civic Engagement Across the Curriculum: A Resource Book for Service-Learning Faculty in All Disciplines.* Providence, R.I.: Campus Compact, 2002.

Bellah, R. N., and others. *Habits of the Heart.* Berkeley: University of California Press, 1985.

Billig, S. "The Impacts of Service-Learning on Youth, Schools and Communities: Research on K–12 School-Based Service-Learning, 1990–1999." [http://www.learningindeed.org/research/slresearch/slrsrchsy.html]. 2000.

Boyte, H., and Hollander, E. *Wingspread Declaration on Civic Responsibilities of Research Universities.* [http://www.compact.org/civic/Wingspread/wings1.html]. 1999.

Campus Compact. *Presidents' Declaration on the Civic Responsibility of Higher Education.* [http://www.compact.org/resources/plc-declaration.html]. 1999.

Campus Compact. *Introduction to Service-Learning Toolkit: Readings and Resources for Faculty.* Providence, R.I.: Campus Compact, 2000.

Campus Compact. *Wingspread Summit on Student Civic Engagement: March 15–17, 2001.* [http://www.compact.org/wingspread/more_wingspread. html]. 2001.

Chronicle of Higher Education, "1998–99 Survey of the Attitudes and Activities of Full-Time Faculty members," Aug. 31, 2001, p. A29.

Dalton, J. (ed.). *Journal of College and Character.* [http://collegevalues.org/journal.efm].

Delli Carpini, M., and S. Keeter. *What Americans Know About Politics and Why It Matters.* New Haven, Conn.: Yale University Press, 1996.

Dewey, J. *Democracy and Education: An Introduction to the Philosophy of Education.* New York: MacMillan, 1916.

Diani, M. "The Concept of Social Movement." *Sociological Review,* 1992, *40*(1), 1–25.

Ehrlich, T. (ed.). *Civic Responsibility and Higher Education.* Phoenix: Oryx, 2000.

Eyler, J., and Giles, D. E., Jr. *Where's the Learning in Service-Learning?* San Francisco: Jossey-Bass, 1999.

Giles, D., Porter Honnet, E., and Migliore, S. *Research Agenda for Combining Service and Learning in the 1990s.* Raleigh, N.C.: National Society for Experiential Education, 1991.

Heffernan, K. *Fundamentals of Service-Learning Course Construction.* Providence, R.I.: Campus Compact, 2001.

Hollander, E., and Hartley, M. "Civic Renewal in Higher Education: The State of the Movement and the Need for a National Network." In

T. Ehrlich (ed.), *Civic Responsibility and Higher Education*. Phoenix: Oryx, 2000.

Hollander, E., Saltmarsh, J., and Zlotkowski, E. "Indicators of Engagement." In L. A. Simon, M. Kenny, K. Brabeck, and R. M. Lerner (eds.), *Learning to Serve: Promoting Civil Society Through Service-Learning*. Norwell, Mass.: Kluwer, 2001.

Howard, J. (ed.). *Praxis I: A Faculty Casebook on Community Service Learning*. Ann Arbor: University of Michigan OCSL Press, 1993.

The Institute of Politics. "Attitudes Toward Politics and Public Service: A National Survey of College and University Undergraduates." *HPR Online, Harvard Political Review,* [http://www.hrponline.org/survey/]. 2000.

Jacoby, B. *Service-Learning in Higher Education: Concepts and Practices*. San Francisco: Jossey-Bass, 1996.

Knefelkamp, L., and Schneider, C. "Education for a World Lived in Common with Others." In R. Orill (ed.), *Education and Democracy: Reimagining Liberal Learning in America*. New York: College Board, 1997.

Kotter, J. *Leading Change*. Boston, Mass.: Harvard Business School Press, 1996.

Matthews, D. *Creating More Public Space in Higher Education*. Washington, D.C.: Council on Public Policy Education, 1998.

Mellman Group. "Memorandum to Leon and Sylvia Panetta, the Panetta Institute" [summary of the results of a national survey of 800 college students], [http://www.panettainstitute.org/poll-memo. html], Jan. 11, 2000.

National Association of Secretaries of State. *New Millennium Project,* Part I: *American Youth Attitudes on Politics, Citizenship, Government and Voting: Survey on Youth Attitudes*. Lexington, Ky.: National Association of Secretaries of State, 1999.

National Commission on Civic Renewal. *A Nation of Spectators: How Civic Disengagement Weakens America and What We Can Do About it*. College Park, Md.: National Commission on Civic Renewal, 1999.

O'Grady, C. R. (ed.). *Integrating Service Learning and Multicultural Education in Colleges and Universities*. Hillsdale, N.J.: Erlbaum, 2000.

Pitkin, H. "Justice: On Relating Public and Private." *Political Theory,* 1981, *9*(3), 327–352.

Porter Honnet, E., and Poulsen, S. J. *Principles of Good Practice for Combining Service and Learning*. Racine, Wis.: Johnson Foundation, 1989.

Putnam, R. D. "Bowling Alone." *Journal of Democracy,* 1995, *6*(1), 65–78.

Putnam, R. D. "The Strange Disappearance of Civic America." *American Prospect,* 1996, *15*(24), 34–48.

Roper Starch Worldwide, Inc. "Public Attitudes Toward Education and Service-Learning." [http://www.roper.com]. 2000.

Sax, L. J., Astin, A. W., Korn, W. S., and Mahoney, K. M. *The American Freshman: National Norms for Fall 1999.* Los Angeles: University of California–Los Angeles, Higher Education Research Institute, 2000.

Sirianni, C., and Friedland, L. *Civic Innovation in America: Community Empowerment, Public Policy, and the Movement for Civic Renewal.* Berkeley: University of California Press, 2001.

Stanton, T. K., Giles, D. E., Jr., and Cruz, N. *Service-Learning: A Movement's Pioneers Reflect on Its Origins, Practice, and Future.* San Francisco: Jossey-Bass, 1999.

Templeton Foundation. *Honor Roll for Character-Building Colleges 1997–1998.* Radnor, Pa.: Templeton Foundation, 1997.

Thomas, N. "The College and University as Citizen." In T. Ehrlich (ed.), *Civic Responsibility and Higher Education.* Phoenix: Oryx, 2000.

de Tocqueville, A. *Democracy in America.* New York: New American Library, 1956.

Vogelgesang, L. J. Unpublished data. E-mailed July 23, 2001, to the Service-Learning Discussion Group. Archived at [http://csf.colorado.edu/mail/service-learning/jul01/msg00076.html].

Walker, T. "The Service/Politics Split: Rethinking Service to Teach Political Engagement." *PS: Political Science and Politics,* 2000, *33*(3), 647–649.

Wallace, A.F.C. "Revitalization Movements." *American Anthropologist,* 1956, *58*(2), 264–281.

Zlotkowski, E. "Civic Engagement and the Academic Disciplines." In T. Ehrlich (ed.), *Civic Responsibility and Higher Education.* Phoenix: Oryx, 2000.

Chapter Fifteen

Building Service-Learning Partnerships for the Future

Barbara Jacoby

The purpose of this book is to encourage the development of strong, democratic partnerships for service-learning that yield substantial outcomes in terms of learning and empowerment for students and communities. As several chapters in this book demonstrate, service-learning partnerships can and should inspire and lead the partnering institutions to enter into broader partnerships to address the most serious issues facing communities and society at large. Previous chapters discuss the multiple partnerships that must serve as the foundation for high-quality service-learning. Each chapter provides principles and examples of good practice and also offers suggestions for how to improve service-learning partnerships, enabling them to achieve their goals, to serve as the foundation for further collaboration among partners, and to become more democratic.

This chapter highlights several essential themes that, taken together, generate a strategy to advance service-learning by building and enhancing partnerships. As advocates and practitioners of service-learning, we must always keep in mind that service-learning is all about partnerships and that reflection has led, and will continue to lead, to wisdom that we must use in our work. We should strengthen the relationships among service-learning, civic education, and institutional citizenship; institutionalize partnerships for service-learning throughout higher education; continue to develop partnerships with elementary and secondary education that ensure a cohesive educational system that is accessible to all; broaden and deepen research on and assessment of partnerships; and push for support for service-learning partnerships on the national level.

Always Remember That Service-Learning Is *All About* Partnerships

For this editor, one of the many joys of working on this volume has been distilling the essence of what we know about outstanding service-learning partnerships and thinking about how to use that essence to develop more authentic, more reciprocal, more beneficial service-learning partnerships in the future. Trying to select lessons neither too specific to be useful in shaping various kinds of partnerships nor too general to be useful at all has led to the following precepts.

Partnerships start with and are built upon personal relationships. In fact, Bringle and Hatcher (forthcoming) illustrate how psychological theories about friendships and romantic relationships can be used to explore and enhance campus-community partnerships. It is critical to put in place mechanisms to sustain service-learning partnerships when key players depart, including, when appropriate, formal governance structures. Even with such structures functioning well, relationships between individuals can make or break a partnership.

Although it is essential to continually focus on the elemental personal relationships that form the basis of all partnerships, it is also critical to emphasize that partnerships that tackle the *big* issues must be among *institutions* rather than individuals. Although the daily work of individuals in a partnership may be on the micro level, such as one student tutoring one child or delivery of food or health care to one person at a time, the institutional members of a partnership should also focus, at the macro level, on the root causes—poverty, crime, educational inequity—of the service needs the partnership addresses. Partners can and should learn together, and from each other, about the social issues that most affect them and work as a partnership on behalf of positive social change while dealing with the here and now.

Although solid partnerships are built on a foundation of personal relationships, they are likewise anchored in shared goals and objectives. However, it is inevitable, appropriate, and even desirable for the individual partners to seek to achieve their own separate goals through the partnership. For example, through their participation in service-learning partnerships, student leaders may wish to acquire experience to build their résumés, young faculty could hope to develop their tenure portfolios, and community partners might be interested in gaining access to university resources for their organizations and their families. On the institutional level, a university may engage with its community to enhance the image of the neighborhood surrounding the campus to be more appealing to prospective students and parents. Likewise, improving the security and physical appearance of the neighborhood might serve a local business's self-interest by attracting customers and employees.

It is worth assuming the risks and taking the time to explore multisector partnerships. Several chapters in this book address the unilateral and mutual benefits as well as the cultural and other differences that partners from various sectors encounter in the partnership process. Although several critics of university-corporate partnerships have warned of the potential "contamination" of higher education by corporate interests, universities and communities must enlist corporate partners in addressing societal problems on all levels. More and more large corporations are entering into partnerships with nonprofits "in addressing the increasing number of complex issues that spill over sectoral boundaries" (Fisher, 2002). Independent Sector urges cross-sector collaboration to tackle major social issues by identifying how driving forces are changing the strategies by which government, business, and nonprofit organizations define and carry out their roles and how these strategies are then changing the relationships among the sectors (Fisher, 2002). Higher education leaders and service-learning educators must enter into these conversations to find ways to enrich and broaden multisector partnerships.

In addition, we should always be on the lookout for new partners in service-learning. What partnership possibilities, for example, does information technology offer? Partnerships that help bridge the so-called digital divide by equipping schools, libraries, nonprofit agencies, and homes in low-income areas with computers and software and training individuals to use them already exist, but many more are needed. Such partnerships clearly benefit all partners, certainly including computer hardware and software companies that stand only to gain if more institutions and individuals acquire access to their products and to the Internet. The Internet offers other partnership opportunities, such as those described in Chapter Eleven, that enable communities to share information about research and development activities so that they can learn from one another's successes and failures. Distance learning is one more avenue of great potential for service-learning partnerships that remains largely unexplored.

Faith-based organizations are another potential partner often shunned by (public) higher education. Although many faith-based organizations provide direct human services, fewer are currently involved in broader community development agendas. Universities and secular nonprofit agencies are in a good position to reach out to religiously affiliated groups and churches, offer technical assistance as needed, and consider partnerships that address common concerns. There is a host of other possible future partners with whom we can and should explore our options, including, but surely not limited to, the media, professional athletics, the music and film industries, telecommunications, mass transportation providers, and public and for-profit gambling enterprises.

In authentic service-learning partnerships, the partners share control of the partnership's agendas. This sounds easier to achieve than it often is in practice. For example, higher education administrators, accustomed to taking charge of agendas, may find it challenging to share control with students. It may be difficult for a faculty member whose experience has been as a solitary researcher to accept nonacademic community members as full research partners. Universities, likewise, may be hesitant to enter into "equal" partnerships with neighborhoods or community agencies. However, as Sandra Enos and Keith Morton explain in Chapter Two, partnerships should be viewed as potentially transformative for all involved and such transformation should not be feared. When partnership synergy occurs, a partnership gains the capacity to think and act in ways that surpass the capabilities of the partners acting individually (Center for the Advancement of Collaborative Strategies in Health, 2002).

In this spirit, it is essential in any service-learning partnership to leave room for serendipity. Partnerships are dynamic and can never be scripted, no matter how hard one may try. They will flow, take unexpected turns, and end up in unpredictable places. Like relationships among individuals, partnerships among institutions have the potential to transcend the sum of the parts.

Finally, one of the most compelling benefits of service-learning partnerships is the ability to tap into streams of funding that would not be accessible to the partners acting on their own. Federal grants from programs such as HUD's Community Outreach Partnership Center and the Corporation for National and Community Service's Learn and Serve America specify in no uncertain terms that successful proposals will be grounded in partnerships. Grants from key foundations and corporations, exemplified in Chapter Twelve by Kellogg and JP Morgan Chase, are available only to multi-sector partnerships.

Institutionalize Partnerships for Service-Learning

In order for partnerships for service-learning to survive in the long run and to enable the partners to reap their rich potential benefits, the partnerships must be integrated into the missions, policies, and practices of higher education institutions. The nature and extent of an institution's engagement in partnerships for service-learning should be mission-driven. Nearly every college or university mission statement includes some reference to citizenship, but this concept is rarely defined clearly or operationally. As the movement to revitalize the civic role of higher education grows, institutions are seeking ways to sharpen their missions and to become engaged universities that intentionally involve themselves in activities related to their missions and "generate, transmit, apply, and preserve knowledge . . . for the direct benefit of external audiences" (Votruba, 1996, p. 31). When documents like the *Presidents' Declaration on the Civic Responsibility of Higher Education* (Campus Compact, 1999) excite college presidents, an opportunity to bring service-learning partnerships to their attention presents itself. Service-learning proponents would do well to establish service-learning in the engaged campus framework.

It is wholely appropriate for institutions with different missions to take fundamentally different approaches to service-learning partnerships. For example, the civic role of the Maryland Institute College of Art can and should be different from those of Loyola University and the University of Maryland School of Medicine, although all are located in downtown Baltimore. Service-learning partnerships can help to both define and fulfill the civic aspect of institutional mission. As such, they should be firmly based and explicitly stated in strategic plans, institutional goal statements, and budgets.

Similarly, service-learning stands to benefit substantially by formalizing its links with civic and citizenship education. Advocates of service-learning partnerships would do well to develop authentic, democratic partnerships that model and engage students in public problem solving, the development of civic judgment, and reflection on the roles of individuals and institutions in building democracy. The civic education frame also has more pragmatic benefits for service-learning partnerships, as the Corporation for National and Community Service's Learn and Serve programs and major foundations have established civic education and democratic participation as desired student-learning outcomes.

The institutionalization of service-learning is clearly dependent on the reorientation of the traditional roles of research, teaching, and service to reflect an ethic of community engagement. Defined as they currently are, the promotion and tenure processes generally fail to recognize or reward faculty involvement in service-learning partnerships as teaching, research, or service. Ramaley's paradigm shift of this triad to the "more multidimensional terms of discovery, learning, and engagement" (2000, p. 233), described in Chapter One, facilitates and supports the development of service-learning partnerships. As president of Portland State University, Ramaley demonstrated how an institution's leadership can make it safe for faculty to orient their teaching and research toward community engagement, not by protecting them but rather by initiating and encouraging campus discourse about the institution's civic role (B. Holland, personal communication, July 2001). Campus Compact and the American Association for Higher Education (AAHE), as well as other national associations, have taken the lead in advancing engaged disciplines and in seeking ways for faculty to work with communities while ensuring academically rigorous research and learning. AAHE's 2002 annual conference on Faculty Roles and Rewards focused specifically on the engaged scholar, community-based research, and the faculty role in community partnerships (American Association for Higher Education, 2002). Developing an ethic of community engagement in graduate education is a strong starting point: "In many cases graduate students are the current and future educators of undergraduates. . . . Even when the intent is not to prepare them as instructors, community engagement is a powerful applied learning tool in many graduate disciplines. . . . Communities can be partners in graduate education by providing consultation and research opportunities that develop professional and scholarly skills" (Reed, 2000, p. 1).

Another critical dimension of the institutionalization of service-learning partnerships consists of confronting the prevailing organizational structures that constrain, sometimes inadvertently, the development of partnerships within the institution and with external individuals and organizations. Both organizational cultures and functional "silos" can stymie interdisciplinary work as well as collaboration between student affairs and academic affairs. In Chapter Four, Cathy McHugh Engstrom highlights how the transformation from a teaching to a learning paradigm is leading to partnerships between faculty and student affairs that recognize that such partnerships are essential for creating seamless learning environments and opportunities for students that transcend the artificial boundaries of the curriculum and the cocurriculum. As all types of institutions are embracing the concept and practice of learning communities, service-learning advocates should work closely with partners in both academic and student affairs to ensure that high-quality service-learning is an integral component. Other intrainstitutional partnerships that address the multiple administrative challenges related to service-learning are critical and too easily overlooked. Alliances with departments that handle functions such as renting vehicles, parking, and room reservations can prove valuable in many ways. A close relationship with legal advisers regarding risk management and liability issues is primary.

Partnerships with offices that work with public relations, fund-raising, and alumni affairs are also important.

An increasing number of prestigious universities are creating offices and positions focused on partnership development. National leaders in service-learning partnerships like Ira Harkavy, director of the Center for Community Partnerships and associate vice president at the University of Pennsylvania, have long been promoting partnerships at their own and other institutions. The staff of the Haas Center for Public Service at Stanford University includes the position of director of public partnerships. Irene Fisher, the longtime director of the Lowell Bennion Community Service Center at the University of Utah, currently holds a new position as special assistant to the president for campus-community partnerships (I. Fisher, personal communication, January 2002).

Finally, colleges and universities must themselves model behavior as good citizens and good partners both internally and externally. This requires a very real culture change along multiple dimensions in our institutions. These dimensions include, but are not limited to, shared governance, open inquiry and public discourse, democratic processes, encouragement for all voices to be heard, private and collective reflection, and elimination of boundaries among institutional constituencies and between campus and community. Hollander notes, "'We can't teach students to be good citizens unless institutions are good citizens themselves, in terms of how they behave on campus and what they do in their communities. This is something that has to be built from the faculty up as well as the president down'" (London, 2000, p. 3).

Service-Learning and Civic Education Begin in the K–12 System

Service-learning partnerships have the potential to engage students in learning about civic responsibility and in acquiring democratic skills as well as to lead institutions of higher education toward more extensive partnerships that address critical social issues. It is becoming increasingly clear that realizing this vast potential depends on the health of K–12 schools, their capacity to partner with colleges, their ability to effectively begin the process of civic education, and the extent to which they can level the playing field by improving the achievement of children in all schools at all socioeconomic levels. As Liane Brouillette admonishes in the *Chronicle of Higher Education*, "Public education in the United States is at a crossroads. Not since the end of the 19th century has there been such a widespread consensus that 'something must be done' about the public elementary and secondary schools" (2001, p. B16). Educational leaders and scholars agree that the higher education and K–12 systems must join forces "to create an educational culture in which both systems think of themselves as being parts of a broader educational system that stretches from kindergarten through university" (Parker, Greenbaum, and Pister, 2001).

In addition, there is general agreement that civic education must begin at the elementary level. The most forthright and powerful statement to this effect, the *Declaration on Education and Civil Society Partnering Initiative: Weaving a Seamless Web Between School and Community*, challenges schools, colleges, and community organizations to work together to foster civic values (Partnering Initiative on Education and Civil Society, 1997). Its call to action is explicit about the greater efforts needed to integrate civic values into the educational process:

> Emphasis should be placed on: 1) expanding opportunities for young people and adults to become more involved in meaningful service with neighborhood and community organizations by making service learning an integral part of the educational experience; 2) encouraging students to explore the twin issues of character development and responsible participation in the civil society by integrating service learning, character education, democratic education, and citizen education opportunities into the classroom; 3) weaving the historical legacy and values of the civil society into a broad range of curricula and community programs; 4) extending the values of democracy and community to the classroom by engaging students in the design of their own learning experiences; 5) eliciting more direct involvement between community organizations, civic associations, and businesses with local schools, colleges, and universities; 6) ensuring that faculty, students, staff, families, and community organizations have a genuine voice in school, college, and university-level policy making; and 7) making every

effort to ensure that the human, financial, and community
resources needed to accomplish these goals be available
[Partnering Initiative on Education and Civil Society, 1997,
p. 1].

In order to create the seamless web for civic values that the Partnering Initiative envisions, it must comprise multiple, cross-sector
service-learning partnerships as described throughout this volume.

Another seamless web that is fundamental to developing the
potential of young people and enabling each to become a full participant in our democracy is that of information literacy. Concerns
about the "digital divide" are endemic; the problem is most often
defined in terms of access to computers and the Internet. However,
a growing number of leaders in education view it more as an issue
of information literacy (Breivik, 2000). Schools with limited hardware and Internet connections necessarily provide fewer opportunities for their students to acquire the information and information
literacy skills that are required for learning and problem solving.
Similarly, the nonprofit sector is experiencing "an organizational
version of the 'digital divide'—the technology gap between large
and small nonprofits" (Independent Sector, 2001, p. 1), and
between those with varying levels of funding. All social sectors,
including government, corporations, private philanthropy, and
higher education, must join together as partners to enable information literacy to support and strengthen democratic participation. There is a clear role for service-learning partnerships in
creating mechanisms for sharing information technology resources
and information literacy skills.

The concluding chapter of *Service-Learning in Higher Education:
Concepts and Practices* asserts that the future of service-learning in
colleges and universities is closely tied to its quality and success
in elementary and secondary education (Jacoby, 1996). Every year
more schools, districts, and municipalities are integrating service-
learning into the elementary curriculum and requiring it for high
school graduation. Students who have positive precollege service
and learning experiences will likely seek and engage in service-
learning in college and, one hopes, make career and life decisions
based on socially responsible values that they have acquired in the

process. On the other hand, those who do not view their service-learning experiences in the K–12 years as worthwhile or clearly linked to their education may shun service-learning in college and fail to understand how social responsibility can be integral to all career or life choices. Service-learning partnerships that are designed to enhance the educational experiences of students at all levels are therefore of paramount importance in securing the future of service-learning.

Advance Research and Assessment of Service-Learning Partnerships

Although the quantity and quality of research on service-learning has increased substantially since the publication of *Service-Learning in Higher Education* (Jacoby, 1996), that book's call for additional research to add to our knowledge of how service-learning fosters academic and civic learning and "how higher education and communities can best collaborate to reach mutual goals" (p. 326) remains current. In recognition of the number and salience of unanswered questions, Campus Compact convened a National Research Advisory Council in 1997 to advance the service-learning research agenda (Howard, Gelmon, and Giles, 2000). Research priorities generated at the meeting included "understanding community impact, pinpointing a range for a conceptualization of service-learning and its impacts, learning from history, encouraging theory-driven research, analyzing faculty roles and rewards, understanding institutional impact, and reviewing the impact of research on such matters as policy and funding" (p. 6). Other topics raised that are of particular import for service-learning partnerships involve learning more about the connection between service-learning and democratic participation and focusing research on partnerships as the unit of study (Cruz and Giles, 2000).

There is no doubt that additional research is required to increase our understanding of the relationship among service-learning, citizenship, and civic responsibility. A series of recent studies of the civic involvement of college students have found that they are more and more active in community service and service-learning but less interested in public affairs than earlier generations (Institute of Politics, 2000; Mellman Group, 2000; National

Association of Secretaries of State, 1999; Sax, Astin, Korn, and Mahoney, 1999). However, other surveys of students have found that service-learning is linked with increased evidence of personal, social, or civic responsibility (Astin and Sax, 1998; Eyler and Giles, 1999; Melchoir, 1997; Rand Corporation, 1996). Eyler and Giles report that "participation in [high-quality] service-learning leads to the values, knowledge, skills, efficacy, commitment that underlie effective citizenship" (1999, p. 164). Kahne, Westheimer, and Rogers argue that researchers now need to "consider how features of higher education institutions (such as size, emphasis on research, religious mission, and funding base) shape the civic mission of these institutions and their use of service-learning opportunities" (2000, p. 42). They frame three broad research questions to guide researchers in exploring the complexity of service-learning experiences and how those experiences relate to citizenship and democracy: "What conceptions of 'good' citizenship drive various service-learning programs? . . . How can service-learning research inform and be informed by broader disciplinary research on citizenship and democracy? . . . How does the civic mission of higher education institutions enable or constrain service-learning?" (Kahne, Westheimer, and Rogers, 2000, pp. 44–47). Along these lines, the Center for Information and Research on Civic Learning and Engagement at the University of Maryland received a grant of nearly $5 million from the Pew Charitable Trusts to study youth civic engagement and the factors that lead to it. It is critical that partnerships between service-learning practitioners and researchers explore and report on specific initiatives that effectively link service-learning and civic engagement.

As each of the chapters in this volume indicates, much remains unknown about exactly what constitutes a successful partnership for service-learning. Undoubtedly, we need to know more about the specific elements that enable partnerships to grow and develop over time so that they may achieve the goals of the partnership and of the individual partners. Groundbreaking new work in this area is very encouraging. In Chapter Three Sherril B. Gelmon proposes an evolving framework for assessing the service-learning partnership itself. In a similar vein, Cruz and Giles propose a new research approach that focuses directly on the partnership as the unit of analysis: "This is based on the assumption that the partnership is the infrastructure that facilitates the service and learning and is both an intervening variable in studying certain learning and service 'impacts' as well as an outcome or 'impact' in itself" (2000, p. 31). In this way, the characteristics of the partnership can be studied in relation to their impacts on service and learning. Fundamental research questions are "Is the partnership better now with service-learning than it was before without service-learning? Alternatively, are service and/or learning better because of the quality of the partnership?" (p. 31).

A study of university-community partnerships by Sandman and Baker-Clark raises additional research questions that should be pursued for greater understanding of how partnerships work: "1. Is there a typology of different university-community partnerships? That is, do partnerships with health, human service, educational organizations differ significantly from those in technical fields such as engineering and business? 2. How are partnerships best framed to insure faculty scholarship as one of their outcomes? 3. Is there a framework for timing of the overall partnership and its phases? 4. How and when are university-community partnerships typically ended? 5. What are major policy issues influencing development of university-community partnerships?" (1997, p. 4).

As the manuscript of this book was being finalized, the Center for the Advancement of Collaborative Strategies in Health launched an easy-to-use web-based "Partnership Self-Assessment Tool" in June 2002. The new tool was designed as a result of the findings of the National Study of Partnership Functioning conducted in 2001. The study revealed that partnerships that have a high level of synergy are characterized by leadership that promotes productive interactions among diverse participants and the ability to use participants' resources wisely. It also found high levels of synergy associated with particular kinds of management and administration capacities and the partnerships' ability to garner nonfinancial resources from their participants, such as skills, connections, and information. Consequently, the tool measures a partnership's level of synergy in terms of these and other key factors. It is intended for use by a broad array of partnerships focusing on any kind of goal, not only those in the area of health. The tool is provided to partnerships at no charge. Information and registration to use the "Partnership Self-Assessment Tool" are available at [http://www.PartnershipTool.net].

Research on partnerships is necessary, but the mere existence of data does not lead to the enhancement of partnerships or to the achievement of their goals. It is encouraging that universities are creating mechanisms to share information with their community partners, as noted in Chapters Ten and Eleven. The University of Pennsylvania recently announced the launch of InfoR, a web-based community information resource on West Philadelphia that includes public data sets, research by faculty and students, research by school and community partners, and other materials. Joann Weeks of Penn's Center for Community Partnerships describes InfoR as "a democratizing way of access to data and recognition that data flows two ways" (2001). InfoR, itself a multisector partnership, was developed collaboratively by representatives of West Philadelphia community-based organizations, Penn's Department of City and Regional Planning, the Center for Community Partnerships, Wharton Real Estate, the West Philadelphia Partnership, and others, with funding from HUD and the W.K. Kellogg Foundation (Weeks, 2000). InfoR can be accessed at [http://westphillydata.library.upenn.edu]. As both an information-sharing resource and a partnership, InfoR provides an excellent example to be followed by all kinds of partnerships for service-learning.

In addition to sharing information among service-learning partnerships, it is critical to raise awareness about partnerships. The reality is that potential partners and supporters, to say nothing of the general public, simply do not know the good that partnerships for service-learning are doing and are capable of doing. As we acquire more data about the benefits of service-learning partnerships, we must make the effort to engage the media in spreading the word about our important work. Higher education leaders often lament the fact that the media tend to focus on colleges and universities when there is something negative to report. We can invite representatives of local and national media to learn about and to observe firsthand the positive outcomes, as well as the challenges, of service-learning partnerships for all involved. Although many National Public Radio stations are housed on campuses, we fail to reach out to them as partners to help us articulate clearly and publicly the urgency of addressing the issues that partnerships are all about (B. Frankel, personal communication, June 2002).

Integrate Partnerships for Service-Learning into National Agendas

Although building the capacity of individual campuses and communities to engage in service-learning partnerships is essential, advocacy on the national level is also necessary to create an additional, broader infrastructure to ensure their ability to survive and thrive into the future. Advocates must constantly be aware of issues on the horizon for national legislation, education associations, foundations, and other policy arenas that can increase support, or not increase support, for partnerships for service-learning. Pollack recognizes the power of laws and policies to "create the legal and bureaucratic frameworks that guide interaction in the social arena by sanctioning and devoting resources to certain types of activities while prohibiting others" (2000, p. 105). He then raises several key questions: "What has been the relationship between research and policy-making in the field of service-learning? Has our growing body of knowledge and expertise informed policy, or, have policy-makers proceeded without benefit of knowledge from research? Are research and policy informing or ignoring each other?" (p. 105). As this book goes to press, there are several examples of major issues on the national agenda that advocates of service-learning partnerships can and should address.

Senators John McCain (R.Ariz.) and Evan Baye (D.Ind.) introduced The Call to Service Act of 2001 on December 10, 2001, to increase the number of AmeriCorps members from 50,000 to 250,000, as well as to require every college and university to devote 25 percent (rather than the current 7 percent) of its federal work-study funds for community-service positions (Campus Compact, 2002a). In his State of the Union address on January 29, 2002, President George W. Bush called on all Americans to serve their country for the equivalent of two years, or four thousand hours, over a lifetime. He announced his request for more than $560 million in new funds for the formation of the USA Freedom Corps, which includes three components: a newly created Citizen Corps to engage citizens in homeland security efforts, an expanded and enhanced AmeriCorps and Senior Corps, and a strengthened Peace Corps ("USA Freedom Corps," 2002). In addition, the president specifically proposed that every college and university be required to devote 50 percent of its federal work-study funds to community service. This proposed increase, twice that of the McCain-Baye bill, would mean that an additional 250,000 to 300,000 students would serve an average of ten hours per week in nonprofit organizations ("USA Freedom Corps," 2002).

These proposals have great potential for increasing and enhancing the work of service-learning partnerships; however, partnership advocates have a critical role to play in ensuring that the legislation and resulting guidelines reflect the principles and accumulated knowledge to enable these funds to achieve outcomes that will be most beneficial to students, institutions, and communities. For example, the material that appeared immediately following the State of the Union address mentioned service but not learning. It referred to promoting "a culture of responsibility, service, and citizenship" ("USA Freedom Corps," 2002) but did not say how this would be done. Leaders of nonprofit organizations immediately expressed concern that they did not have the capacity to manage a huge, rapid influx of volunteers. They also noted that volunteers alone were not sufficient to address social problems. Chuck Gould, president of Volunteers of America, explained, "We're always a little cautious of volunteerism as the magic bullet that's going to solve these systemic issues . . . such as affordable housing" (Salmon, 2002, p. A1).

From the perspective of higher education institutions, there is fear that for many colleges, especially smaller and less wealthy ones, the dramatic increase in the requirement for use of the federal work-study program to fund community-service positions would drain an essential labor source from on-campus departments that depend on work-study students to accomplish essential functions. In addition, many would not be able to find the resources to develop high-quality programs to enable students to earn their work-study awards through community service work off-campus. For rural institutions in particular, there may simply not be enough community-service placements in their areas. Likewise there is concern that an increase in the federal work-study community service requirement would place an unfair burden on low-income students to do community service work without doing anything to encourage service involvement by wealthier students (Hebel, 2002). It is clear that national service and university-community partnerships have achieved bipartisan support in Congress and, as such, are key national agendas that higher education must help to shape.

Another Bush administration initiative with potential relationship to service-learning partnerships is support for an increased role of faith-based organizations in delivery of direct service to communities. In his administration's early days, President Bush proposed legislation to enable churches to obtain federal contracts for social services and created the White House Office of Community and Faith-Based Initiatives. In July 2002, the U.S. Department of Health and Human Services announced the availability of $30 million to intermediary organizations that provide technical assistance to faith-based and community organizations in developing their capacity to create programs that address issues such as hunger, homelessness, transition from welfare to work, and the needs of at-risk children and those requiring intensive rehabilitation, such as addicts or prisoners (U.S. Department of Health and Human Services, 2002). Although these initiatives have faced opposition in Congress and from a variety of organizations, they remain important to the administration (Allen, 2001). As a result, practitioners, researchers, and advocates of service-learning partnerships should actively consider how to effectively partner with faith-based organizations.

Yet another Bush administration initiative is a post–September 11, 2001 attempt to revive civic education in elementary and secondary schools. Although the subject is potentially controversial with some conservatives likely to oppose any form of government mandate to schools and with some liberals equally likely to view such federal efforts as encouragement of blind obedience or as garnering support for the current administration, expansion of service-learning classes is anticipated to be part of any proposal (Milbank, 2002). As such, service-learning proponents should view the federal government as a serious partner and should advocate for the development of the civic education initiative to create a rich and seamless P–16 civic education curriculum.

In January 2002, the National Commission on Service-Learning, chaired by Senator John Glenn, released its report, *Learning in*

Deed: The Power of Service-Learning for American Schools. The report issues a strong call to schools to embrace service-learning as a proven method of instruction that promotes academic achievement as measured by testing programs already in place and reverses trends of youth disengagement by preparing them for active roles as citizens (National Commission on Service-Learning, 2002). The report recommends that colleges of education partner with associations and government agencies "to create a comprehensive and integrated system of ongoing professional development that helps teachers to forge stronger linkages between service-learning and curriculum knowledge" (National Commission on Service-Learning, 2002, p. 44). Some of the professional development strategies mentioned are incorporating service-learning into teacher and administrator preparation and in-service education, including service-learning in the completion criteria of teacher certification programs and state licensing boards, and creating multimedia professional development resources. In this chapter and in Chapter Nine it is urged that advocates for service-learning in higher education should seek more and deeper partnerships with K–12 education. As reports like *Learning in Deed* attract the attention of government officials, education organizations, foundations, and the media, proponents of service-learning partnerships should take advantage of these opportunities to advance their agendas.

Several major foundations have provided significant funding for service-learning partnerships and civic engagement, including the Pew, Ford, Johnson, Kellogg, and Carnegie foundations. They generously support and promote cutting-edge work in these areas. It is essential that advocates for service-learning partnerships continue to develop relationships with national foundations, demonstrate clearly how foundations' support enhances the quality of partnerships and the achievement of their objectives, and propose new ways in which foundation support can address social problems, increase student and community learning, and build democracy in the United States and around the world.

Throughout this volume, chapter authors highlight numerous ways in which national education associations advance partnerships for service-learning. These include the establishment of principles of good practice, proposing agendas for research and assessment, creating models for building the infrastructure of colleges and universities to support partnerships, urging the development of the capacity of community organizations, setting service-learning in the frames of civic engagement and civic education, and transforming the very culture of higher education from its traditional "holy trinity" of research, teaching, and service to embrace the broader concepts of discovery, learning, and engagement suggested by Ramaley (2000).

An excellent example of how proponents of service-learning can partner with a national association in the advancement of related agendas is the previously mentioned 2002 AAHE Conference on Faculty Roles and Rewards on the topic of engaged scholarship. Several well-respected service-learning educators and advocates were featured on the program, including Elizabeth Hollander, Edward Zlotkowski, Mary Walshok, Robert Bringle, Mark Langseth, Barbara Holland, Amy Driscoll, Sherril Gelmon, Ira Harkavy, Richard Battistoni, and John Saltmarsh, to name but some of the featured speakers (American Association for Higher Education, 2002). Other higher education associations, such as the American College Personnel Association, the American Association of Community Colleges, the Council of Independent Colleges, the National Association of Student Personnel Administrators, and the Association of College Unions–International are featuring service-learning more prominently in their publications, conferences, and grant programs. In 1999, Campus Compact and the American College Personnel Association joined together to offer a daylong conference on service-learning as a precursor to the latter's annual convention. In both 1999 and 2001 the Association of College Unions–International partnered with the American College Personnel Association and the National Association of Student Personnel Administrators to present the Forum on Volunteerism, Service, and Learning. Advocates of service-learning partnerships who are members of these and other associations should become even more actively involved in integrating topics related to partnerships into association activities.

Another set of national agendas that can and should support service-learning partnerships relate to institutional classification and accountability. As this volume goes to press the Carnegie Foundation for the Advancement of Teaching is in the process of revising its scheme for the classification of higher education institutions. The foundation plans to issue two revisions of the Carnegie Classification. The second revision, scheduled for 2005, will replace the single-classification system with a series of classifications, each of which will highlight different dimensions of institutional variation. Discussions have already begun about incorporating elements of civic mission into the revisions for 2005 and initiating pilot efforts to develop a new set of criteria for civic engagement (Campus Compact, 2002b).

Accountability has become increasingly prominent on the higher education scene during the past two decades, and it is highly likely that this trend will continue. A number of reports by experts inside and outside of higher education demand that it specify outcomes for student learning and public service and to what extent they are being achieved (Jacoby and Jones, 2001). The accreditation process is one mechanism through which colleges and universities are held accountable. What if the extent and success of an institution's involvement in partnerships for service-learning were criteria for accreditation? Advocates of service-learning partnerships would do well to be part of these national conversations.

Conclusion

What is the future of partnerships for service-learning? Those of us who believe in the power and potential of such partnerships have many reasons to be optimistic. Higher education continues to reaffirm its responsibility for responding to social issues locally, nationally, and globally. Educating students to be lifelong learners, active citizens of our communities, and builders of democracy are becoming clearer missions of colleges and universities. Partners in service-learning are increasingly able to demonstrate the benefits they gain from their involvement.

Partnerships for service-learning, although they may begin with well-delineated boundaries, a small number of participants, and finite goals, need set no limits on future growth in duration, place, or scope. In fact, their virtually limitless potential may go untapped for years until its unpredictable benefits are realized. Who knows what far-reaching partnerships the CEO of a global corporation might form based on a rewarding college experience within a multisector service-learning partnership? What about a young teacher in a K–12-higher education partnership who eventually becomes a superintendent or the U.S. Secretary of Education? Could not a homeless person learn enough through involvement in partnership activities to eventually head a nonprofit organization that would join with schools, colleges, government agencies, and other nonprofits to create an innovative welfare-to-work program? On the institutional level, might partnerships for service-learning eventually lead to the fundamental transformation of how universities use knowledge? Moving to the next level, can cross-sector partnerships generate enough new energy and creativity to solve social problems? Is it not possible that sustained partnerships among equals can redefine the very process of positive social change?

As we continue to develop principles for authentic, democratic service-learning partnerships and to design partnerships accordingly, more and better models will result. I am confident that participants in partnerships—students, K–12 and higher education faculty and administrators, community members, community agency staff, corporate leaders, government and foundation officials, and others—will use these models to enhance the democratic process in many organizations and in many ways. This will, in turn, create and sustain institutions and environments that will enable future generations to join together in dynamic partnerships to engage in mutual learning, enhancement of the common good, and fulfillment of the public purpose of higher education.

References

Allen, M. "Bush Aims to Get Faith Initiative Back on Track." *Washington Post,* June 25, 2001, pp. A1, A5.

American Association for Higher Education. "Knowledge for What? The Engaged Scholar," Conference on Faculty Roles and Rewards. [www.aahe.org]. January 2002.

Astin, A., and Sax, L. "How Undergraduates Are Affected by Service Participation." *Journal of College Student Development,* 1998, *39*(3), 259–263.

Breivik, P. S. "Information Literacy and the Engaged Campus." *AAHE Bulletin,* 2000, *53*(3), 3–6.

Bringle, R. G., and Hatcher, J. A. "Campus-Community Partnerships: The Terms of Engagement." *Journal of Social Issues,* forthcoming.

Brouillette, L. "How Colleges Can Work With Schools." *Chronicle of Higher Education,* Feb. 23, 2001, p. B16.

Campus Compact. *Presidents' Declaration on the Civic Responsibility of Higher Education.* [http://www.compact.org/resources/plc-declaration.html]. 1999.

Campus Compact. "Current Legislation Affecting Community Service and Higher Education." [http://www.compact.org/national/legislation.html]. July 2002a.

Campus Compact. "Initiative: Revising the Carnegie Classifications to Include Civic Engagement." [www.compact.org/mapping]. July 2002b.

Center for the Advancement of Collaborative Strategies in Health. "Partnership Self-Assessment Tool." [http://www.PartnershipTool.net]. June 2002.

Cruz, N. I., and Giles, D. E., Jr. "Where's the Community in Service-Learning Research?" *Michigan Journal of Community Service Learning,* Special Issue, Fall 2000, 28–34.

Eyler, J., and Giles, D. E., Jr. *Where's the Learning in Service-Learning?* San Francisco: Jossey-Bass, 1999.

Fisher, S. R. *Working Better Together: How Government, Business, and Nonprofit Organizations Can Achieve Public Purposes Through Cross-Sector Collaboration, Alliances, and Partnerships.* Washington, D.C.: Independent Sector, 2002.

Hebel, S. "National-Service Program Turns Critics into Fans." *Chronicle of Higher Education,* Apr. 26, 2002.

Howard, J.P.F., Gelmon, S. B., and Giles, D. E., Jr. "From Yesterday to Tomorrow: Strategic Directions for Service-Learning Research." *Michigan Journal of Community Service Learning,* Special Issue, Fall 2000, 5–10.

Independent Sector. " The Impact of Information Technology on Civil Society: How Will Online Innovation, Philanthropy, and Volunteerism Serve the Common Good?" *Facts and Findings,* 2001, *3*(2), 1.

Institute of Politics, Harvard University. "Attitudes Toward Politics and Public Service: A National Survey of College and University Undergraduates." *Harvard Political Review,* Fall 2000. [http://www.hpronline.org/survey/].

Jacoby, B. "Securing the Future of Higher Education." In B. Jacoby (ed.), *Service-Learning in Higher Education: Concepts and Practices.* San Francisco: Jossey-Bass, 1996.

Jacoby, B., and Jones, S. R. "Visioning the Future of Student Affairs." In R. B. Winston Jr., D. G. Creamer, and T. K. Miller (eds.), *The Professional Student Affairs Administrator: Educator, Leader, and Manager.* New York: Brunner-Routledge, 2001.

Kahne, J., Westheimer, J., and Rogers, B. "Service-Learning and Citizenship: Directions for Research." *Michigan Journal of Community Service Learning*, Special Issue, Fall 2000, 42–51.

London, S. *Seminar on Higher Education and Public Life.* Washington, D.C.: Kettering Foundation, 2000.

Melchoir, A. *National Evaluation of Learn and Serve America School and Community-Based Programs. Interim Report.* Washington, D.C.: Corporation for National Service, 1997.

Mellman Group. "Memorandum to Leon and Sylvia Panetta, the Panetta Institute [summary of the results of a national survey of 800 college students]," [http://www.panettainstitute.org/poll-memo.html]. Jan. 11, 2000.

Milbank, D. "Revival in Civics Education Is Explored." *Washington Post,* May 12, 2002, p. A14.

National Association of Secretaries of State. *New Millennium Project—Phase I.* Washington, D.C.: National Association of Secretaries of State, 1999.

National Commission on Service-Learning. *Learning in Deed: The Power of Service-Learning for American Schools.* [www.servicelearningcommission.org/report.html]. Feb. 2002.

Parker, L. L., Greenbaum, D. A., and Pister, K. S. "Rethinking the Land-Grant Research University for the Digital Age." *Change,* Jan.-Feb. 2001, 12–17.

Partnering Initiative on Education and Civil Society. *Declaration on Education and Civil Society Partnering Initiative: Weaving a Seamless Web Between School and Community.* Washington, D.C.: American Association of Community Colleges, 1997.

Pollack, S. "The Role of Research and Policy in Constituting the Service-Learning Field." *Michigan Journal of Community Service Learning,* Special Issue, Fall 2000, 105–112.

Ramaley, J. A. "The Perspective of a Comprehensive University." In T. Ehrlich (ed.), *Civic Responsibility and Higher Education,* Phoenix: Oryx, 2000.

Rand Corporation. *Coupling Service and Learning in Higher Education: The Final Report of the Evaluation of Learn and Serve America, Higher Education Program.* Santa Monica, Calif.: Rand Corporation, 1996.

Reed, J. *Campus Compact: Building Lasting Bridges Between Campuses and Communities.* Midwest Collaboration of Campus Compacts, 2000.

Salmon, J. L. "Nonprofit Groups Cool on Call for Volunteers." *Washington Post,* Feb. 8, 2002, pp. A1, A5.

Sandman, L. R., and Baker-Clark, C. A. "Characteristics and Principles of University-Community Partnerships: A Delphi Study." Presentation at Midwest Research-to-Practice Conference, East Lansing, Mich., Oct. 1997.

Sax, L. J., Astin, A. W., Korn, W. S., and Mahoney, K. M. *The American Freshman: National Norms for Fall 1999.* Los Angeles: Higher Education Research Institute, University of California–Los Angeles, 1999.

"USA Freedom Corps." [http://usafreedomcorps.gov]. Jan. 2002.

U.S. Department of Health and Human Services. [www.hhs.gov/news/press/2002press/20020605a.html]. July 2002.

Votruba, J.C. "Strengthening the University's Alignment with Society: Challenges and Strategies." *Journal of Public Service and Outreach,* 1996, *1*(1), 29–36.

Weeks, J. [weeks@pobox.upenn.edu]. "Penn's InfoR Website." In service-learning listserv. [sl@csf.colorado.edu]. July 16, 2001.

Name Index

Subject Index